Path through the Wilderness

BECOMING WHO YOU WERE MEANT TO BE

THE REVEREND BOB RAGAN

Published by Shell Shocked
For more information, contact PaththroughtheWilderness@gmail.com

Printed in the United States of America

Library of Congress Cataloging-in-Publication Data

ISBN: 978-0-578-58152-1

Cover design and interior layout design by Epic Life Creative
(www.epiclifecreative.com)

Acknowledgements

This book is the culmination of what I have learned through my journey regarding my struggles, addictions, and years in devoted ministry to the sexually and relationally broken since 1988. I cannot find enough words to express my eternal gratefulness to the Lord. He drew me from utter darkness, not once but twice, into His marvelous light.

I am indebted to so many who have mentored and ministered to me. They include Paul Morgan, Alan and Willa Medinger, Rev. David and Margie Harper, Sally Blankingship, Leanne Payne, Rev. Mario Bergner, Clay McLean, Andrew Comiskey, Rev. Rick Wright, the Right Rev. Martyn Minns (who ordained me), the Right Rev. John Guernsey, Rev. John Yates, and Rev. Nicholas Lubelfeld.

The Lord has brought four significant men into my life as close and trusted friends. They are Dr. Randy Newman, Bob Perdue, Henry Orejuela, and Stoney Noell. They have been a much needed source of encouragement. I feel honored to call them my friends and brothers.

I am grateful to Bob and Terri Perdue, Joyce Smith, and Kyle Bowman for the generosity of their time to write five chapters in this book. My thanks to Jane Campbell, for her wonderful gift of editing. I also want to thank Dr. Linda Seiler for her valuable insight.

It was these godly men and women who helped shape, develop, and further my becoming and calling. Like Aaron and Hur, who upheld Moses' arms when they were weak, these individuals have done the same for me on multiple occasions.

Contents

Introduction

AND IT WILL BE SAID: "BUILD UP, BUILD UP, PREPARE THE ROAD!

REMOVE THE OBSTACLES OUT OF THE WAY OF MY PEOPLE.

ISAIAH 57:14

Path through the Wilderness (Path) is the fruit of my experiences in ministry beginning in 1988. I have read many books, attended numerous conferences around the world, and been the recipient of healing prayer ministry through various pastoral leaders. As I entered my process, I initially got sidetracked, having the wrong focus. Eventually, I realized the following:

- Behavior modification is not the ultimate goal.
- Trying to be pure and holy through my means fails.
- Trying to live life through a set of rules places my focus on doing and striving rather than resting and being.
- I cannot become the individual God created me to be without community.
- Transparency and honesty are not an option but a necessity.

Although behavior modification and striving for perfection looked good at first, it did not bring the peace and endurance for which my soul yearned. Looking for a cause for a particular attraction or brokenness often results in an ego-centric focus. We search with our own understanding, thinking healing is based on finding the cause for our brokenness.

It was through trial and error that I began to let go and let God be Lord of my process. He had to define what healing meant and what was the true goal of my process. I had to keep an upward focus, allowing God to expose what lay beneath in my mind and heart.

The goal of Path is for you to grow in intimacy with God and to become more the man or woman God has created you to be. Each chapter addresses a specific area in this lifelong becoming process. It is not about striving, desperately trying to figure out how to absorb each chapter. It is, with the Lord's help, letting Him reveal how each chapter applies to you. God will remove the obstacles in your path, which hinder your becoming process. It is not about your trying to be perfect. It is about the Lord perfecting His work in you.

> Teacher, which is the greatest commandment in the Law?" Jesus replied: *"'Love the LORD your God with all your heart and with all your soul and with all your mind.' This is the first and greatest commandment. And the second is like it: 'Love your neighbor as yourself.' All the Law and the Prophets hang on these two commandments.*
>
> – Matthew 22:36–40, italics added

In the Scripture above, Jesus answered the question regarding the greatest commandment by providing two of them. Upon first reading, although there are two commandments, we see that there are three relationships involved. The first is our relationship with God. The second is our relationship with others. And, third, how can we have whole relationships with others if we are not in a whole relationship with ourselves? These three relationships, therefore, provide the structure for *Path*.

Path has four sections:
Section 1: Loving God Aright
Section 2: Loving Ourselves Aright
Section 3: Loving Others Aright
Section 4: Loving Our Process Aright

Each section will explore those things that prevent us from being in whole relationships. Each chapter builds on the content of the ones preceding it. Each section provides a foundation for the next section.

Getting Started

Because God orders our steps, I believe He has led you to obtain this book. I recommend you to set aside this time of study for a season to let the Lord take you deeper into knowing Him and others. Before you begin to read each chapter, choose a time when you will be able to focus and concentrate. Pray before you begin to read. Read at a pace that allows you to absorb the content. Ask the Lord to center you in His will and purpose. Allow the Holy Spirit to bring revelation to your soul, addressing those areas that He knows are in need. Trust in His commitment to you and your process: "Being confident of this, that he who began a good work in you will carry it on to completion until the day of Christ Jesus" (Philippians 1:6).

How to Read Each Chapter

As you read each chapter, be sensitive to the following three occurrences:

1. Be sensitive to any deflective reaction. If you finish reading a page and cannot remember what you just read, stop. You may be reading too quickly, be too tired, or perhaps you deflected due to the content. My greatest concern is deflection. The content may hit too close to your personal story, and your heart may have shut down. Pray and ask the Holy Spirit if you deflected. Ask Him to reveal what about the chapter content evoked a reaction whereby you were no longer present to it. Seek His help to process this deflective reaction.

2. Stay present to your emotions. Stop if you suddenly feel angry, anxious, happy, joyous, etc. Your heart is responding to the content. When your emotions become stirred, ask the Holy Spirit, what evoked that particular emotion. This process joins your head and your heart. An important aspect of going through this book is to obtain both a head and heart knowing. Emotions frequently trigger addictions and broken behaviors. Being able to identify our emotions is an important aspect of our becoming process.

3. Stay present to your memories. Our minds contain millions of memories. Why, when you are reading a specific section, does a memory surface from your past? It is because a connection occurred with the chapter content. Ask the Holy Spirit to reveal the significance of the memory. Often when a memory arises, it is due to an emotion associated with that memory.

If you are reading the chapters too quickly, you may be missing something the Lord desires to reveal. Once again, set apart your time with *Path* as a season for the Lord's deeper healing and revelation. Let Him be Lord of your process and stay present to His presence as you go through *Path*.

There is a glossary of terms at the end of this manual to assist you.

A Final Important Recommendation

As stated earlier, the goal of *Path* is to have an increased level of intimacy with God. Therefore, an important step after reading *each chapter* is to reflect on how the chapter content correlated to your capacity to experience healthy relational intimacy. This not only applies to your relational intimacy with God but also with others and yourself. What blocks did the chapter expose to knowing God, others, and yourself aright? Seek the Holy Spirit to identify these hindrances and to reveal how to remove them. Looking at Isaiah 57:14 once more, "Remove the obstacles out of the way of my people." it expresses the Lord's desire for your path to be clear. Seek Him to assist in removing any obstacles which limit you becoming the man or woman He has created you to be.

SECTION 1
LOVING GOD ARIGHT

Our relationship with God is of primary importance

Loving God Aright

We start *Path* by addressing our relationship with God. This relationship is of primary importance. He is the source of our healing and any blocks to Him will hinder our process of becoming, becoming the man or woman God has created us to be. Through our broken relationships, we often transfer our broken reactions onto God. We must let Him reveal whatever blocks us from entering into deeper intimacy with Him.

Another important aspect of growing in our depth of intimacy with God is knowing Him in the fullness of His Trinitarian expression. We must know Him as Father, Jesus, and the Holy Spirit. I am not referring to a *doctrinal* knowing of Him, but a *personal, relational* knowing. Jesus' death and resurrection made a way for us to know God as Father. We become new creations when we invite Jesus into our hearts as Lord and Savior. We now have an identity as defined by God and not by the world or our sin. The Holy Spirit, as the Spirit of truth, makes the love of the Father and the Son experiential and real in our lives. We need to know the fullness of His image as manifested in the Trinity.

It may seem odd to include the chapter on shame in this section. Shame is a powerful reaction and emotion that can greatly diminish our capacity to receive and extend love. Shame, therefore, can significantly decrease our capacity to know God. Shame also interferes with our being present to others in community. The topic of shame is one we will refer to throughout *Path*.

Remember to reflect on what blocks did the chapter expose to knowing God, others, and yourself aright.

ONE

What's Your Problem?

A BRUISED REED HE WILL NOT BREAK, AND A SMOLDERING WICK HE WILL NOT SNUFF OUT.

ISAIAH 42:3

All of us are on a journey, a pilgrimage to our true home. We are sojourners and aliens in a strange land. We are traveling to a sacred place. Jeremiah 6:16 states, "Stand at the crossroads and look; ask for the ancient paths, ask where the good way is, and walk in it, and you will find rest for your souls." We are following the ancient path of those who have gone before us. We are on our way. The Bible confirms that we truly desire rest for our souls; and we know from John 10:10 that we long for the "life to the fullest" that Jesus promised us. The fact that you are reading these words is evidence of your longing, and it is that longing that creates hope within you. Hope will allow you to lift up your head out of "what is" and move toward what is "not yet."

But we are living in the present, with the "what is." We experience the current moment with all its challenges and difficulties. Do you ever feel like the "bruised reed" or "smoldering wick" of Isaiah 42:3 (above)?

A reed can be used for a musical instrument. However, if it is bruised, it cannot function for this purpose. A smoldering wick indicates that there is minimal wax present and that the wick is being consumed by the flame. It is no longer of use to provide light. Both the reed and the candle, as far as these uses are concerned, are now worthless. They no longer serve a purpose. Has your past resulted in bruising? Have you felt as if your candle is about to go out? We carry burdens that affect our emotional, mental, spiritual, and physical well-being. From a human perspective, we feel like the reed and wick, no longer fit for any purpose. We lose hope and begin to despair. We must let God define hope for us and reveal how we respond or react when despair knocks at our door. We must allow Him to identify the real problem with our souls and grant to us His divine knowledge and understanding.

Most who search for a resource like *Path* have reached a crossroads in their lives. They realize something must change. Either they stay on the existing path, or they make the intentional choice to change direction. Some are so sin-aware that they have lost their God-consciousness. The eyes of some have become so downcast that they can no longer look up to recognize that they are still part of God's greater plans: "I know the plans I have for you," declares the Lord, "plans to prosper you and not to harm you, plans to give you hope and a future" (Jeremiah 29:11).

Before God created the world, He knew you were going to be reading *Path*. Your steps are sovereignly ordered. No matter what your relational or sexual brokenness, God has a plan for your life. However, it is hard to embrace hope for your future when you cannot see beyond the present circumstances. God seems distant. You ask if this pain will ever stop. *How long will I remain in bondage to my sin?*

God has made a path for you. He has not abandoned you. He will never give up on you. To face the days ahead, we must embrace the virtue of hope.

The Reality of Hope

God fully welcomes and loves us where we are. However, He does not accept our sin apart from the cross of Jesus. He is holy and righteous and therefore, does not accept sin. Our culture uses the word "acceptance" as an indication that one's behaviors are perfectly okay or even encouraged. What God feels for us is not "sloppy *agape*" (one of the Greek words for love), as if we can go on willfully choosing to embrace sinful and broken patterns. He desires that we become something greater, the men and women He designed us to be.

We must not limit our vision to the present moment, but know there is something much greater ahead. God is the One who creates and reveals what is "not yet," He is the author of our

HOPE IS NOT AN EMOTION; IT IS THE CONVICTION THAT ALL WILL TURN OUT WELL FOR ME.

hope. He puts it into our hearts to move forward, away from sin and brokenness and toward life and rest. Hope is evidence of God's pursuit of us and His presence with us.

We are making progress toward the "not yet." It is a goal set before us. There is a place of glory for us that is beyond our imagination. So we must make the often-challenging choice to look beyond the "what is" toward what is higher, greater, and when we will be with Jesus.

We are not merely human beings on a spiritual journey; we are also spiritual beings on a human journey. Our identity in Christ is not earthbound but heavenly centered. Therefore, our journey is a spiritual one, which we walk in the temporal reality of our shared humanity.

Caught up in brokenness, we have a hard time seeing beyond our humanity. Focusing on our human brokenness in the "what is," we lose sight of being a new creation destined for the "not yet." A holy tension exists between these two realities. To live within this tension, we must embrace the virtue of hope. Hope keeps us moving forward through the tension. This movement is called *life*!

If hope is simply an emotion, when we experience a good day, our hope is high; and when we encounter a difficult day, our hope is low. However, hope is not an emotion; it is the conviction that all will turn out well for me. The reason it will turn out well for me is that the very Creator of the universe lives in me! The God who knows me is alive in me. John 14:20 says, "On that day you will realize that I am in my Father, and you are in me, and I am in you." The realization, knowing our relational connection with God, is incarnational reality: God indwells, inhabits, and is living in me.

My Story

Before rededicating my life to the Lord in 1987, I struggled with an addiction to pornography and masturbation for seventeen years. I threw out my collection of pornography but wrestled with established habits. The worst times for me were right before I fell asleep. Instead of using my hand as a member of unrighteousness, I would place my hand on my chest and practice the presence of Jesus. Speaking to my troubled heart, I would say, "Jesus, You are just as close to me as You have ever been. You know my next thoughts, my next words, my next breath. You live in me! You are right here at my center. Jesus, would You enter into the places where I am struggling at this moment? Would You inhabit my anxiety and pain?"

As I prayed these prayers, Jesus would sustain me and meet me in my anxious heart. I was practicing the incarnational reality that Jesus lives in me. He was not standing far off, ready to strike me with a lightning bolt. Instead, He wanted my permission and invitation to come and meet me in my time of need.

Knowing that God lives in me creates holy anticipation in me for the "not yet" ahead. In times of distress or anxiety, I know that God will work everything for my good (Romans 8:28). Faced with a daunting challenge, I know that nothing catches God by surprise. In a quiet time, Father God spoke to my anxious heart, saying, *The unknown is not unknown to me*. As my intimacy and trust with God deepened, I began to anticipate how the Lord would meet me in my need. Instead of fearing what was ahead, I knew God had proved Himself faithful to me.

Through the empowering of the Holy Spirit, I can look up and out of myself, recognizing that my present circumstances are truly temporary. I choose to anticipate my future fulfillment rather than focus on my current absence of fulfillment. Josef Pieper writes, "In hope, man reaches 'with restless heart,' with confidence and patient expectation, toward the … arduous 'not yet' of fulfillment."[1] On our pilgrimage home, we must press through days of rain along with days of sunshine.

[1]Joseph Pieper, *On Hope* (Ignatius Press, 1986), p. 27.

The Nemesis of Hope

When consumed by our circumstances and sin, we turn easily inward on ourselves. Instead of practicing the presence of God, we practice the presence of self as expressed in our brokenness. Leanne Payne calls this "diseased introspection." We allow our self-conscious, diseased attitudes and emotions to dominate our thinking. This negative-self talk often sounds like this: *What kind of Christian are you? Why don't you just give up? You're beyond any hope. You are tainted and defiled. Who could love you?* These thoughts constantly play like old recordings in our subconscious minds, sometimes surfacing in our conscious thought. We stop being able to rest in who we are in Christ and start placing barriers to our union with God. We split off, embracing non-being, believing we are separated from God, which centers us in our sin and broken behaviors.

This incessant negative self-talk results in self-hatred and loathing such that the "what is" feels overwhelming and hopeless, and the "not yet" feels unattainable and beyond our capacity to become. Without hope, we become preoccupied with "what is" and lose sight of the "not yet." The "not yet" turns into the "never will be." Without hope, our patient expectancy becomes anxious control as we seek ways we think we can be fulfilled—or fulfill ourselves. Our heavenly vision becomes earthbound.

By cutting ourselves off from God, we focus on ourselves. We shift our center from being in Christ to being "in me," and we begin to live out of our personal resources and strength. This living out of our strength is what we call living in the flesh. When our spirit loses hope, our flesh takes over, striving for solutions that we can make happen. Instead of being Spirit-led, we begin to determine for ourselves what is best for us. We lose sight of our real problem (which we will discuss at the end of this chapter) so that the path we take results only in frustration and disappointment. Separated from our spirit and our consciousness of God, our flesh rises to resolve the problem, resulting in striving—our vain attempts to find a resolution.

In the diminishing presence of hope, at least two long tendrils choke our hearts.

Despair

One of these tendrils is despair. As the antithesis of hope, despair believes that it will turn out badly for me. Despair causes me to embrace a fatalistic mindset or a victim mentality. Leanne Payne, referring to a person caught in diseased introspection, writes:

> Richard stood, as if it were, outside himself, analyzing, hating, rejecting, pitying, despairing over himself. If we think of this in terms of a complex of inferior, negative feelings about the self, we can see that he was living from a locus of an inferiority neurosis. That was his home, his center.[2]

Despair centers us in non-being. This non-being goes beyond the mere feelings of despair; it is a mindset telling me that I am beyond hope. Josef Pieper writes, "Despair [is] a perverse anticipation of the non-fulfillment of hope."[3] Negative self-talk spirals us downward, so our minds become consumed by vain imaginations, with thought after thought embracing non-reality. We become centered in an illusionary world of our own design. We continue to distance ourselves from the reality of being centered in Christ. Embracing despair gives rise to the lie that we are beyond God's help.

Have you felt this pull to withdraw from God into the creation of your illusionary matrix?

Sloth

The pull to withdraw sets the stage for the other tendril that begins to choke our hearts: sloth. It is hard to determine which grows first, despair or sloth. But once they begin to grow, they weaken the human will and its power to choose what is right.

Sloth is an antiquated word that having lost its deeper meaning is merely associated with laziness. Laziness or idleness reveals the presence of sloth. However, laziness is the outer expression of what has become an inner stronghold. Sloth is the process whereby I stop becoming. I begin to abdicate my will and embrace passivity. I allow my earthbound vision to limit my potential. "One who is trapped in sloth (*acedia*) has neither the courage nor the will to be as great as he really is," writes Josef Pieper. "He would prefer to be less great in order to thus avoid the obligation of greatness." [4]

I start to avoid God's presence. The "not yet" becomes obscured as I put it out of view. Consumed by feelings of inadequacy or inferiority, I run from God. I believe all God can see is my failure. I wish He would leave me alone. I lose sight of incarnational reality—that I am a new creation and hidden in Him. An uneasy restlessness begins to emerge, combined with an ever-

[2]Leanne Payne, *The Healing Presence* (Baker, 1995), p. 83.
[3]Pieper, p. 47.
[4]Ibid., p. 56.

present sadness. Growing indifference to the truth allows cynicism to rise, causing me to focus on my behaviors to judge my "success" or "progress." Each failure rebuffs grace and mercy. Why should I bother? I am only going to fail again.

Striving

An alternate reaction to despair and sloth is for us to rise in our own strength—that is, striving. To battle non-becoming, we embrace restless activism. We may pursue avenues of healing that seem right to us: *If only I could read that insightful book, attend that anointed seminar, or find that perfect counselor, then I would be healed.* Looking only to behavior modification sidetracks us—for instance, focusing on sobriety, assuming our behaviors are the problem—without gaining an understanding of what is driving our behavior. We pursue knowledge restlessly, believing it will bring the healing our heart's desire. The danger is we have chosen yet another path that will result once more in despair. We keep pursuing the gaining of knowledge, which we erroneously believe will save us.

To summarize: Self-focus leads to negative self-talk; negative self-talk leads to self-hatred; self-hatred leads to despair; despair opens the door for either sloth or striving.

Where do you find yourself in this chain of events?

The Tree of Knowledge

The way of fools seems right to them, but the wise listen to advice.

–Proverbs 12:15

We seek a resource like *Path* because we have a particular problem or issue we would like resolved. You would not be reading this book if the previous paths you had chosen had brought you the solution you seek. What was the first action you took when you realized there was a problem in your life? Did you decide to pray more? Did you devise a plan to try harder? Did these actions work for you? Often we jump into action trying to modify our behaviors.

Several years ago, I heard pastor and author Timothy Keller say in a sermon, "God is not

ALL TOO OFTEN WE STRIVE TO DO SOMETHING RATHER THAN REST IN BEING SOMEONE.

after a morally restrained heart, but a supernaturally changed one." All too often, we strive to *do something* rather than rest in *being someone*. As a result, we get caught up in our thinking and pursue a path based on what we think is right. All too often, however, what we think is the problem is not. The actions and plans we make, therefore, are doomed to fail because we have not identified the correct problem.

True freedom is the result of repentance (*metanoia*), which is a change—not solely in our doing but also our thinking. The Pharisees were extremely familiar with the Scriptures; the problem was how they knew or interpreted them. Over many years we have absorbed much knowledge. Knowledge in and of itself is not the issue; the issue is how we have absorbed that knowledge. Because of our past experiences, we have created filters in how we see, hear, and receive. We need to go back to the Garden to grasp the deeper reality of our situation.

Genesis 2:9 tells us, "In the middle of the garden were the tree of life and the tree of the knowledge of good and evil." God told Adam and Eve not to eat the fruit of the tree of knowledge. But Satan enticed Eve into eating of its fruit, thereby disobeying God. In Genesis 3, we find the narrative that addresses the consequences Adam and Eve had to face as a result of eating the fruit (Genesis 3:16–19). Those consequences were the result of the Fall of humankind brought about by Adam and Eve's ignoring of this command.

Not one of the nine Hebrew words for *sin* occurs in the Genesis 3 Fall narrative. With no mention of sin, was there another problem for which Jesus came to earth? Did it involve something more than sin? Was there something even deeper that Jesus accomplished for you and me?

When Adam and Eve ate of the forbidden fruit, according to Genesis 3, they took into themselves the knowledge of good and evil. Doing so, their source and foundation of reality changed. Why did God not want them to have a knowledge of both evil and good? God wanted Adam and Eve to trust Him as their source of the knowledge of good and evil. He did not want them to create their own standards for good and evil, but to look to Him for clarity and delineation.

After the Fall, however, they viewed everything through the lens of knowledge—their way of thinking. We have inherited the same lens. Bob Hamp, in his book *Think Differently Live Differently* indicates that the significant reason Jesus came to earth may not have been for the breaking of a rule, but for what changed as a result. The gaining of knowledge replaced relationship with Jesus as the tree of life.

Jesus' greater purpose in coming to earth was to be the connection—the way for us to get into right relationship with the Father. Adam and Eve's capacity to see and hear rightly changed in a moment when they ate the fruit. In that very moment, as their spiritual eyes closed, their soulish eyes were opened; they went from life to death! The knowledge of good and evil replaced their true source of life.

Knowledge in and of itself cannot impart life in any capacity, apart from Jesus. Doctrines cannot produce life in us. Not being centered in Jesus, we pursue "good" knowledge to overcome "evil" knowledge, which in the end, will not yield life. Only through the Person of Jesus can we find life.

The problem Jesus came to solve was not just to address bad behavior, then, but to restore the true source and foundation of life. The Pharisees believed that their knowledge made them good and gave them the strength to be good. They chastised Jesus for His lack of knowledge. Jesus, however, using bread as an example, warned the disciples about "the leaven of the Pharisees" (Matthew 16:6, NKJV)—although the disciples missed what He was saying by focusing on literal bread. Jesus healed the woman bent over for decades (Luke 13:11), but all the Jewish leaders could focus on was that He did so on the Sabbath. They chastised Jesus, who restored life to this woman—His very purpose for coming!—because they could not see. All these examples represent the knowledge of good and evil: seeing without sight.

Our frantic pursuit of knowledge can eclipse our love of God. Do we truly know what our problem is? Have we shifted our focus onto our behaviors rather than on the real issue? Have we begun to understand that our outward behaviors reflect an inner problem? What are the filters that prevent me from seeing aright? We are easily distracted, believing the goal is merely behavior modification. We need the capacity to see that there is something within us that needs the healing presence of Jesus.

So What *Is* our Problem?

We search and hope for something more. We sense that there has to be something beyond our daily pain and struggles. We can come to the point of making the courageous choice to believe God will meet us. It is a fearful and difficult choice to believe and to hope. Believing entails the relinquishing of our control. We must face the unknown and what lies beneath in our hearts.

There is a place within you that wants to believe; otherwise, you would not be reading these words at this very moment. Choosing to believe means, you can face your fears regarding God. It means you can allow God to remove the distorted filters through which you see and know Him.

I often pray for God to expose any area in which I am remaking Him into my image. Many of us make "designer gods" that fit our preferences. We need to enter a true relationship with the real God. The God I seek is He who is always there, who knows my voice, who knows my heart, who always sees me. God always sees me—not with eyes searching for what is wrong, but with eyes that yearn to draw me toward His healing word for my aching soul.

We are more than merely a problem waiting for God to solve. Rise up, beloved daughter, and precious son! Your struggles do not make you chronically unique. They make you human. We are one body, struggling together with multiple relational and sexual issues. Our struggles do not separate us but join us because of our shared humanity. All of us are broken in some capacity and need a Savior. Your need is no greater or no less than the need of those who surround you.

The way to wholeness and freedom is the same for all: following Jesus, who is our path through the wilderness. Understanding this is a *metanoia* moment, a change in our thinking. We stop letting our behavior, our temptations, and our circumstances define us. God's intervention enables us to see and know Him aright. In so doing, we will eventually see and know others and ourselves aright.

In the early years of my "process"—beginning to face and address my brokenness within—I

I WAS PURSUING THE HEALING OF MY SOUL RATHER THAN THE HEALER OF MY SOUL.

was pursuing the healing of my soul rather than the Healer of my soul. As I began to relinquish control of my process into His hands, deep, almost imperceptible changes began to occur within me. The constant presence of God's love began gently to break down my walls, the barriers I had created over many years. Slowly He lifted my eyes to see into His face, a face full of grace and mercy. Looking up and out of myself, I waited for His healing word for my soul.

He does speak to us, you know. The mighty and majestic Creator of the universe is waiting to speak to you. Will you risk believing He will? Will you let Him reveal Himself to you in whatever way He chooses? God does not fit us into a box; neither should we try to fit Him into one.

Do you see in yourself the progression of self-focus that leads to sloth or striving? Did you obtain this book as another attempt to get healed or to change your behavior? Are you only searching for the "right" knowledge that will somehow help you achieve your idea of perfection? Right now would be a great time to shift your focus from striving to do better to focus on knowing Him better, which is my hope for you! Shift your focus from your behavior to the Savior who longs to connect you to the Father as your source. This shift will create hope, and hope will lead you forward on this journey.

As you begin this path through the wilderness, choose to make hope a belief. "His divine power has given us everything we need for a godly life through our knowledge of him who called us by his own glory and goodness" (2 Peter 1:3). The knowledge of Him is not just knowing the Bible, the book of the Lord, but also knowing the Lord of the book. I hope you will read the following chapters not to merely gain knowledge, which has a practical application but to seek God's deeper, intimate, relational knowledge.

Prayer

Lord, You know my innermost thoughts and struggles. You are acquainted with my pain, grief, and sorrow. You know right where I am when I lack the words to describe my circumstances.

I need Your discernment to define and reveal my brokenness. Lord, show me where my problem truly lies. How have I pursued wrong paths that led only to disappointment and fear?

I turn to You. I need Your presence to lead and guide me. Impart to me Your grace and mercy as I enter this dedicated season of seeking You more deeply. Help me to lay down any restless activism in my pursuit of healing rather than the pursuit of You as my Healer. Reveal where I am striving instead of resting in Your care. Please help me to yield and release control trusting in Your plan for me. May I truly come to know that my hope is secure in You because You dwell in me. Lead me in Your way everlasting.

Soul Work

1. How have despair and sloth been present in your life?

2. In what ways have you pursued the healing of your soul rather than the Healer of your soul?

3. Draw a picture of God and include yourself in the picture. You do not have to be a great artist here; stick figures are acceptable! You may use whatever media you like. Please do not make this a doctrinal expression or a theologically correct image. Make it an expression more of the way you see or image God in your heart. Save this picture for future reference.

Journaling Moment

Set aside a time when you will not be interrupted or disturbed to complete this assignment. Dedicate the time to the Lord and invite the Holy Spirit's direction. Most of us suffer from some form of self-hatred. Ask the Holy Spirit to reveal any deep places of self-hatred and how it has limited your relationships and capacity to be an image-bearer of God. Write down what comes to mind, no matter how foolish or meaningless it may seem. Sometimes memories, feelings, or images may come to mind. Write them down. Then ask the Holy Spirit for His truth and revelation as to why these things came to mind. Write down whatever you feel He is speaking to your heart and let His words sink in.

TWO

The Big Picture

BY BOB PERDUE

Congratulations! You have embraced hope enough to push forward into this next chapter of the journey. Remember the truth we learned in chapter 1—that we are spiritual beings on a human journey. That human journey is complicated by negative self-talk, despair, sloth, striving, and more, as well as by behaviors and attitudes and mindsets that have led us to this path in the wilderness. At this point, these behaviors and attitudes and mindsets may be your focus. But to find deep healing and get to the root issues, we must step back to see the bigger picture, the larger story.[5]

Let's return to the beginning, back to the Garden of Eden. When God created Adam and Eve, you and I were in our spiritual parents—part of God's plan from the beginning—and His plan for us was good. But because of the entrance of sin, we never got to experience the life God intended for us. Even so, we were in the heart of God, and He created us in His image. He made us His sons and daughters. He gave us good hearts, and He longs to commune with us as He did with Adam and Eve.

This interactive, affirming, ongoing relationship with the Father is called life. (See diagram 1) Because our hearts are good and we are loved unconditionally, we are free to live out of our hearts and to trust them. We are free to express ourselves, grow, explore, risk, question, and live. Life expresses what is in our hearts. This is the life we were always meant to live. This is the self we were always meant to be. This is our true self—the self as God intended it. This is the life we want and the life God urges us to choose.

[5]A large part of this chapter is taken from Bob Perdue, *Ten Life Choices* (CrossHouse Publishing, 2010).

Diagram

LIFE

Good sense of value, community, power, male/female and true identity

But let's pause here for a moment. Go back and reread the previous paragraph, substituting *we*, *our*, and *us* with *I*, *my*, and *me*. For example, *This is the life I was always meant to live.* Does it sound too good to be true?

Let's take it another step. Go back and cross out the singular pronouns and write in your own name: For example, *This is the life* ______ *was always meant to live.* That whole paragraph becomes foundational for your hope. God created you for more!

What Constitutes Positive Identity?

One of the benefits of living in relationship with the Father is that He gives His children a positive identity. We know who we are, and it is good. This positive identity differs from what psychologists call positive self-esteem. Self-esteem is how we feel about ourselves; positive identity is who we really are. As we read through God's creation of man and woman in Genesis 2, it is clear that positive identity was part of the original creation.

There are four components to positive identity:

1. Value

This is the sense that we have spiritual value and worth. Our value is derived not from good things we do for God, but from the fact that we are created in the image of God. God created Adam and Eve and called them good. What had they done to deserve that affirmation? Nothing. Their goodness was part of the way God made them—their true selves. Knowing our true value is a vital part of positive identity.

2. Community

This is the sense that we belong, that we are part of something bigger than ourselves, and that we have something to offer. God created us out of community ("Let us make mankind in our image," Genesis 1:26) and for community ("It is not good for the man to be alone," Genesis 2:18). An infant is "we" with its mother before he or she becomes an "I." Knowing that you belong to a caring community is a vital part of positive identity.

3. Power

This is the sense that we have choices and the ability to choose. God created us with a choice and the power to make that choice. He created two trees, the tree of life and the tree of the knowledge of good and evil, and He gave man and woman power over which of those trees to choose. Limits to our power by God-given boundaries help keep that power from destroying our virtue. Knowing that we have the power to make good choices is a vital part of positive identity.

4. Man/Woman

This is the sense of how comfortable and secure we are with our sexuality. God created humankind specifically as "male and female" (Genesis 1:27). The difference between the sexes is part of the design. The unique ways God created men and women allow them to complement each other as they move together toward intimacy. Being comfortable with who we are as men and women a vital part of positive identity.

Since all four of these qualities are part of the true self that God created us to be, it stands to reason that any movement away from these qualities indicates that we are moving away from the life God intended for us. In fact, any time we move away from life, our positive identity suffers because we are trying to find life in something other than God; and since God gives us our positive identity, we lose sight of it as we wander from Him. These components of positive identity become good criteria, therefore, for judging whether we are living in this intimate relationship with God called life.

This is a good time for us to pause and ask a few probing personal questions:

Do I understand my value as a person or do I tend to base my value on performance or behavior?

Do I enter fully into community and feel part of something bigger than myself or do I tend to isolate from others and "perform" in public?

Do I use my power carefully to make good choices, or do I tend to play the victim, as if I have no power to make positive choices?

Do I feel the need to use my power to control those around me?

Am I comfortable with being a man or woman, or do I tend to act as though I have something to prove?

Results of Wounding

Life and positive identity go hand in hand. By asking the above questions about our positive identity, we can take a regular inventory of our lives.

Our tendency, however, is to judge the quality of our lives by other criteria: Am I happy? Am I getting what I want? Am I achieving all my goals? These criteria actually grow out of a view of God as a resource to make my life work the way I think it should rather than viewing God as life itself.

In the Garden of Eden, Adam and Eve lived out of their true selves and enjoyed a relationship with God, seeing Him as life itself. He was their life, and they enjoyed life … until sin.

Sin separates us from God and interrupts the relationship called life. (See diagram 2) The Bible says, "Your iniquities have separated you from your God" (Isaiah 59:2) and "All have sinned and fall short of the glory of God" (Romans 3:23). Since we all were born into sin, we were born outside the experience of life that God intended. As sinners, without life but still created in the image of God, with a God-given passion for life, we are driven to try to find life on our own terms.

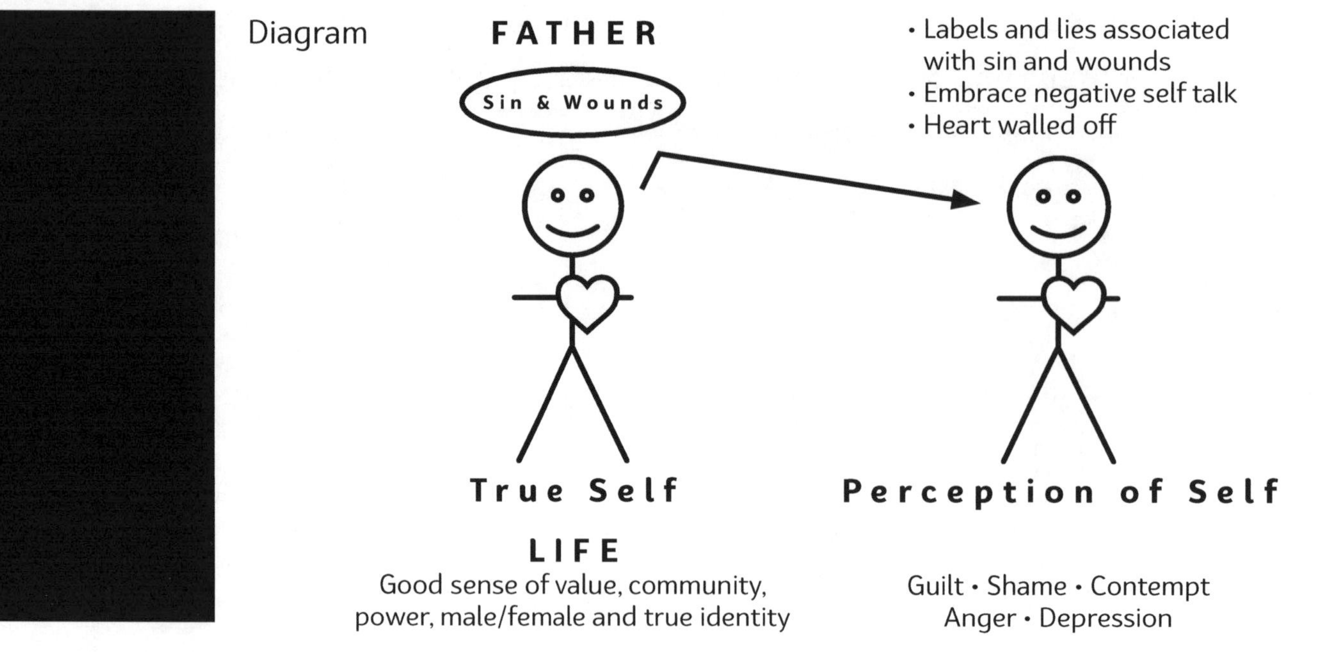

Our individual sins grow out of the many ways we try to draw life out of things other than God. Unfortunately, these attempts just increase the separation. Our original sin, inherited from Adam, separated us from life as God intended it; and our own sin furthers the separation. This makes it impossible for us to see ourselves as a reflection of the Father, created in His image. Instead, we begin to see ourselves as a reflection of our sin. (See diagram 2)

Complicating this scenario is the introduction of wounds. (See diagram 2) Wounds are sins that are committed against us by others. These wounds include all forms of abuse, rejection, abandonment, and neglect. They carry with them specific attacks on our positive identity. Here are four of these attacks resulting from wounding.

1. Worthlessness

As a wounded person, I feel devalued. The violation of me by another leaves me feeling abused and worthless. Since my sense of value is damaged, I strive to prove that I am okay (performance) or else I sink into the idea that I have no value (victim).

2. Distrust

Since wounds are usually inflicted by someone in my community—a trusted family member, authority figure, or friend—my sense of community is shattered by an overwhelming feeling of distrust. I cannot be part of the community because I cannot trust anyone to get too close. I begin either to isolate from others or to develop a public persona that people will accept. (More on this later.)

3. Powerlessness or Control

In my wounding, I usually experience being overpowered by the one who inflicted the wound. Things happened (abuse, abandonment, rejection, humiliation) that were outside my control. I felt that I had no power. As a result, my sense of power is affected adversely. I react by either giving up all power and letting others rule me completely (victim) or by developing the attitude that I must always be in control in order to be okay.

4. Sexual Confusion

Sexual wounding (through abuse, exposure to inappropriate sexual situations or images, or imbalance in the parental example of opposite-sex relationship) causes confusion about sexuality. Feelings of insecurity as men or women, same-sex attraction, rejection of sex, or obsession with sex—all result from the loss of sexual identity through wounding.

Men who are wounded in this way may overcompensate and become machismo to prove they are men. Or they may become passive, or reject aspects of being a man altogether and move toward homosexuality. Women who are wounded in this way may overcompensate by becoming overly syrupy sweet, or they may become militant to prove the power of women, or they may reject aspects of being a woman altogether and move toward homosexuality.

Let's pause for a moment and look again at the diagrams. Do you tend to see yourself as the person in diagram 1, living out of your heart with a positive identity? Or do you tend to see yourself as the person in diagram 2, living with a broken identity as a reaction to your sin and wounds? If you see yourself as the person in diagram 2, which parts of a positive identity have been broken for you? Identifying these at the beginning of this process will aid you greatly as you move forward to choose life.

Negative Self-Talk

Our sin and wounds separate us from the affirming voice of God, and thus from our positive identity. We are left in confusion about who we really are. In this void, the powerful voice of our sin and wounds speaks up to put a label on us—a label that identifies us or connects us with our sin and wounds. This is the negative self-talk in our minds that we referred to in the last chapter. It tells us things like this:

I am a pervert.
I am a failure.
I am inadequate.
I am so undisciplined.
I am a terrible parent.
I am a disappointment.
I am a loser.
I am damaged goods.
I am stupid.

These labels and many more represent the false perception of self that we may adopt because of our sin and wounds. The labels we wear are reinforced by the lies of the enemy that circulate in our minds as more negative self-talk:

I will never amount to anything.
I will never overcome this habit.
I have nothing to offer others.
If people know who I really am, they will not want to be with me.

Satan is "the father of lies" (John 8:44) and introduces, then fuels, these lies. In time they become a stronghold in our minds and empower the labels we have chosen. We not only "become" what we fear, but we act out of that identity.

Sheryl's Story

I received a phone call from Sheryl, a beautiful young mother of three. She could barely make it through a sentence without breaking down and sobbing into the telephone. The only line I could understand amidst the sobs was, "I'm a terrible mother." When I met with Sheryl later, she began to share that she could not seem to love her children the way other mothers did. She did not want to hold or hug them. Although they wanted to cling to her, she would not allow it. She saw other mothers cuddling their children and knew this was what she *should* do—so she must be a bad mother.

As we talked about her relationship with her heavenly Father, she revealed that years before, as a teenager, she had had an abortion. It was apparent to me that she was completely broken over the choice she had made in a desperate situation. But she did not realize that, as a result of that sin, she had accepted a label. What kind of mother would kill her unborn baby? A terrible mother. She had labeled herself a terrible mother before she ever gave birth to her first child. She was deriving her identity from her sin and was now living out of that identity.

Sheryl had to make several life choices to cast off this label and begin to believe in who she really was—a precious daughter of the Father and a loving mother.

Our separation from the affirming voice of God and our acceptance of the powerful message of false labels and lies convince us of our negative identity. The end result of embracing this negative identity is a deep sense of shame. (See right portion in diagram 3) Shame is the overwhelming feeling that there is something wrong with me. Other people are okay and have it together but not me. Lewis Smedes, in his book *Shame and Grace*, explains:

> The feeling of shame is about our very selves—not about some bad thing we did or said but about what we are. It tells us that we are unworthy. Totally. It is not as if a few seams in the garment of our selves need stitching; the whole fabric is frayed. We feel that we are unacceptable. And to feel that is a life-wearying heaviness. Shame-burdened people are the sort whom Jesus had in mind when he invited the "weary and heavy laden" to trade their heaviness for his lightness. [6]

Shame is an extremely powerful emotion that elicits various responses in us.

[6] Lewis Smedes, *Shame and Grace* (HarperCollins, 1993), p. 6.

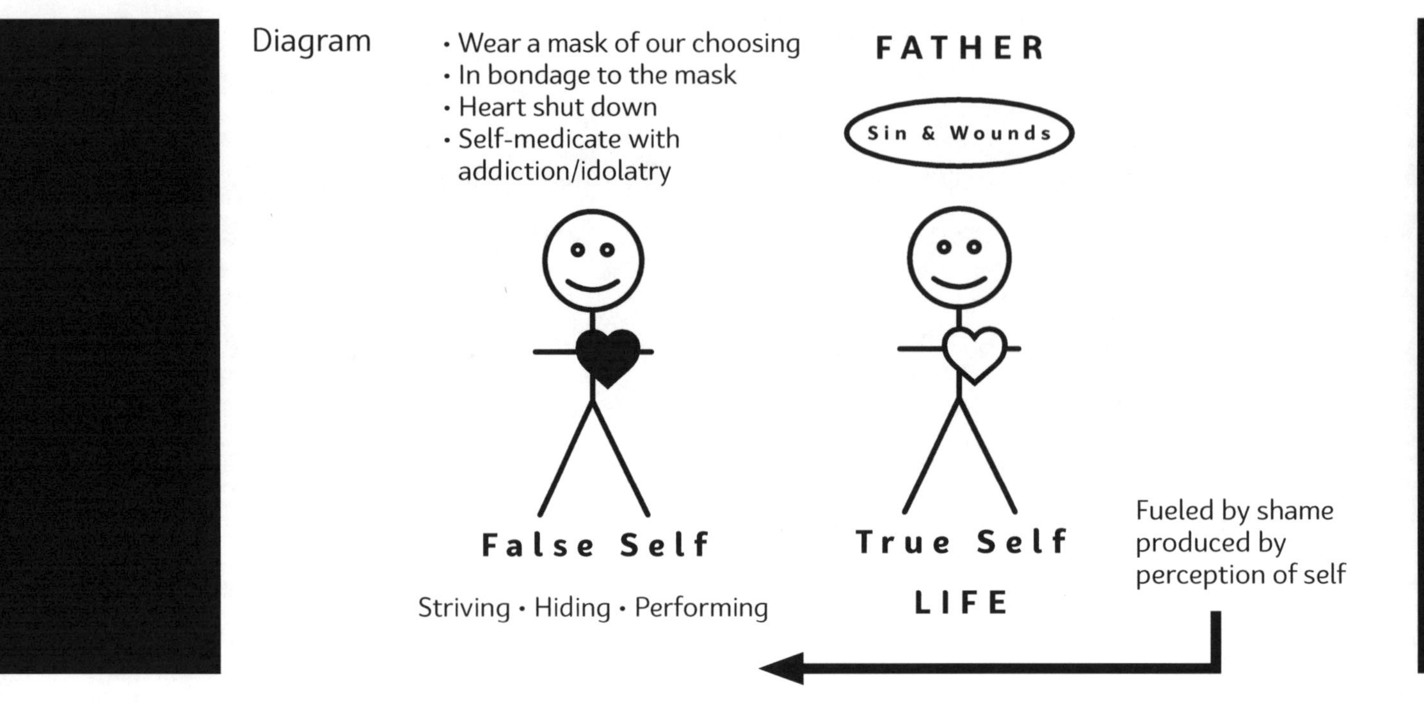

Repentance

The first possible response to shame is repentance. Adam and Eve experienced shame when they sinned against God in the Garden. God's subsequent conversation with them seems to indicate that the purpose of their shame was to lead them to repentance. He asked them questions to which He already knew the answers in order to get them to confess their sin and seek forgiveness: "Where are you? Who told you that you were naked? Did you eat the forbidden fruit?"

God knew the answers to these questions. He knows everything. He wanted Adam and Eve to turn the shame that caused them to hide from Him into contrite hearts that returned to Him in honesty and repentance.

Contempt

Adam and Eve did not choose to turn their shame into repentance. Instead, they chose the path of contempt. Contempt is the energy of shame directed against someone we feel is responsible for our sin and wounding. It is a powerful feeling of malice against another. Adam blamed Eve for his sin, and Eve blamed the serpent. When we choose the path of contempt, we are basically saying that our problem, sin, wound, or label must be someone else's fault and that someone else must pay.

This type of contempt directed against others interferes with our relationships and makes it hard for us to get along with others. We expect others to hurt us, so we find reasons not to enter into close, meaningful relationships, even with God. If we are rebelling against authority, loners, hard to get along with, or critical, we probably struggle with a deep contempt for others that comes out of shame. Community is impossible for us if we choose this route, and we are destined to live in either shallow relationships with others or in isolation.

Self-Contempt

If we see ourselves as the ultimate cause of our wounding, self-contempt is the third way we may deal with our shame. Self-contempt interferes deeply with the positive identity God gave us. We blame ourselves for the bad things that have happened to us. Our label is our fault, which increases the power of our negative self-talk.

Abuse victims often feel there must have been something about them that caused them to be chosen for the abuse. Deep inside they think, *It's my fault*. The end result of self-contempt is self-hatred that shows itself in various ways: depression, suicidal thoughts, poor hygiene, self-mutilation, passivity, unhealthy lifestyle choices (like drug or alcohol abuse or unprotected sexual activity), and others. All of these can be linked to self-contempt that comes out of shame.

Wearing a Mask

Everyone has sin and wounds, so we must all learn to deal properly with shame. Shame that leads to repentance is the path to life. Shame that leads to contempt is a detour away from life and ultimately leads to hiding. Most find it easier to hide than to repent. Hiding behind fig leaves, and then behind trees, was the first response of Adam and Eve to their shame.

The identity that rises out of our sin and wounding does not feel acceptable and drives us to hide. (No one enters a room and announces, "Hi, I'm Bob, and I'm a pervert!") We cannot be who we believe we are, so we must create another persona. The easiest way to hide is to find a way to present ourselves in public that is both believable and fairly easy to maintain.

This public image or false self is a reaction to our shame. (See diagram 3)

The false self is like a mask we choose to wear in order to keep others from knowing what we really look like—what we see as the real truth about us. Our choice of mask is based on what we are familiar with, what works in our social setting, and what best fits our abilities and personality. The athlete, the student, the religious zealot, the fixer, the control freak, the success, the performer, the clown, and the know-it-all are all examples of the false self.

The longer we wear our masks, the farther we get from our true selves. Soon we find ourselves hiding not only from others but from ourselves and even from God. The freedom to live out of our hearts is completely gone. Our hearts hold a dark secret that cannot be revealed. Ashamed of who we are, we must also shut down our emotions, which are the keys to the heart, so that nothing of the secret is revealed. We cannot afford to feel because our feelings will take us back to the labels and lies. We are now forced to live out of our masks. People come to expect us to be smart, athletic, funny, or successful. We are bound to a certain role, while the grip of the mask gets tighter and tighter. *Bondage*, *drudgery*, *boredom*—these are words that describe our life. It does not resemble the life we were created to live. And the self-talk begins: *There has to be more to life than this.*

And there is!

Carla visited a Bible study at church with the wife of a friend of mine. As the women shared concerns and prayer requests, it became apparent that Carla was suffering from severe exhaustion and slipping into depression. As the group began to uncover the root of the problem, they found that Carla was holding down a part-time job while keeping her three elementary-age children involved in all the extracurricular activities they wanted and doing all she could to support them—taking them to practices, serving as team mom and room mother, making snacks for every group.

It seemed simple to suggest to Carla that she slow down, but even the idea was unthinkable for her. She depended on her performance as "Super Mom" to feel good about herself. At the same time, it exhausted her, keeping her from celebrating her children and trapping her in an endless cycle of doing. But that was her identity, and she was unwilling to change it.

Over time, we begin to seek relief for the pain of wearing the mask and the exhaustion that comes from performance. Our lives are not flowing freely from our hearts; they are forced, performance-driven, and hard to maintain. (See diagram 3) We spend all our time and effort striving to make life work and keeping the mask in place.

Self-medication becomes the only way to survive the pain and exhaustion. The medicine we choose is a combination of what appeals to us and what is part of our lives. Pornography, alcohol, drugs, work, money, possessions, sports, church, sexual exploits, travel, food, relationships—any of these, or others, or a combination, yields the good feeling that allows us to keep going. (See diagram 3)

Addiction to any of these contributes to our feeling of shame—which we will look in more detail in chapter 4—and only fuels the cycle. For now, we see that the weakness of giving in to addiction reinforces our negative identity and binds us more deeply to the mask. We now enter a cycle of striving and indulging, striving to prove we are okay and living behind the mask. When exhausted, we indulge in something that brings us pleasure, it also drives us to strive harder to prove we are okay.

Any attempt on our part to reconnect with God without taking off the mask will end up in religious performance. But if we are unwilling, to be honest before the Lord, we reduce our relationship with Him to a system of religion that maximizes "doing" and minimizes "being." We cannot "be" in relationship with God because of our negative identity; we can only "do" things to appease Him and try to convince Him (and others and ourselves) that we are okay.

The Good News

Do you see the cycle? Does this sound like the life Jesus died to give us? Didn't He promise rest? Does He really want us to grin and bear it until heaven when all our striving will cease? Churches today are caught in this cycle—desiring life, desiring God, but powerless to get there because of our inability or unwillingness to take off our masks. The result is empty, powerless religion in which we end up judging others for what we ourselves are doing or not doing, instead of enjoying life and inviting them into it. We have reduced the good news of the Gospel to rules and regulations.

But the Gospel is good news; it really is! The really good news is that we can choose life. Jesus said, "I have come that they may have life, and have it to the full" (John 10:10). And He said, "I am the way, the truth, and the life. No one comes to the Father except through me" (John 14:6). How we come to know Him is the subject of our next chapter.

Prayer

Lord, You see what I cannot. You know what I do not. I welcome Your presence to begin the process of seeing and knowing that which will enable me to embrace the journey ahead. I invite you to start the deeper healing necessary for my soul. I acknowledge that I have allowed my wounds, sins, and thinking to influence my choices and to limit my becoming.

I thank You, Lord, for being with me on this path through the wilderness. I thank You that it is not up to me to figure out what is wrong, to identify every wound or injury, or to strive in my own strength for perfection. I admit I have already been walking down those paths, and they have not yielded what I had hoped. I choose in this moment to release my control, to the best of my capacity, into Your capable hands. What seems impossible for me is not impossible for You. Please help me trust You more with my process. Help me let You determine my steps.

Lord Jesus, help me choose life. When I face the challenges that lie before me, remind me that life is always the choice I can make because You are with me. Holy Spirit, I need Your truth when the enemy or my areas of self-hatred are speaking lies to me. I need Your discernment and wisdom not to diverge from this path—Your path, Lord Jesus.

I release to You, Lord, my hopes and expectations. I welcome Your centering Holy Spirit that I may rest in this journey and not strive. May I know more and more what it means to abide in You and Your love. I am forever grateful to You for Your promise never to leave or forsake me. I am my Beloved's, and He is mine.

Soul Work

1. The four components of positive identity are value, community, power, and man/woman. How have your life experiences influenced these four components, which resulted in your having less than a positive identity? How have you reacted to the wounds in these four areas?
2. How has your perception of self created pathways into bondage (as seen in the diagram on the left side)?

3. Describe your negative self-talk. What are your areas of self-contempt? What masks do you wear and when do you wear them?

Journaling Moment

As you read in this chapter, we have the tendency, due to the Fall, to reflect our wounds and sin rather than the image of God. We view ourselves through a filter of brokenness. For this journaling assignment, ask the Holy Spirit to reveal to you how you see yourself. What image(s) comes to mind? How do you reflect your brokenness rather than the face of God? Now ask the Holy Spirit to show you how the Father sees you. What image(s) comes to mind? Write down what He shows you.

THREE

Knowing Jesus

'FOR IN HIM WE LIVE AND MOVE AND HAVE OUR BEING.' AS SOME OF YOUR OWN POETS HAVE SAID, 'WE ARE HIS OFFSPRING.'

ACTS 17:28

The Creator of the universe has placed within us the desire to know Him. The deepest desire given to us by God is to know and be known by Him. Because of this desire, we are compelled to search for God. This search becomes an ache and a drive. Our response is either to draw nearer to God, seeking true intimacy (a heart-knowing relationship), or to walk away from Him, seeking false intimacy (for example, through fantasy, addiction, codependency, or other means).

Jesus Christ is the embodiment of life itself, life as God intended us to experience. And Jesus longs for us to know Him.

How can I describe the One who is so beyond my comprehension? If He were to appear suddenly before us, we would fall as if dead due to His holiness and righteousness. Yet Jesus asks you and me to draw near to Him, even with our sin and brokenness! Jesus is enthroned majestically in the heavens, far above us, yet He calls you and me by a name both intimate and personal: *Beloved.*

Throughout the gospels, Jesus used multiple illustrations to enable us to understand the deeper, spiritual ways of knowing Him. One such example is when He identified Himself with bread and wine, saying, "Take and eat; this is my body... Drink from it, all of you. This is my blood…" (Matthew 26:26–28). In the simplest of terms, Jesus was associating hunger for food with a hunger for Himself.

But the hunger for Him goes even deeper.

Jesus As Bread and Water

I am the bread of life. Whoever comes to me will never go hungry, and whoever believes in me will never be thirsty.

– John 6:35

What comes to mind when you think of bread? Do you think of a sandwich, with bread as just the outer covering for the tasty content? Or is it an optional part of a larger meal: "Would you like bread with your meal?" "No, thank you, I'd rather not fill up on bread." In our carb-conscious culture, bread is undesirable and avoided. Bread no longer has the significance it had in centuries past.

Two thousand years ago, bread was not an optional side dish but could be the main meal. If people lacked bread, they would starve. When Jesus indicated that He was the bread of life, those hearing His words understood them far differently than we do today. Jesus was saying, "I am a necessity." The promise that those who came to Him would not go hungry, moreover, went beyond the physical. Jesus was saying, "I will satisfy your deepest hunger—to know and be known by God."

Jesus also identified Himself with living water. Like bread, without water, life would cease. One of the meanings of the word believes (pisteuo) in the above Scripture signifies "to have a reliance upon." Just as those in centuries past relied on bread for life, we likewise must rely on Jesus for life.

We must follow God for who He is and what He intends, not for what we want and what we prefer.[7]

– Ravi Zacharias

Today we have many options for bread and water. Would you like rye, sourdough, or whole grain? Would you like filtered, sparkling, or flavored water? We can choose whatever suits our fancy. These designer options align with our personal preferences. But they do not apply to Jesus. He says, "I am the way and the truth and the life" (John 14:6). Scripture's use of the definite article *the* is significant, indicating that there is no other way, truth, or life. There are not many ways, only one—the One. When we try to pigeonhole Jesus to fit our conditions, we are in danger of conforming Him to our image or preferences.

We must follow Jesus based on His principles and not our preferences. The Scriptures are

[7]Ravi Zacharias, @RaviZacharias, Twitter, May 26, 2016, 2:39 A.M.

not a buffet where we pick and choose what we like, taking them out of context. The Bible should be studied in its entirety; each book took in the context relating to the whole.

When Jesus invites us to believe, He is not teaching a doctrinal concept but an intuitive way of knowing—head and heart joined, left and right brain working together.

And there is yet a deeper understanding that we must grasp. Jesus desires to be our inner reality, the core identity in which "we live and move and have our being" (Acts 17:28).

Jesus As Our Identity

Identity in our culture is significant. Social media provides multiple boxes to check for defining who we are. We find any number of categories from which to choose, an ever-expanding variety. "I am" statements reveal aspects of personal identity: I am a teacher. I am a Christian. I am an addict. I am damaged goods. These "I am" statements are an outward communication of an inner identification we have determined over time and with experience.

How you identify yourself is crucial. Your identity is the focal point of how you live your life. "For as he thinketh in his heart, so is he" (Proverbs 23:7, KJV). Identity motivates you to search not only for connection and recognition but also for security.

Knowing Jesus affects your identity significantly and, hence, your security. If you have made Him your Lord and Savior, He has become your true center. Lacking security in Jesus as the core of your identity (identity = self), you will turn to the temporal rather than the eternal to define your "self." "In our culture, the three gods we do trust for security are possessions, power, and human relationships. To a greater or lesser extent, all of us worship this false trinity."[8] But if you find your identity in anything apart from Christ, you are living in a self split off from Him (that is, the false self); whereas when you are secure in your identity as centered in Christ, you will live in and through Him (that is, the true self).

Once we invite Jesus into our lives, He regenerates our center, making it one with Him. God has established His divine core in us, replacing the broken core that earlier defined us. Centered in our spirit, we are living in our true self. "On that day you will realize that I am in my

[8]Gerald G. May, *Addiction and Grace* (HarperOne, 2007), p. 32.

Father, and you are in me, and I am in you" (John 14:20). Before Jesus lived in you, your spirit was dead to God. Now you are truly a new creation, your spirit alive in Christ.

A significant aspect of repentance (metanoia) has to do with a change in your thinking. For you to experience the life Jesus desires, requires you to make an important realization. Your broken relationships and the dysfunctional or abusive experiences of your past can no longer define who you are. They no longer have the power to limit who you can become. But it is a challenge to change years of "stinking thinking" (faulty belief systems and lie-based identity) to believe this spiritual truth and reality.

> The fallen self cannot know itself. We do not know who we are, and will search for an identity in someone or something other than God until we find ourselves in Him.[9]

Living out of the false self centers our focus in our emotions, thoughts, and experiences. We give power to our earthbound past to shape us. We give authority to the world, the flesh (that is, the false self), and the devil to define who we are. Our sexual and relational brokenness, instead of being an aspect of our past, often becomes a label to describe who we are now. Sin, rather than the Son, is the authority that defines us. Rather than being transformed into His image, we allow the world to be the source that shapes and defines us.

Are you not weary of living this way?

> I have been crucified with Christ, and I no longer live, but Christ lives in me. The life I now live in the body, I live by faith in the Son of God, who loved me and gave Himself for me.
>
> – Galatians 2:20

OUR SEXUAL AND RELATIONAL BROKENNESS, INSTEAD OF BEING AN ASPECT OF OUR PAST, OFTEN BECOMES A LABEL TO DESCRIBE WHO WE ARE NOW.

[9]Leanne Payne, *The Broken Image* (Crossway, 1981), p. 149.

When you invited Jesus into your heart, He did not come in to spackle the large cracks in the walls of your heart. He was not adding a new coat of paint to cover up the old stains. Jesus created a new foundation. He came to exchange your finite existence with infinite reality. "For you died, and your life is now hidden with Christ in God" (Colossians 3:3). Do you get it? Your false self died, but you are now wonderfully alive, connected to your core with the Creator of the universe, who calls you friend.

We are tripartite beings consisting of body, soul, and spirit. In this way, we reflect the Trinitarian being of God, to which Paul refers in 1 Thessalonians 5:23: "May God himself, the God of peace, sanctify you through and through. May your whole spirit, soul and body be kept blameless at the coming of our Lord Jesus Christ." Our beings also reflect the tri-fold design of the Tabernacle (and later Temple) of the people of Israel, which contained the outer court (representing the body), the Holy Place (representing the soul), and the Holy of Holies (representing the spirit). Paul emphasized this by indicating that we are living temples (2 Corinthians 6:16).

Your body connects with your exterior surroundings. Your soul—containing your mind, emotions, and will—connects you with God, others, and yourself. Your spirit is the deepest part of you, the true self, which intimately connects you with the very Person of God. God is no longer just a concept; He has become a relational actuality. We are to live from this true self.

This new identity is a gift—an extension of God's grace to you—that cannot be earned or formed through your own strength. You do not have to do righteous things to become a righteous man or woman. Through faith in Jesus Christ, God makes you a righteous man or woman, which results in our capacity to do righteous things. Behavior does not determine identity; identity determines behavior. By giving us the gift of a completely new identity, Jesus creates the capacity for us to change our behavior.

Are you beginning to comprehend the deeper reality of God's marvelous design and image within you? How have you allowed your attractions or behaviors to determine your identity?

Let me state once again that you are not merely a human being on a spiritual journey; you are a spiritual being on a human journey. Your identity is in your spirit, centered in Christ. The marvelous work of the cross of Jesus invalidates any identity based on attachment or sources other than Jesus. You died but are now alive in a way foreign to the world's comprehension.

Here is an everyday example. A cup of boiling water and a tea bag are two separate entities. But place the teabag in the water and the water changes by taking into itself the essence of the tea leaves. It is no longer water but has become tea. In spiritual terms, Jesus is the tea bag, and you are the water. The very essence of Christ now permeates your being and becomes one with your spirit. *You are changed.* Your center has shifted. Every aspect of your old identity, the false self, has shifted from being centered in the flesh (living a self-focused life, centered in the soul) to your true self now being centered in your spirit. You have been born again.

Water baptism is a physical expression of a spiritual reality. Certain denominations recognize baptism as a sacrament—an outward and visible sign of an inward and spiritual grace. The submerging under the water symbolizes the false self, as now crucified and buried (see Romans 6:3–5). Rising out of the water, we partake of the same power that raised Christ from the grave.

Are you grasping this profound spiritual reality? Your sin, your broken relationships, your family of origin, your addictions, your job, or whatever noun you place after the pronoun your—none of that is who you are! Is this not cause for radical rejoicing? This is the reality of being alive in Jesus. To know who you are, you no longer have to trust in the tree of the knowledge of good and evil—as if knowledge alone were the source of definition and security. Personal relationship—being one with Jesus—goes far beyond mere knowledge.

You have gained the incredible reality of who you are. But because you are a Christian, that knowledge and understanding stem from your relationship with Jesus and by the revelation of the Holy Spirit. This personal knowledge connects the split between head and heart, divine knowledge forever linked with divine relationship. You are no longer the frozen chosen, cut off from the heart.

In the process of sanctification—being set apart for God—the Holy Spirit reveals those things that prevent you from knowing who you are in Christ. Allowing Him to change your thinking results in the erasing of the old tapes recorded from your past (tapes like "You'll never amount to anything!"). Those tapes limited your becoming who God created you to be. This is part of what the Apostle Paul meant when he urged us to renew our minds (Romans 12:2; Ephesians 4:23). The positional identity we have in Christ manifests itself relationally through the process of sanctification.

Growing in trust, transparency, and honesty with Jesus over time allows His healing presence to permeate the wounds of our hearts. Often those wounds blocked us from experiencing true intimacy with Him. As our trust in Jesus grows, it increases our capacity to trust others, too, thereby creating a community. When we enter into safe community, we can begin to experience healthy and holy relational intimacy. Our brokenness was often the result of broken relationships. Our healing process occurs, therefore, through the development of whole relationships.

During the process of sanctification—that lasts the rest of our lives—we bring our thoughts, emotions, and wounds into the presence of the Father, Son, and Holy Spirit. God wants us to do so. Because our relational and sexual brokenness developed over time, so also time is necessary for us to allow God's gentle access into the deeper wounds of our souls. He will never force Himself upon us but will always wait for our invitation. "Here I am! I stand at the door and knock. If anyone hears my voice and opens the door, I will come in and eat with that person, and they with me" (Revelation 3:20). Note how Jesus is inviting us once again to dine with Him.

As we gain an understanding of God's true nature, we begin to realize that His revelations of our areas of brokenness are not to shame us. Rather, these revelations are opportunities for us to experience greater depths of God's love, grace, and mercy. When I invite Jesus' healing presence into my exposed brokenness, I am allowing Him to bring His holy order into the chaos of my soul.

Do you see your brokenness as a place of shame or as a place that God Himself wants to inhabit? We can stop coping, making allowances, and come out of denial.

I wish these were easy choices. If only these changes could happen overnight or with a simple prayer! But the extended process of choice builds character, which increases the fruits of the Spirit within us (see Galatians 5:22–23). This is both sanctification and spiritual development. The rebirth that occurs within us is the result of the sacrifice of Jesus on the cross.

Jesus As Our Salvation

> Unless I understand the cross, I cannot understand why my commitment to what is right must take precedence over what I prefer.[10]
>
> – Ravi Zacharias

Jesus, taking on flesh, entered into our humanity and took our place on the cross. In so doing, He broke the grip of the power of sin and death. Through the suffering of Jesus and His obedience unto death, when we put our faith in Him, He becomes our way to eternal life. This is a great mystery: Jesus was fully human and fully God. Through the excruciating work of the cross, Jesus, as the Son of Man, expressed our humanity to the Father. As the Son of God and Messiah, Christ wrought salvation for us.

Crucifixion for criminals was an extreme punishment and instrument of shame. Jesus was stripped naked on the cross before those present—a form of sexual abuse. I consider the crucifixion as seen in Mel Gibson's movie *The Passion of the Christ* as the most accurate depiction of the horrific suffering Jesus endured for us. In addition to His physical suffering, we have no concept of what it was like for Jesus to bear the weight of the sin of the world on Himself. Deuteronomy 21:23 makes a significant point regarding punishment inflicted by hanging a man on a tree: "Be sure to bury [the body] that same day because anyone who is hung on a pole is under God's curse." The Jews believed that God cursed those who were crucified.

But this instrument of torture and shame became the way of your salvation and the restoration of your relationship with the Father. The cross is the place where God welcomes your every sin, every idol, and every wound. Do you hear what I am saying? The foot of the cross beckons you to bring every aspect of your brokenness and sin. In Luke 7:36–50, Luke describes an unnamed woman who sought Jesus contritely, just as she was, in the house of Simon the Pharisee. We, too, can come contritely and humbly to the cross of Jesus, just as we are.

The obedience of Jesus from birth to crucifixion facilitated the release of grace to us—receiving what we do not deserve. Jesus bore the full judgment and penalty for every sin we have committed. "He was pierced for our transgressions; he was crushed for our iniquities; the punishment that brought us peace was upon him, and by his wounds, we are healed" (Isaiah 53:5). His cross allowed mercy (not receiving what we do deserve) to be extended to us. Every sin you have ever committed and ever will commit has been forgiven! Pause for a moment and let this truth permeate your thinking and your emotions. Through our confession, seeking God to expose and cleanse our hearts, we have access to that forgiveness.

A word of warning: A dangerous doctrine called antinomianism states that the moral law no longer applies to Christians by God's grace as outlined in the Gospel. The dispensation

[10]Ravi Zacharias, *I, Isaac, Take Thee, Rebekah* (Thomas Nelson, 2005), p. 43.

of grace, according to this heretical thinking, releases us from the obligation of adhering to any moral restrictions. Based on the principle that all sin for a Christian is forgiven, this way of erroneous thinking allows believers to live immorally. When we choose to embrace sin, there is always the likewise embracing of its consequences.

God forbid! As Jesus stated to the woman caught in adultery, "Go and sin no more" (John 8:11, NKJV). We must make no allowance for sexually or relationally immoral lives. It is one thing to fall into sin as part of our overcoming process. But embracing sinful behavior as acceptable misinterprets God's Word and demeans His grace.

I could write much more about the cross of my Beloved. As you read the subsequent chapters in this book, I pray that the cross of Jesus Christ becomes a source of comfort and healing that you will embrace. Here is a redemptive invitation for you to release any pain, shame, and suffering. Here is a place to free you of your brokenness, allowing it to come up and out of you, going into His broken body. "The Spirit and the bride say, 'Come!' And let the one who hears say, 'Come!' Let the one who is thirsty come; and let the one who wishes take the free gift of the water of life" (Revelation 22:17).

Becoming the Beloved

Our spiritual journey home is a deepening of the reality that we are the *Beloved of Jesus.* There are many obstacles which hinder that becoming. The enemy of our souls will do all that he can to prevent us from entering into the spiritual reality of being the Beloved. Our broken and wounded hearts also battle accepting that reality (i.e., deflection due to feelings of self-hatred).

We need discernment to determine which voice is speaking to our souls. With the help of the Holy Spirit, we can begin to discern when it is the voice of Jesus in our hearts, drawing us into greater intimacy with Him. The more we listen to and receive Jesus' healing words, the more we desire to seek His Presence to increase our knowing of Him. This is the process of becoming; becoming who we were meant to be from the beginning of creation.

Knowing we are the Beloved is the very foundation which enables us to enter into whole and healthy relationship with God, others, and ourselves. Our becoming must go beyond a doctrinal understanding and have the realization that it impacts every aspect of our lives. As the Beloved of Jesus, we can know His peace in every circumstance, situation, or trial. It is to know that every part of our daily lives stems from our center in being the Beloved.

Many of us pursue our healing process with much zeal and focus. In a frenzied pace, we seek multiple resources to attain psychological knowledge of our broken lives. Henri Nouwen posed a significant question regarding our healing journey.

> "My question is whether it is possible to be as articulate about our spiritual journey as we are about our psychological journey. Can we come into touch with the mysterious process of becoming the Beloved in the same specific way as we can come in touch with the dynamics of our psyches?"[11]

We must find a balance and have a clear focus for the road ahead. Our goal is not to understand every aspect or supposed cause of our brokenness. The goal is to become like Jesus. The goal is to know who He is in us and who we are in Him. It is knowing that I am my beloved's, and my beloved is mine (Song of Songs, 6:3). In that becoming process, in our deepening of *knowing* we are the Beloved, Jesus will provide all the insight and understanding we need for our process.

Wrapping Up

In this chapter, I have discussed three important mysteries that will change or may already have changed your life:

1. Jesus is not only a necessity for life; He is life.
2. Your identity is no longer based on the past, but is alive and centered in Jesus.
3. Jesus bore every sin on the cross that you, as a believer, have ever committed and will ever commit.

These three truths are the bedrock of your faith. Jesus made a way for you to enter into the eternal life that the Father has planned for you since the beginning of the universe.

[11]Henri Nouwen, Life of the Beloved, (Crossroad, 1996), p. 41.

Seek God for His divine objectivity, seeing your own life through His eyes. Ask the Holy Spirit for the gift of faith to believe that you are a new creation. Pursue Jesus for a deeper understanding of who He is in you and who you are in Him. He sees you with eyes of compassion. He knows exactly where you are in your process. When you lack the words to describe what is in your heart, Jesus knows exactly what you are feeling. He longs to come into the deep places within your being. All He awaits is your invitation.

Will you let Him in?

Prayer

Holy Spirit, I welcome You to come and expose where I am lacking in knowledge of Jesus as my center and my life. Jesus, please show me where I have embraced knowing You as more of a doctrinal belief, and lacking in true relational connection.

Jesus, where am I hesitant or resistant to allowing You to go deeper into my soul? What walls or barriers prevent me from embracing You with greater intimacy? Please help me enter into a deeper relationship with You. Open the eyes of my heart to truly see and know You, not only as my Redeemer but also as my Friend, Brother, and Beloved.

Thank You, Jesus, for Your life and death on the cross. Impart to me greater knowledge and understanding of Your crucifixion and resurrection. Help me grasp the reality of the forgiveness of my sin. May I enter into the reality of accepting my complete cleansing and restoration through Your sacrifice. Thank You for making the way for me back to the Father.

Lord Jesus, I offer my life up to You. I lay at the foot of Your cross all my perfectionistic striving. The only way I can live Your life in and through me is by Your presence and strength. Show me where I try to obtain security in anything apart from You.

Jesus, may I truly come to know that "neither height nor depth, nor anything else in all creation, will be able to separate [me]" from Your love (Romans 8:38).

Soul Work

1. Read Galatians 2:20 and answer the following:
    a. What does Paul mean that we have been crucified with Christ? Answer this with direct examples about your life.
    b. Paul says, "I have been crucified with Christ," and that "I no longer live": yet he also mentions "the life I now live in the body." Define what Paul means regarding these two I's and how this applies directly to you and your struggles.
2. Read Romans 6:3–7 and answer the following:
    a. Explain in your own words what it means personally to you that you have been buried, are living a new life, and are united with Jesus in His resurrection.
    b. How do you define the "old self" as it pertains to your life?
    c. What does Paul mean when he states that our old self (man) has been crucified with Jesus?
3. What does it mean to "live and move and have our being" in Jesus (Acts 17:28)? How do you incorporate this into your daily life?

Journaling Moment

Reflect on the reality of your true self. Use the Scriptures in the Soul Work section above to help you focus. Ask the Holy Spirit to help you define your true self. Ask Him to expose whatever hinders you from standing in your true self. Also, seek the Holy Spirit to show you what your false self looks like. Ask Him to show you where and how you practice the presence of the false self.

FOUR

The Garments of Shame

SHAME IS THE RAINCOAT OF THE SOUL, REPELLING THE LIVING WATER THAT WOULD OTHERWISE ESTABLISH US AS THE BELOVED OF GOD. IT PREVENTS US FROM RECEIVING GRACE AND TRUTH WHERE WE NEED THEM THE MOST.[12]

- ANDREW COMISKEY

Our souls and bodies are constantly active, whether we are going about our daily activities or sleeping. Our senses are aware of our surroundings. Our minds are never completely disengaged. Likewise, our emotions are active in response to our thoughts and experiences, even when we are asleep. Consciously or unconsciously, we are imaging and responding to the world around us. Multiple stimuli affect the way we think, feel, and act.

Our earliest experiences and relationship with Mother and Father begin the process of our emotional formation. In our infancy, we respond emotionally without the benefit of cognitive understanding. We are like sponges, soaking up our environment. Our eyes and ears are like a video camera, recording the world around us without comprehension. Children are the greatest recorders of information but the poorest interpreters.

These familial environments contribute to our varying levels of shame—the overwhelming

[11]Andrew Comiskey, *Strength in Weakness* (InterVarsity, 2003), p. 69.

feeling (as we saw in chapter 2) that there is something wrong with me. Shame may develop from the actions of others and our perception of circumstances. But it goes back much farther than that.

Our Inheritance of Shame

Let's trace the lineage of shame back to its primary source.

From the Garden

In the beginning, Adam and Eve maintained no façades in their relationships with each other and God. They lacked a diseased self-awareness—which for us is rooted in insecurity, comparisons, or control—and enjoyed whole relationships, centered in perfect love. I believe they ate from the tree of life, knowing and living the life God intended. They related directly to God without any hindrance or barriers.

But eating the fruit of the forbidden tree, the tree of knowledge of good and evil, caused a broken self-consciousness in Adam and Eve and the loss of their integration with God. Cloaked with shame after sinning, they hid, reluctant to be vulnerable with Him. In the Garden of Eden, we read the first recorded question that God voiced to humankind: "Where are you?"

The powerful result of the shame Adam and Eve experienced was a breach in relationship with God. And when God turned them out of the Garden, keeping them from the tree of life, there were profound consequences.

We come into this world with shame as an inheritance. We long for Adam and Eve's original relationship with God and each other. All of us have an inner ache, an inner drive to be in true and whole relationships. But we hide our weaknesses, imperfections, and inadequacies behind designer fig leaves (for example, jobs, accomplishments, and possessions)—whatever works best to prevent others from seeing beneath the surface.

From Our Families

All of us experience some degree of dysfunction in our families. No family is perfect, able to meet all our love needs as God intended. Our intimacy deficits—not having all our love needs met in childhood—result in shame, which turns us inward.

The family is the first environment where shame is formed, interpreted, and internalized. The development of the core of shame takes place in our unique family system, layer by layer, applied like heavy garments of lead, or even death shrouds.

Early in life, before we are cognitively aware, we absorb our experiences intuitively. Shame develops before we have the language to define it. Later, however, shame gains residence in our minds and affects the neurobiology of our brains.[13] Our negative thinking filters our experiences, which then can give rise to emotional reactions.

Our family of origin can create shameful attitudes and perceptions for situations out of our control. External issues such as poverty, the level of education, employment, community, and location contribute to shame. Internal issues such as abuse, domestic violence, addiction, misogyny (the hatred of woman), and misandry (the hatred of men) also contribute to the shame core. Adding to the core are physical issues associated with mental illnesses, chronic disease, or handicaps.

Dysfunctional families have unspoken shaming rules: *Do not think, talk, trust, or feel.* They may also convey shaming messages: *I wish I never had you. Why can't you be like So-and-So? You never get anything right. You'll never amount to anything.* We absorb these rules and internalize the "You are" statements (such as "You are stupid"), which later become "I am" statements (such as "I am stupid"). All this becomes an unconscious belief system, which I refer to as our "stinking thinking," that determines our identities and eventually governs our lives.

From Our Environment

A third source of shame is the level of pain and wounding we experience from our environments. Shame originates in relationships. "Although we experience our shame response emerging wholly and independently within us, it does so *in response to an encounter we have with someone else*."[14] We react emotionally to a relational stimulus, be it a momentary glance, a negative word, or outright abuse.

[13]Shame involves a significant level of neuropsychology. There is a flow in the neurobiology of the brain connected with our experiences. Deeply internalized shame influences the functional capacity in the brain. It is beyond the scope of this chapter to address this topic, but I highly recommend Curt Thompson's The Soul of Shame, which provides in-depth understanding.

[14] Curt Thompson, *The Soul of Shame* (InterVarsity, 2015), pp. 68–69.

Wounds beget wounds; cracks in the heart may eventually become a gorge of pain. Misdirected passions seek false sources of love, acceptance, and the fulfillment of unmet needs.

A pull develops, beckoning us to retreat into shame-filled darkness. Pain, loss of true intimacy, and shame become a three-branch vine, growing within me, which encircles and strangles my heart. My core of shame creates patterns influencing my relationships and behavior choices. My core of shame is a filter through which I view my life, which gives rise to my belief system. I view myself, God, and others through these filters of shame.

I add secondary layers of shame to the earlier developed central shame core. These secondary layers are for the shame I feel regarding the behaviors I choose to suppress, avoid, or pacify my pain. I may also integrate shame for my race, or who I am as a man or woman.

Do you fear to have your inner pain and shame exposed? Like Adam and Eve, do you stay in the shadows wearing fig leaves to hide from God or others?

We embrace self-protective mechanisms. I take control of my life, believing I need to be in charge. I build an image that I am okay and looking good to prevent others from detecting my deficits. I walk with an underlying fear that someone will detect how shameful I truly am.

Perfectionism is a mask often worn to hide shame. If I can appear to be perfect, keeping others at a distance, they will not see the imperfection or pain within. Perfectionism can lead to four "should" beliefs that reinforce the appearance of perfection:[15]

I should always look good.
I should never rock the boat.
I should never get angry.
I should always be strong.

These "shoulds" are exhausting. They mean I am constantly aware of my surroundings, anxious to deflect attention from myself. I sacrifice my well-being to maintain peace and security around me. Whatever my emotions, opinions, or personal needs, I sacrifice them all for the sake of remaining hidden and safe.

The question arises: If I acknowledge my wounds and pain, will someone be there to help me?

[15]Kathryn W. Chamberlin, *From Shame to Glory* (Xulon, 2014), p. 188.

Living with Shame

> Shame is a sense of being uniquely and hopelessly flawed. Shame leaves a person feeling different from and less valuable than other human beings.[16]
>
> – Sandra D. Wilson

Shame is rooted in both our emotions and our thinking. Shame connects with our thinking, but it expresses the reality of its presence through our emotions.

Our first reaction to shame is often to cope by choosing control. We make vain attempts trying to hide, fix, or ignore it. Nevertheless, shame remains rooted in the deep recesses of our hearts and minds.

My internalized belief system tells me I am flawed, damaged goods, inadequate to survive in the world. Shame keeps me self-aware and turned inward, which creates barriers to God and community. In my diseased introspection (the self-consuming, inward focus on my faulty beliefs, diseased attitudes, and unresolved emotions), I concentrate on my negative self-talk and thinking. I remind myself continually of my imperfections. Shame gives rise to deep-seated feelings of self-hatred and self-loathing.

Feelings of shame result from a spectrum of experiences. Shame as the byproduct of trauma or abuse is readily understandable. When dramatic events occur that place us in uncomfortable situations, we can often identify the resulting shame. But what about the shame that occurs from less obvious situations? Shame may accumulate slowly over time through the neglect or inability of our parents to provide for our basic emotional or physical needs (e.g., the lack of words of love or affirmation, inability to provide food and shelter, etc.). Shame in a subtle form continues to grow. Its presence influences our relationships and behaviors. But because it accrues slowly, it goes undetected because we have grown numb to it.

Shame is a uniquely personal experience. Our temperaments and life experiences result in varying reactions to shame. For one individual, a particular event may result in only momentary concern. For another, the same event has a deeper impact, due to internalization, and becomes toxic over time. It is wrong to judge another's level of shame by imposing our interpretation of how we would react if placed in a similar situation. No matter what one's level of shame, it is valid

[16]Sandra D. Wilson, *Released from Shame* (InterVarsity, 2002), p. 10.

because it is what he or she feels.

Having lived for many years with internalized shame, we may be unaware of its influence. It can be subtle and unconscious. Other emotions like anger, self-hatred, or envy can keep shame hidden, covering it in our depths. We need the presence of the Holy Spirit to reveal our core of shame, bringing it out of the shadows into His marvelous light.

How aware are you of shame in your life?

We recognize that shame has strong connections with our emotions. Indeed, our emotions express the power of shame. Shame also produces strongholds in our thinking, creating faulty beliefs associated with our behaviors. In my moments of "stinking thinking," after I have failed in some capacity, instead of accepting that I *made* a mistake, I believe that I *am* a mistake. Shame gives my experiences the power and authority to define my self-worth. In these situations, feelings of inadequacy, and not having what it takes, shift my focus inward, with condemnation reinforcing my core of shame. Layer begets layer.

"Shame is deeply committed to exploiting the machinery of attachment in creating states of aloneness within us and between us, and most substantially between God and us."[17] Shame hinders our capacity to develop healthy attachments with God and others. We design masks, façades, which keep God and others at a distance. The greater that distance, the more we are alone. As relational beings, shame sabotages our capacity for becoming known. Shame limits and destroys community. It imprisons us in isolation. Secluded, I give credence to my diseased introspection, blocking out any healing words from God or others.

The enemy loves shame. Satan incorporates any means that will prevent us from walking in the fullness of knowing we are God's beloved daughters and sons. He wants to separate us from community and God. He encourages us to turn inward, so we lose sight of the beauty of the Lord and His creation. Most of all, Satan wants to block us from knowing God's goodness and loving-kindness. He wants to rob us of our capacity to know God's true character and nature.

Another of Satan's goals is to disrupt the expression of our calling and giftedness. Do you realize you have a calling from God and the gifts to accomplish that calling? Satan fears who you are becoming! One of his primary objectives is to blind you to your role in bearing God's image and advancing His Kingdom purposes. Satan desires to undermine the expression of the Father's will through you.

[17]Thompson, p. 54.

In summary, here are some reasons why we must address shame in our lives:

Shame creates a barrier to receiving God's love, mercy, and grace.
Shame blocks us from entering into whole relationships.
Shame obscures the presence of appropriate self-love.
Shame keeps us prisoners of diseased introspection.
Shame prevents us from embracing the full calling and gifts God has given us.

Released from Shame: Embracing Liberating Truths

Those who look to him are radiant; their faces are never covered with shame.

– Psalm 34:5

Adam and Eve's original vulnerability before the Fall allowed openness with God and each other. Later, however, they viewed their vulnerability as something negative. So they hid.

Vulnerability (being open and willing for healthy and whole relationships), is an absolute necessity. The very nature of shame motivates us to cover and conceal it. Fearing rejection or humiliation, we avoid disclosure, choosing not to be transparent and honest. Instead, we choose a behavior that is the direct opposite of what will be the most beneficial. To overcome shame, we must be willing to become vulnerable, letting God and others behind our mask or façade. By being vulnerable, I am not suggesting that we open ourselves to abuse, becoming a doormat for others. Healthy vulnerability is letting our barriers down, so we are open to the good that God and others offer us.

Have you ever wanted to hide when you felt vulnerable and exposed?

Shame and self-hatred cause us to detach defensively from God and others. We resist believing that we can go beyond and become greater than who we are in the present moment. Ultimately, we abandon hope and embrace despair. We run from God Himself, the One who knows us best—the One who names us according to His divine plan for us.

SHAME AND SELF-HATRED CAUSE US TO DETACH DEFENSIVELY FROM GOD AND OTHERS.

God wants us to bring our shame and deficits into His light. He searched for Adam and Eve, fully aware of their disobedience and where they were hiding. Likewise, God searches for us, wanting us to welcome Him into the very places we keep hidden from Him. However, we wear many identity labels, based on our faulty beliefs and brokenness, and we avoid His healing presence and touch.

God longs to inhabit us with His truth wherever the lies of shame limit and constrain us. But we must deal with shame directly and not merely try to manage it. If I am trying to manage it, I am making allowance for it to remain.

Because of our wounds, we must address the shame associated with the sin committed against us. Forgiveness is a necessary component, therefore, in processing those wounds. (We will talk about forgiveness in detail in chapter 13.) We must also address the faulty beliefs and attitudes of the heart that keep us locked in the grip of shame.

Release from shame in our thinking requires the need for accepting the liberating truths that expose the lies or misbeliefs hiding beneath.

The Liberating Truth of Your Worth

If you had a diamond and wanted to know its value, you would take it to an expert jeweler. Let us say the jeweler valued that diamond at ten thousand dollars. That would become its price tag. On one side of a scale of worth, sits the diamond, and on the other side, balancing out the gem sits ten thousand dollars—what someone would pay for it. The value of something is what one is willing to pay for it.

Who would you seek out to determine your worth? Father God is the One who created you and the only One who knows your worth. To find out your price tag, you must place yourself on God's balance scale. What are you worth? The Apostle Paul gives us a hint: "You were bought at a price. Therefore honor God with your bodies" (I Corinthians 6:20). Placing Jesus—, which is the price on your price tag— on the other side of the scale, would balance it. I am not saying we are equal to Jesus, but He is your price tag as determined by the Father, and your true worth to the Father.

Stop for a moment and ponder this remarkable truth. Father God has established a blood covenant with you, as a believer, through the cross of Jesus. Due to His character of truth and faithfulness, he cannot renege on that covenant. He desires your freedom and is fully committed to your process. Yet how often do we fall short of our commitment to Him?

When shame or brokenness suggests that you are flawed and damaged goods, remember your price tag. Will you believe this spiritual fact in spite of your feelings?

The Liberating Truth of His Grace

We invest a lot of energy, creating our façade of what I call the Christian four-letter F-word—being "fine." For years we have hidden our imperfections and concealed our shame behind fig leaves. God's mercy is not receiving what we *do deserve*. However, God's grace, receiving what we *don't deserve*, is a challenge when we are cloaked with shame.

We conceptualize God in response to our shame and create a religious false self. To accept His grace, we must acknowledge and confess any religious perfectionism that blocks our capacity to admit we are fallen and in need of grace. The Pharisees are a good example. "They were so busy being in the world for God that they failed to be in God for the world."[18]

We must lay down our religious "doing." We need to lay down our performance, achievements, and restless activism (the inability to remain still and enter into rest). Restless activism takes the form of doing the "correct" Christian activities. We construct a life that we hope convinces others, God, and even ourselves of our committed religiosity. Instead of living under grace, we place ourselves under the law. We have made God into our image. Shame-based repentance, living under the law, says, "I have broken God's rules." Shame-free repentance, living under grace, stems from the realization that "I have broken God's heart."[19] One is relational, the

[18] M. Robert Mulholland Jr., *The Deeper Journey* (InterVarsity, 2016), p. 47.
[19]Chamberlin, *From Shame to Glory*, p. 206.

other bondage.

I have heard some use the terminology "good-shame." However, they usually are referring to conviction, as imparted by the Holy Spirit. This is not shaming, but a form of Godly sorrow for what I have done. There is only one form of shame, and it is never good!

Adam and Eve covered up their nakedness due to shame. On the cross, Jesus was stripped naked on our behalf, bearing our shame. He did this to identify Himself with our shame and abuse. He became completely vulnerable on the cross that we might be completely vulnerable with the Father. Jesus modeled the way for us; He made the way for us approach the Father.

So stop trying to be who you think you need to be. Let go of your control—not an easy choice! Ask the Holy Spirit to enable you to lay down all your vain attempts and simply rest in Him. Seek the Lord to expose any areas that block you from resting in His grace, mercy, love, acceptance, and forgiveness.

Will you take the risk of being open and vulnerable before Him?

The Liberating Truth of Your Potential

Magnanimity is the virtue of realizing that I can become so much more than I could ever imagine. Experiencing magnanimity is possible because of the reality of Jesus Christ's presence within me. However, I must have the courage to become that person.

The Bible is full of examples of those who wrestled with God, thinking He had the wrong person. But He does not have the wrong person. Just as God spoke to Joshua, He also speaks to us: "Be strong and very courageous" (Joshua 1:7). Note that He did not say, "I will make you." He said, "Be." God desires us, with His strength and power, to rise in courage.

Accepting that we have flaws is the primary step in releasing ourselves from shame. This does not mean we ever condone sin. We are admitting, rather, our human frailty and need of a Savior. Refusing to acknowledge our brokenness and weaknesses keeps us earthbound and blocked from God. However, confessing our brokenness and weakness enables us to accept our potential for becoming much more than we could ever imagine.

So we leave our inadequacies and flaws at the foot of the cross, looking up and out of ourselves, offering them to Jesus. We see His incredible sacrifice, which enables us to become all the Father has intended since the creation of the world. The acceptance of our imperfections connects us with the Body of Christ, which, like us, has human frailty.

The Liberating Truth of Community

Accepting our humanity connects us with community. Since our brokenness arose from dysfunctional relationships, our healing and release from shame will come through the establishment of whole relationships. "To be fully loved—and to fully love—requires that we are fully known."[20] We all have wounds, and we are all in the same boat. So although our healing process may start with books, programs, ministers, or counselors, its fullest expression and flourishing will take place in community.

When Jesus called Lazarus from the grave (as recorded in John 11), Lazarus walked out of the tomb still wrapped in his grave clothes. Jesus told those around Lazarus to come and take off his grave clothes, which identified him with death. So Lazarus' friends did so. In the same way, we will find those in the Body of Christ to come alongside us and assist in the removal of our death clothes—our garments of shame.

We need one another other to walk in freedom from shame.

Through community, God expresses Himself through flesh and bone. The faces, voices, and embraces from your Christian brothers and sisters represent God's love for you. To enter into the fullness of love, as exemplified in the Trinity, you must learn to receive and then give love back in return. Never forget you are an easier target for the enemy when you are alone and isolated. Through community, you enter into family. You enter into transforming relationships. You enter into the reality of becoming.

Wrapping Up

Years ago, I ran across this quote from pastor and author Danny Silk: "It takes practice to believe the truth when you have momentum in a lie." The Holy Spirit will release us from the lies, behaviors, and misbeliefs we have about God, others, and ourselves. We must identify our fig leaves, asking God to empower us to become transparent and vulnerable before Him. Our garments of shame, which we have worn for a lifetime, need removal. We need to confess our self-hatred as sin and embrace the virtue of healthy self-love.

[20]Thompson, *The Soul of Shame*, p. 126.

Jesus has made the way and the place for you to deal with your shame. Will you allow Him to call you out, as he did Lazarus, from your tomb of shame?

Prayer

> I praise you because I am fearfully and wonderfully made; your works are wonderful, I know that full well.
>
> – Psalm 139:14

Lord, I come before You just as I am. I thank You that You do not label me according to my past, my present, my circumstances, or my behaviors. You saw me in my mother's womb. I thank You that You knit me together. You tell me that I am fearfully and wonderfully made, but too often, I do not "know that full well." I need Your healing presence to surround me as I seek Your face.

I welcome You, Holy Spirit, to expose my garments of shame. When did I allow these garments to be placed upon me? What lies have I believed about myself that allow these garments to remain? These are like the grave clothes Lazarus wore when he came out of the tomb. I long to be freed from them. The weight of them has worn me down. They have hampered me, preventing me from standing upright in my true self.

Lord, what are the specific areas for which I bear shame? I invite You to search me and bring these areas to mind. What are the labels I wear that do not line up with who I am in my true self? How have I allowed shame and labels to prevent me from entering into deeper intimacy with You and from those around me? Where have I believed the lie that I am permanently flawed or less than other human beings? Expose where I have taken broken words spoken over me and turned them into "I am" belief statements. How have I limited myself from becoming who You created me to be?

Lord, what are my inner thoughts that limit me? I am willing for You to go deep within to surface and cleanse me of any words that prevent me from rising as Your true son or daughter. I will wait upon You, remaining still in Your presence as You do this deep work within me.

Lord, what is Your healing word for me? What words, Father, would You speak to replace those words that have bound my personhood to lies and misbeliefs? How would You manifest Yourself to me at this moment? You are my Creator. You knew me when I was first conceived when I drew my first breath. You were there and rejoiced over me. Please help me not to deflect that which You desire to impart to me in this holy moment. Please write Your words on my heart that I may not forget them. Please help me see myself with divine objectivity, to see as You see me. Help me have the courage to receive Your blessing and to walk in accordance with how You have named and created me to be. I am Yours, and You are mine. I am Your beloved. I am forever grateful for Your healing and life-changing work in me.

Soul Work

1 As quoted in this chapter, Sandra Wilson states, "Shame is a sense of being uniquely and hopelessly flawed. Shame leaves a person feeling different from and less valuable than other human beings." How have you felt this way in the past or today?

2. When we make a mistake, shame says, "I *am* a mistake," and we allow our behaviors to identify who we are as a person. If I believe my very being is flawed, I can easily slip into self-hatred and self-loathing. How have you allowed your behaviors to define your worth? Where do you allow self-hatred and self-loathing to be part of your life?

3. The common unspoken rules in dysfunctional families are *Do not think, talk, trust, or feel.* How were these rules present in your family to maintain equilibrium or the status quo? How are they still present in your family? How do you still feel the impact of these rules?

Journaling Moment

In your journal or on a sheet of paper, draw a line down the middle of the page. Once again, read the prayer written at the end of this chapter. In the left column on the page, write down any words, lies, or faulty beliefs that have been part of your life. Ask the Lord to reveal the words you typically use to define yourself during your weakest moments, when you make a mistake, or when you fail to live up to an imposed standard of perfection. Offer those words back to Jesus at the foot of His cross.

Now ask the Holy Spirit to enable you to hear the words that the Father would speak to you in place of those you just offered. Write these words in the right column opposite the words in the left column. Ask for the Holy Spirit's help to hear Him aright. Ask for help to rise above self-condemnation or feelings of rejection. Meditate on the words in the right column. Ask the Lord for the strength not to deflect but to receive His healing words for you.

FIVE

Sense of Being

THOU HAS MADE US FOR THYSELF, O LORD, AND OUR HEART IS RESTLESS UNTIL IT FINDS ITS REST IN THEE.

– AUGUSTINE OF HIPPO

The deepest desire given to us by God (as we said at the beginning of chapter 3) is to know and be known by Him. Ultimately our hearts yearn to experience oneness with God Himself. But we cannot become who we are destined to be by remaining in a relational vacuum. The deep desire to be known by others motivates us to be in relationship. Reading an autobiography allows us to know facts about an individual without knowing that individual personally. To be known requires the presence of a *relational* connection.

Our identity and sense of self begin early in life. Even in the womb, we are forming a natural connection with Mother. We sense her voice and heartbeat. Later we look instinctively into her face, and then those of others, searching for a sense of who we are. Intuitively we want to know, *Am I lovable? Do I have value or worth? Am I acceptable?* We are in a receptive, responsive position to those around us.

Our early relationship with Mother plays a pivotal role in our lives. She influences how we relate to others, to God, and our environment. Through our connection with her, we grow in our capacity to connect with those around us. Relationally there are two polar extremes: a self that welcomes others and a self in isolation. Our connection with Mother lays the foundation for the development of our awareness of self—that is, our sense of being and well-being.

Before continuing, I would like to encourage you to take a moment to stop and pray. Grasping the fullness of this topic goes beyond mere intellectual comprehension. Understanding your sense of being requires you to join your head and your heart. Having a sense of being connects you with the deep longings of your soul. Ask for the Holy Spirit's revelation and clarity as you continue to read. Will you permit Him to manifest Himself in those areas of need within you?

Sense of Being and Well-Being

We come into this world at a deficit due to original sin (the result of the disobedience of Adam and Eve). We are born dependent on those around us. The newborn, separated from the womb, is looking to find a home again. He or she is looking for an attachment to another human being. Curt Thompson writes, "Technically, attachment refers to the process by which the immature infant brain accesses and utilizes the strengths of the mature adult brain in order to learn how to organize and regulate itself."[21] The newborn is sensing his or her environment, searching to find a connection, to thrive and flourish.

When we are born, our cognitive, left-brain faculties are still in development. For the first year or two, the development of the right brain is greater. It is functioning, observing intuitively, and absorbing its surroundings. The right brain is also connecting with the experience of emotions. As infants, we respond intuitively to the coos and gentle words of our mothers and fathers. We look into our parents' faces, observing their expressions, and receiving their love. This receiving is not an analytical, cognitive thought process, but one that is responsive and internalized emotionally.

The left brain, on the other hand, focuses on the linear and analytical processing of thought. Early in life, infants may hear words spoken to them, but they cannot comprehend their meaning. Parents communicate that they love their babies. However, the babies are connecting with the parents' facial expressions, not the meaning of the words themselves. When an infant

[21]Curt Thompson, *The Soul of Shame* (InterVarsity, 2015), p. 52.

starts to use language, connecting meaning with words, the left brain is expressing itself and being functional. Quoting Curt Thompson again: "…Over time, the left brain works to make sense of what the right brain is sending it."[22]

Mother's womb was your first home. In the womb, your need for nourishment, warmth, and security was met. You had awareness within the confines of the womb. Biblical precedent confirms this: Jacob and Esau wrestled in the womb; God knew and called the prophet Jeremiah in his mother's womb; John the Baptist leaped for joy in Elizabeth's womb. The preborn child is receptive to the mother's emotions. He or she can also be aware of what is occurring outside the mother's body. Here are the beginnings, which later develop into a sense of self.

What is your earliest memory of Mother?

Tom, Vicki, and Joyce's Story

My friends Tom and Vicki were expecting their first child, a daughter named Joyce. As Joyce was growing in the womb, Tom routinely spoke to her. Leaning close to Vicki's abdomen, Tom would speak blessing over Joyce and talk to her with gentle words of love. Vicki shared with me that Joyce, in her early infancy, was very aware of Tom's voice. When Tom walked into a room and spoke, Joyce turned and looked for him. Even when Joyce could not spot Tom, she would search for him when she heard his voice. Joyce knew Tom's voice because of the communication that happened before her birth.

Immediately after birth, it is common practice to place the newborn on the mother's breast. The baby, having come through the traumatic birthing process, is comforted to hear the mother's voice—the voice he or she has come to know while in the womb. The newborn senses the familiarity of Mother and feels that she is still near. Cradled in her arms, *I am safe*.

Later, the infant expresses a hunger for not only food but also for connection. Breastfeeding addresses both needs. In the early stages of infancy, the child's field of vision is relatively limited. But as the infant's hunger is satiated with Mother's milk, he or she can see Mother's face and

[22]Ibid., p. 43.

make eye contact. A strong bonding develops. This bond communicates intuitively to the child, You are welcome, you are safe, connecting him or her with the life of another. This connection results in what we call a sense of being.

Our sense of being radiates from an inner core of warmth, acceptance, and connection. The child intuitively senses they are cherished and welcomed, creating a sense of peace. I am simply loved for who I am, not for what I do.

The sense of being develops through rootedness in the life of another. In this early stage of life, I cannot differentiate myself from Mother. Mother and I are one; Mother is my life. Intuitively I gain an inner sense of security through her love.

Your sense of being is the foundation on which your capacity to relate to others is built.

Well-being—your capacity to know you are okay—grows from this foundation as well. A good sense of well-being is one where I find contentment, peace, and rest derived simply knowing I am God's daughter or son.

How secure and loved did you feel early in your life?

Healthy relationship and connection with Mother increase our capacity for later separation from her. Confidence built on the security we experience with her increases our capacity to become independent and trust others. Our early experiences also build confidence in who we are—our growing healthy sense of self. Having a solid, inner sense of self influences how we later receive and extend love. Having a good sense of being and well-being enables us to enter into community.

Separation Anxiety

Numerous factors can interfere with the development of our sense of being and well-being. Whenever circumstances limit or prevent the development of our sense of being, anxiety and fear frequently result. When the preborn child senses rejection—perceived or real—he or she may enter the stages of separation. In utero, a child may sense rejection due to emotions surrounding the pregnancy, if he or she is unwanted.

Infants may also sense disappointment when they are not the biological sex desired.

As stated in chapter four, children are the greatest recorders of information, but the poorest interpreters. The still-developing left brain does not allow for an established point of

YOUR SENSE OF BEING IS THE FOUNDATION ON WHICH YOUR CAPACITY TO RELATE TO OTHERS IS BUILT.

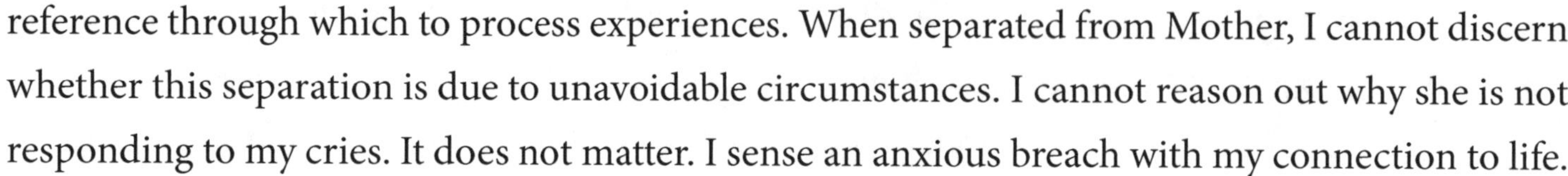

reference through which to process experiences. When separated from Mother, I cannot discern whether this separation is due to unavoidable circumstances. I cannot reason out why she is not responding to my cries. It does not matter. I sense an anxious breach with my connection to life.

Separation can occur due to health issues of the mother or child. Years ago, premature babies placed in sterile metal incubators experienced minimal physical touch. The infant went from the tactile confines of the womb and hearing the mother's voice, to an environment of silence and lack of contact. Neonatal intensive care units today have made significant changes in the treatment of preemies. The babies experience tactile, stimulating connection through placement on wool bedding. Parents today visit and speak to their children, to help lessen any separation anxiety.

Medical complications post-delivery may require removal of the baby from the mother, thereby breaking the connection. Although preemies today experience better care, separation anxiety may still occur. Infants who experience this separation may refuse to breastfeed upon returning to their mothers; they have detached themselves emotionally from her.

Mark's Story

Mark was born in the 1950s. As a preemie, and he was placed in a sterile, brightly lit incubator, separated from his mother for an extended time. Later as a young child, Mark would awaken in the night nervous and anxious. He would quietly slip out of his bedroom and sneak into his parent's bedroom. Mark did this to observe his Mother's face. Once he saw she was breathing, a sense of calm would flood his being. He could then return to his bedroom and enter into a peaceful sleep. Mark's anxiousness had origins in the separation anxiety he felt at birth.

Seeing his mother breathing meant he was okay, restoring a sense of being and well-being.

Separation anxiety can result by following the damaging advice routinely given to mothers in the past, urging them not to respond to their crying babies. In reaction, these infants can internalize anxious feelings of abandonment.

Infants experiencing separation anxiety go through three stages:

Stage 1: Protest. The infant cries in reaction to the absence of Mother.

Stage 2: Despair. The infant begins to lose hope, becoming unresponsive and withdrawn.

Stage 3: Detachment. Although the infant remains responsive to the environment, he or she has lost responsiveness to Mother.

As infants, we expect our mothers to respond to us. What happens if she is incapable of responding? A woman, due to her dysfunctional family history, may be deficient in her capacity to mother or be present to her child.

What was the result if your mother could not respond to your basic need for touch, warmth, and connection?

Our home environment may lack safety and stability. As infants, due to our particular temperaments, we can internalize these experiences as varying levels of rejection, especially as the rejection of self. "Not seldom, self-rejection is simply seen as the neurotic expression of an insecure person. But neurosis is often the psychic manifestation of a much deeper human darkness: the darkness of not feeling truly welcome in human existence. Self-rejection is the greatest enemy of the spiritual life because it contradicts the sacred voice that calls us Beloved."[23] Addressing the lack of a sense of being therefore, is crucial so we may enter into healthy community and a deeper, intimate relationship with Jesus.

Since no family is perfect, to some extent, we all experience imperfect bonding with Mother. We need divine objectivity—the capacity to see our mothers through God's eyes. We do not want to minimize overt sin (for example, abuse) when it is present. However, it is not the intent of this chapter to make accusations or point fingers. No Mother or Father is perfect and has deficits due to their upbringing. We need to recognize where we lack a healthy sense of being or well-being. We need to identify our culpability—how we reacted to Mother, as well as the resulting emotions and

[23]Henri Nouwen, *Life of the Beloved* (Crossroad, 1966), p. 28.

beliefs (e.g., *I am not lovable; I am not wanted; I have no place in the community or this world*).

A diminished sense of being may result in a lack of security or confidence in our identity, affecting our capacity to relate to others healthily. It can also shift our focus onto achievements, accomplishments, or possessions to help us derive personal value and worth. A drive may arise within us to combat our insecurity, which attempts to take control. We may also experience a tendency to "bend" into unhealthy relationships, making selfish connections to fill or deflect the void within.

To whom or to what are you turning, seeking to find out who you are?

The following indications may be the result of a diminished sense of being:

Do you feel detached from human existence, not seen or not heard?

Do you have a pervasive feeling of emptiness?

Do you feel you have no value or that you are unacceptable?

Do you isolate relationally or have difficulty receiving love from others?

Do you have a fear of being alone, abandoned, or left behind?

Do you live with a predominant sense of fear, anxiety, or inner dread?

Do you find yourself bending into others, looking to them to define who you are?

Letting God Enter In

Without a sense of being, we can walk alongside ourselves, in effect, criticizing and judging our actions. Here we practice the presence of the false self, listening to old tapes that

RESTLESS ACTIVISM DIMINISHES ME AS A HUMAN "BEING" BUT INCREASES MY BECOMING A HUMAN "DOING."

focus us inward on inadequacy, shame, or self-hatred. We see ourselves through the lens of our brokenness, deflecting any healing words from our Creator, our Beloved, and the One who loves us unconditionally

We may also practice the presence of restless activism—a constant state of busyness and doing to avoid feeling our emotions or the emptiness inside. I cannot rest. I must keep busy. Restless activism diminishes me as a human "being," but increases my becoming a human "doing." It can also result in a lack of meaning and purpose in my life. Instead of living life in the present, I fixate on the future, which never seems to arrive.

Here is where we need the Lord to come with His peace that passes all understanding:

> Can any one of you by worrying add a single hour to your life? And why do you worry about clothes? See how the flowers of the field grow. They do not labor or spin. Yet I tell you that not even Solomon in all his splendor was dressed like one of these.
>
> – Matthew 6:27–29

God created time and is Himself outside of it. Your past is present to Him and poses no limitation for what He can do. Your future is also in God's hands and under His sovereignty.

Jesus can enter any existing void within your soul, regardless of when or how it came about, and fill it with His presence and blessing. He who spoke the universe into being can speak into your being, affirming and calling forth your value and giftedness. He can also enter your sense of aloneness, which often accompanies feelings of separateness and anxiety. Not only *can* He enter in; He longs to!

Do you believe He does?

"In the Presence," writes Leanne Payne, "is the power to receive healing into the deepest deprivations, even that failure to gain in those first few months of life, in a mother's arms, that most basic sense of *being* and *well-being*."[24]

The most conducive way to enter the Lord's presence is to limit the distractions that surround us. We invite the Holy Spirit to center us, bringing us from the outer court into the Holy of Holies.

Jewish culture believes that the bowels are where our deepest emotions reside. For that

[24]Payne, *The Healing Presence*, p. 55.

reason, people today praying for the sense of being in others, place their hands on the middle of their abdomens. First, the individual receiving prayer places their hands on their abdomen. Then the people praying for them place their hands on top of theirs. They are inviting God to enter where the person experiences any sense of separation, fear, or lack of connection. The key to receiving from God is being vulnerable to His presence.

One implication of the word *vulnerable* is "becoming open to hurt or wounding; exposing a weakness." With Jesus, we can become vulnerable, open to the presence of the One who became vulnerable for us. Jesus became vulnerable by not defending Himself justly against false accusers at His trial, and by allowing Himself to be stripped naked and hung on a cross. He endured the jeers and taunts of those around Him. He humbled Himself for our sakes. His example of making Himself vulnerable for us, even unto death, we can make ourselves vulnerable to Him.

Jesus' vulnerability to the will of the Father enables Him to enter into and redeem our pain and fear. Here is redemptive suffering, allowing my pain to rise and go into the redemptive wounds of my Beloved.

> Deep calls to deep in the roar of your waterfalls; all your waves and breakers have swept over me.
>
> – Psalm 42:7

As our deep calls to His deep, we invite the depths of the Lord to enter our depths of being. We invite the *Being* of God to inhabit our emptiness or void.

Wrapping Up

> "Can a mother forget the baby at her breast and have no compassion on the child she has borne? Though she may forget, I will not forget you!"
>
> – Isaiah 49:15

Having a healthy sense of being is foundational for our becoming whole. Our connection with Mother has a direct and significant impact on our emotional and relational development. Knowing we are part of a greater purpose and community is vital.

Lacking a sense of being, we can bend into others, looking for them to tell us who we are or whether we have value. Where there has been "bentness"—our broken capacity to lean into others for our identity, security, and peace—we seek the Lord to restore our uprightness. "With ears alert to catch His every word, we are brought to the place of *becoming*. It is the free state of listening-obedience where we find healing, completion, and our true identity. In this posture, our arms are stretched straight up to the Father, our palms opened wide to receive all that is good."[25]

Prayer for the sense of being is not a one-time cure, but it can be prayed anytime anxiety or fear rises within us. When we invite Him in, Jesus fills our cup through His presence. When that cup is poured out and emptied, we return, seeking God's infilling once again.

Through prayer, we ask God to do what our mothers did not or could not do. We seek God to sovereignly create the connection with Him and others that have been lacking. Starting with Jesus, we invite Him to meet us in our deepest need to know and be known by Him. These prayers help us experience and know God, thereby creating a deeper intimacy with Him. They provide discernment to recognize what keeps us rooted in the false self. They assist in releasing us from any attachments or entanglements that limit our identity from being in Christ Jesus. The more we practice the presence of God, the more we become the man or woman He created us to be.

Ask the Holy Spirit for the gift of faith to believe that the Lord will meet you in every place of need. Like the beseeching father in Mark 9:24, you may even start with this simple prayer: *Lord, help me to be willing to be willing! Help me with my doubt. Help me with my unbelief.*

The journey is one step at a time.

Prayer

Lord, You knit me together in my mother's womb. You saw me grow and develop. You were present when I drew my first breath. You are aware of every connection I had or did not

[25]Ibid., p. 53.

have with my mother. You knew her capacity and limitations to impart to me a sense of being and well-being. Lord, I recognize that my mother had her areas of brokenness, which may have limited her capacity to connect with me as an infant. I release her to You, seeking Your grace, enabling me to do so.

I come before You, entering Your presence, seeking Your healing touch in those areas where anxiety has lived within me. You have not forgotten me. Your heart is toward me. You longed to bring Israel under Your wings as a mother hen covers her chicks. Jesus, You wept over Jerusalem at the early stages of Your crucifixion and resurrection. You see and know my deficits and pain. You are the compassionate One to whom I can bare my soul.

I offer my soul up to You with its fears, dread, and anxieties. [Place your hands on your abdomen.] As deep calls to deep, Lord, I invite Your healing presence into these emotions that have troubled me in the depths of my being. I no longer desire to meet my insecurity and angst through attachment to false sources of life. I release to You the coping mechanisms I sought to assuage my feelings of being disconnected and separate. I now renounce these attachments which I established by not seeking Your presence. Where others could not fully affirm and bless my existence, I now turn only to You. I welcome Your presence to fill any places within me that were lacking in the sense of being.

I invite You to secure me in Your love. I ask You to establish Your Lordship in the core of my being. Be my foundation. Secure me in the hope that it will turn out well for me. May I know that I am secure in Your love and have a purpose for my life.

Soul Work

1. How present was your mother in your early life? How did she relate to you emotionally? How would an objective outside observer describe the relationship between your mother and you?

2. How connected do you feel as part of God's creation? How involved is God in your everyday life? Answer these from your heart and do not give the "right" scriptural response.

3. What is blocking you from letting God enter any deep areas of anxiety or fear?

Journaling Moment

In a place of quiet reflection, ask the Holy Spirit to give you the divine objectivity to see your mother as He sees her. If your relationship with her is or was strained, ask Him to show you how she imparted good to you. Write out and bring to the Lord the healthy expectations you had regarding your mother. Ask Him to meet any unmet needs. Begin to ask Him to fill any void that was the result of a broken relationship with her.

SIX

Knowing the Father

YOU ARE LOVED BY YOUR MAKER, NOT BECAUSE YOU TRY TO PLEASE HIM AND SUCCEED OR FAIL TO PLEASE HIM AND APOLOGIZE, BUT BECAUSE HE WANTS TO BE YOUR FATHER.[26]

- MAX LUCADO

We had discussed how, in the Garden of Eden before the Fall, Adam and Eve enjoyed an unhindered relationship with the Father. Nothing blocked their capacity to receive His love. Their identity was secure in His love and in the love they shared. They knew true intimacy with God and one another. This is the relationship God created and designed for each of us to experience!

We have also talked about John 14:6, which identifies Jesus as "the way and the truth and the life." He is not only a necessity for life; He is life itself. Christians routinely profess their relationship with Jesus. Our identity is no longer based on the past, but is alive and centered in Him. Indeed, this connection is foundational to the Christian faith. However, the latter part of John 14:6 is just as crucial: "No one comes to the Father except through me."

Jesus was pointing the way to His Father. As we see in the second Garden, the Garden of Gethsemane, Jesus came to fulfill the will of the Father: "Not my will, but yours be done" (Luke 22:42). He made the way, through Himself, for us to know our heavenly Father.

[26]Max Lucado, *Wild Grace* (Thomas Nelson, 2012), p. 141.

Knowing Jesus, then, is but the first step in this pilgrimage to our true home. Knowing God as Father is paramount to our becoming who He created us to be from the very beginning. How often do we acknowledge God as Father? If a relationship with God as Father is lacking in our Christian walk, we have not yet come to the full realization of why Jesus became a man.

Unfortunately, due to family dysfunction, our image of *father* may be askew. We often transfer onto God our broken images of father or authority figures in our lives. It takes little discernment to recognize the unfortunate portrayal of fathers in the media. Doesn't the constant presence of these broken images reveal a wounding and underlying hunger for a true father?

In multiple Bible references, Jesus refers to His relationship with God the Father. Our earthly fathers were to pave the way for us to relate to God as Father. The love we receive from our earthly dad's influences how we receive love from Father God.

Let's examine for a moment the relationship Jesus has with the Father, and the relationship the Holy Spirit has with the Father and Son as well.

The Trinitarian Expression of God

The concept of the Trinity is difficult to comprehend. It goes beyond being a mere doctrinal statement. It is not tri-theism—three separate gods who are best buds. Nor is it unipersonalism—only one god with multiple expressions in different situations. Rather, it is Trinitarianism: one God in three Persons who are in a relationship with one another. God is not fundamentally more one than He is three, nor is He fundamentally more three than He is one.

I think you see the challenge of trying to explain this crucial aspect of our faith.

Let me try another way to define the Trinity. God is not just a cognitive or conceptual idea; He is love. For love to be authentic, it cannot be solely unto itself. Genuine love expresses itself actively by extending itself to others. For love to be real, therefore, relationship has to be present.

Christopher West best describes the expression of love through the relationships within the Trinity:

> … No explanation of the Trinity suffices. Nonetheless, we can discern from revelation that the Father eternally "begets" the Son by giving Himself to and for the Son. In turn, the

Son (the "beloved of the Father") eternally receives the love of the Father and eternally gives himself back to the Father. This ever-shared, ever-spirating love is the Holy Spirit who, as we say in the Nicene Creed, "proceeds from the Father and the Son." Amazing. Stop to think about it. Perfect love—perfectly and eternally given, perfectly and eternally received, perfectly and eternally returned—that's God.[27]

During the seventh century, John of Damascus spoke of the Trinity as perichoresis—literally, "the circle dance." C. S. Lewis talked described the Trinity in *Mere Christianity* in a similar way:

> What does it all matter? It matters more than anything else in the world. The whole dance, or drama, or pattern of this three-Personal life is to be played out in each one of us.... There is no other way to the happiness for which we were made.

The Trinity expresses the reality of love in its fullest dimension.

You may be asking, why is this understanding crucial? It is crucial because the cross of Jesus has made way for you to participate in the holy dance contained within the Trinity. The door is open for you to know the Father. You can—and must!—come into a real relationship with Him. Knowing Father God is not an option. The Holy Spirit (as I will discuss in the next chapter) enables you to experience the love of the Father and the Son in your life.

The Father and the Son

> Philip said, "Lord, show us the Father, and that will be enough for us." Jesus answered: "Don't you know me, Philip, even after I have been among you such a long time? Anyone who has seen me has seen the Father. How can you say, 'Show us the Father'?"
>
> – John 14:8–9

[27]Christopher West, *Theology of the Body Explained* (Pauline Books & Media, 2nd revised edition, 2008), pp. 10–11.

Deep within Jesus lay the purpose and necessity of performing the will of His Father. Jesus was all about the Father. His core mission, manifested through His obedience, was to do the will of His Father. Jesus longed to see the will of the Father accomplished: "I have come down from heaven not to do my will but to do the will of him who sent me" (John 6:38).

The life of Jesus flowed from the Father. Jesus drew His meaning and purpose from the Father. Even as a child, when Joseph and Mary had lost Him and, three days later, found Him in the Temple, Jesus explained that He had to "be about My Father's business" (Luke 2:49, NKJV). Reflect on this for a moment. The young boy Jesus made this statement to His earthly parents! The motivation to do God's will went beyond His being an obedient son; it originated in the deep love Jesus had for His Father. The obedience of Jesus was the love of the Father made manifest. Likewise, the source of our obedience must be similarly grounded in our love for God and not out of performance-based-acceptance.

The relationship Jesus had and has with God the Father is profoundly personal. It is rooted in the core of Jesus' being. Not only did abandonment to the Father's love not negate who Jesus was, but the very Personhood of Jesus was rooted in His oneness with His Father. Abandonment to the Father's love resulted in the fullest expression of the relationship of Father to Son and Son to Father.

Throughout the gospels, Jesus clearly indicated His deep and individual relationship with the Father, leading to the ultimate expression of oneness in John 14:23: "Anyone who loves me will obey my teaching. My Father will love them, and *we* will come to them and make our home with them" (italics added). That holy *we* indicated in this scripture, reflects the incredibly intimate relationship of Jesus with the Father.

Being one with Jesus, you, too, can enter this level of intimacy with Father God. Are you beginning to understand how knowing Jesus more deeply will ultimately result in your knowing the Father? Do you want to know the Father as Jesus does?

The Role of Father

The role of Father God in our lives is a significant part of our becoming the men and women He created us to be. But we exist in a fallen world. We experience broken relationships

FATHER MODELS HEALTHY LOVE FROM MEN AS HAVING THE CAPACITY TO CALL FORTH, AFFIRM, AND BLESS.

on varying levels, going back to childhood. No family meets all our love needs perfectly. To enter the deeper connection Father God desires for us, we must determine if any blocks exist in our relationship with Him.

Children need the presence of both Mother and Father to feel loved and valued. Mother provides a sense of being—that I am okay, connected, and welcomed. Father provides a safe environment and covering, helping me as his child to discover who I am. Father teaches me how to risk, explore, and question, so I can grow and become all God intends for me. Together, Mother and Father provide the form and structure that assist in the mental, emotional, physical, and spiritual development of their children.

At birth, as we have seen, we identify with Mother. Reaching the age of two—commonly called "the terrible twos"—we learn to use the word *no*. This is the age of individuation. Here I begin to sense that I am separate from Mother, that I am an individual with an identity different from hers. I can voice my opinion and say no to anything that does not appeal to my agenda.

At this stage of development, Father's voice plays a crucial role. Father is bigger than I am. I physically look up to him (as I do with Mother). I view him as an authority figure. His role (along with Mother's) is to provide safe and healthy boundaries for me. His presence, expressions, and words affect my developing core of self.

Father also influences the development of a healthy sense and comfort with my being male or female. Mother does so as well, but Father impacts me uniquely because of his male voice. The presence of his voice imparts inner affirmation that differs from that of Mother.

There is a testimony of a young girl who wore a special dress for the first time. Although her mother told her how beautiful she looked, she could not wait until her father came home to see her. Unfortunately, when he did, he failed to notice her. This crushed her. Even though her mother had tried to affirm her, she desired words of affirmation from the male voice, from her dad.

Father models healthy love from men as having the capacity to call forth, affirm, and bless. What is the psychological and emotional impact on me as a child when Father blesses and affirms me? I feel secure and loved. I learn how to love and relate healthily from a place of confidence inside. The more I am inwardly secure, the greater my confidence to relate to my environment and others.

What is your earliest memory of Father?

Father demonstrates his love and affirmation through being present, loving, and engaging in the life of his child. By being emotionally and spiritually present, he "names" who I am, validating and blessing my developing sense of self. His words and healthy boundaries increase my capacity to feel secure in my maleness or femaleness. This adds to the foundation Mother established earlier. Father calls forth my gifts, skills, and interests, which affirms me as an individual. If Father does not "name" me—a legitimate need—I may seek others to name me.

My acceptance of Father influences my relationships with others and with God. Initially, I depend totally on him. Later, he releases and empowers me to become independent, even while I remain connected with him relationally. Through his actions, he reveals that he is trustworthy and true. This foundation will enable me later to enter a relationship with God as Father, knowing that He likewise is trustworthy, loving, and true.

Father Wounding

Due to their brokenness and family history, fathers may create emotionally unstable environments. Their children internalize his degree of presence, ranging from being too absent to too present. Our temperaments influence the way we process our fathers' choices. Some of us may deeply internalize his actions, while others of us compartmentalize them, sequestering them away. We all react or respond uniquely to our family structures.

Too Absent

Father's absence during his children's formative years, from birth to age five, leaves an ache, a longing, and a search for male affirmation. Deficits here can contribute to insecurity in how we feel as male or female. If he is absent while his son is between ages six to twelve, the boy may shift his focus onto appearance without inward confidence that he is male. Father's absence during the same age range for his daughter may leave her insecure and vulnerable to look to other men to find this security. She may also shut down her heart toward men. Insecurity can result in vain attempts by both daughters and sons to compensate for the lack of their fathers' male voice to bless them.

An outwardly demanding father frequently bases his acceptance of me on what I do, not who I am. He often stifles communication, with the common result that I bury my emotions. Unfortunately, this leads me to deny my true feelings and tend to define my value through performance or accomplishment. I am more comfortable with false intimacy— seeking to know and be known via attachments to unhealthy and false life sources—hiding my true feelings and wearing a range of masks. I remain in control, determining how far I let others know me. I limit my capacity to experience true intimacy—that is, being real in healthy relationships—by creating a façade.

When Father is absent, either emotionally or physically, he cannot relate on a heart level with his child. Here, wounding can be found in what remains unspoken. A child missing the presence of an outside voice often responds by turning inward. The result can be an unhealthy, heightened state of self-awareness. Underlying feelings of abandonment develop with accompanying low self-esteem, worthlessness, and rejection. To survive, I self-protect, creating walls and limiting my capacity to trust others.

A passive father is unable to relate healthily with his wife and child. His lack of voice creates an atmosphere of unrest and insecurity in his child. Mother often steps into the void, trying to take Father's place. She cannot replace him, however, which may result in her child's resentment of her. That resentment can later give rise to feelings of hatred toward women (misogyny)—resentment generalized and transferred onto all women. This reaction can occur in both women and men. Other consequences may include viewing men as weak; having poor boundaries; lacking self-discipline, and harboring resentment toward authority

Too Present

A father may also be too present, exerting power through control or abuse. Rather than being demanding, he uses emotional manipulation. As a result, I lack a healthy sense of self and have a confused view of intimacy. My father's feelings invalidate my emotions, so I shut down emotionally, which cripples my emotional development. I learn to create barriers to connecting with others. Isolated children are more vulnerable to enemy attack and seeking self-comfort.

"The real issue isn't how deeply you were wounded," writes Dr. Harry Schaumburg, "but what you've done to protect yourself from further wounds by turning to false intimacy. The issue is also whether or not you'll allow your woundedness to prevent you from loving God and others."[28] As we will see in chapter 9, we were created to experience true intimacy. However, our wounded past opens the door to false intimacy. It also hinders our entering into genuine, loving relationships.

Our Reactions

We must view our fathers through God's eyes. When sin has been committed against us, we seek the Lord's help to forgive. We also seek God's revelation for how we reacted to our fathers. These reactions, with their generalized misbeliefs, limit our capacity to enter into healthy relationships. We are culpable for how we choose to react to the wounds of our past.

Have you transferred onto God as Father any unresolved emotions toward your earthly father, mother, or other authority figures?

Transference occurs through the unconscious redirection of feelings from a person or event in our past to a person or circumstance in the present. Below is a list of misbeliefs, possibly related to transference issues. Can you connect any of them to a specific hurtful occurrence from your past? This realization will be beneficial when we discuss forgiveness and surrender in later chapters. Ask the Holy Spirit to reveal which of the following may apply to you:

God is cruel and capricious.
God is demanding or unforgiving.
God is selective and unfair.
God is distant and unavailable.
God is simply not there when I need Him.
God is kind but confused.
God is present, but incapable.
God is impotent or passive, unable to effect change truly.
God is _______.

[28]Harry W. Schaumburg, *False Intimacy* (NavPress, rev. ed. 1997), p. 65.

The Father's Blessing

> Be there … care… and put your children first in your life. When you are given the awesome responsibility of being a father, that is the most important responsibility you can have. God wants us to have a loving relationship with our kids and help them grow … just like God's relationship with us.[29]
>
> – John Harbaugh, head coach, Baltimore Ravens

God as Father is constantly extending His love toward you, whether you can sense Him or not. His very heart's desire is that you know He has reclaimed you as His child. He wants you to experience the depths of intimacy that exist in the Trinity.

What is preventing you from knowing Him?

The Father will not force His will on yours, but He will do everything He can to reveal His heart for you. He is committed to your knowing His true character and nature. He desires to identify and remove anything blocking your capacity to know Him. The Father longs for you to stop resisting His love through expressions of fear and control.

Have you experienced glimpses of the Father's pursuit of you? Are you willing to begin opening your heart to the truth of His love and pursuit?

God, as Father desires that we foster intimacy with Him, as He has with Jesus. We cannot do that merely by changing our behaviors or by trying harder. Rather, we can foster intimacy with Father God by permitting Him to pinpoint in our hearts where we are reacting to any previous wounding. Spending quality time with Father God increases intimacy with Him. With the help of the Holy Spirit, we seek a deepening awareness of God, free from the dysfunctional relational experiences of our past. To embrace this deeper knowing and true intimacy with God requires the difficult choice of rising above the limitations of our past. God will strengthen our capacity to do so. He is not like our earthly fathers; He is a true Father.

Paul writes in Romans 8:15–16,

> The Spirit you received does not make you slaves so that you live in fear again; rather, the Spirit you received brought about your adoption to sonship. And by him, we cry, 'Abba,

[29]John Harbaugh, quoted in Kurt Faust, *"Happy Father's Day: Blessings to All Committed Fathers,"* Midland Daily News, June 21, 2015.

Father.' The Spirit himself testifies with our spirit that we are God's children.

The word *sonship* is not one of biological determination but of positional identity. Through the work of the cross, as believers, we now, male or female, have the full inheritance of sons. We are no longer in the family of Adam, but we enjoy, through this adoption, full rights as daughters and sons of the Father.

One of the associations of Paul's use of the word testifies (*summartunreo*) is with martyrdom. It means to give a significant witness, like those who were martyred. The Apostle is strongly affirming us as the Father's sons and daughters and providing compelling evidence that we are standing before a new and true Father. It is a dynamic, powerful reality, grounded in spiritual truth. This is not about how we feel but the reality of *who we are*.

Are you starting to make the connection that your feelings or circumstances are not the indications of your identity?

The Father desires us to experience the fullness of His love as extended to Jesus at His baptism. The Father's blessing of Jesus was not a deductive thought process, nor was it a warm, sentimental Hallmark moment. The Father ripped open the heavens to pour a blessing down on His Son. The blessing of Father God, confirmed Jesus' identity as imparted by the Holy Spirit.

The Holy Spirit wants us to have the same consciousness that we are in the family of God. Beyond any doubt, this is a factual, spiritual reality.

According to Galatians 4:4–7, we have within us the Spirit of Jesus, enabling us to cry, "Abba, Father." *Abba* is a personal word of endearment for *father*. Jesus cried out to the Father as Abba when He sweated blood in Gethsemane. This is deep relational devotion.

Have you ever cried out like this to the Father? God has placed within the depths of your being the capacity for you to cry out to the Father as Abba, Papa, Daddy. Blocks to God as Father may hinder this level of intimacy.

God the Father is a good Father. By His divine nature, this is who He is. Through His goodness, He shapes you by words of affirmation, discipline, and admonishment. Knowing Him as true Father, you receive His challenging words as words of love. They are words of love because His correction is an opportunity for removing whatever limits your becoming. Father God knows what is best for you because He designed your innermost being. He sees what you cannot. He knows what you do not.

Knowing the Father

"Our understanding of the Father's fullness is progressive," writes Andrew Comiskey, "and essential to our integration as persons. Theological fullness results in psychological wholeness."[30] Some may resist the word *progressive*, but this is the reality of the process of sanctification. To build our knowledge of and trust in God as Father requires ongoing experience.

The Creator of the universe will prove His trustworthiness to you. I am humbled that He is more committed to me than I am to Him. How is it possible that your Creator pursues you, watches for you, and longs for you to enter the depths of knowing who He truly is? When we come into knowing the amazing character of God, it helps provide greater clarity in our thinking (for example, destroying any false conceptions or misinterpretations about Him) and thereby results in our greater wholeness. Once again, changing our thinking brings about outward manifestations regarding our behavior.

Wrapping Up

We must stop looking for the dad we never had. Father God is more than able to repair any breach that occurred with our earthly fathers. He will step into any void created by a stolen or limited relationship with our dads. For some of us, Jesus' cry on the cross, "Father, why have You forsaken me?" echoes a similar cry buried in our hearts. The cross of Jesus made the way to fill every missing component with our earthly fathers. The affectionate authority of God the Father replaces any broken authority figures in our lives. Feelings of abandonment have a place to go in the cross of Jesus. He will never leave or forsake you. Because Jesus is in the Father, and because you are in Him, the Father is present to any feelings of isolation, loneliness, or seclusion.

> I will be a Father to you, and you will be my sons and daughters, says the Lord Almighty.
>
> – 2 Corinthians 6:18

> I will say to the north, 'Give them up!' and to the south, 'Do not hold them back.' Bring my sons from afar and my daughters from the ends of the earth.
>
> – Isaiah 43:6

[30] Andrew Comiskey, *Restoring Relational Integrity through the Broken Body of Christ* (Desert Stream, 2013), p. 62

Both of these verses reveal the heart of God for you. He wants you to know Him as Father, as Abba. Will you let Him into your damaged, internalized beliefs and wounds? Will you allow the removal of the words and labels that have limited and plagued you? Will you allow God to do this process so He may renew your mind?

If your image of fatherhood is tainted, the Holy Spirit can resymbolize that image, especially for how it interferes with relating to God as Father. As you embrace Jesus as your core identity and pursue intimacy with Him, He reveals the Father to you. Jesus will take you to the Father's house.

The Father is waiting for your invitation. Please stop and, at this very moment, ask the Holy Spirit to release from the core of your being the ability to cry out for God as your Abba, your Father.

Prayer

Heavenly Father, I come before You seeking Your presence. You know my inner struggles. You are aware of every connection I had with my father. You knew his capacity and limitations to impart the good of a male voice and blessing. Lord, I recognize that my father had his own areas of brokenness, which may have limited his capacity to connect with me. I release him to You, seeking Your grace, enabling me to do so.

Holy Spirit, I welcome Your truth to expose where I am in reaction or resistance to Father God. Show me where I have transferred the past hurts onto Father God, which prevents me from entering into deeper intimacy with Him. Where am I fearful of Him? Why can't I trust Him? Please show me the dysfunctional filters through which I see God as Father.

Father God, please meet me in the exact place of my need. Where do I lack a father's blessing? Where have I blocked out the capacity to be affirmed by You or by the whole men in my life? Please alleviate my fears or enable me to lower my walls of defense toward You.

Father God, I desire to receive Your blessing. I long to hear the words *Well done, good and faithful servant.* May I begin to believe I am Your beloved daughter or son. May this reality grow ever more real within my being.

Soul Work

1. How present was your father in your early life? How did he relate to you emotionally? How would an objective outside observer describe the relationship between your father and you?

2. How has the lack of the presence of your father's voice impacted your confidence, your sense of security being a man or woman, and the capacity to be in whole relationships?

3. Read Galatians 4:4–7. Describe how your life and relationship with God reflect the reality of this Scripture?

Journaling Moment

Write down the words *mother* and *father* in your journal. Ask the Holy Spirit to reveal and name the emotions you feel when you see these words. What images come to mind? Write them down. If this is an emotionally difficult exercise for you, invite Jesus into the midst of your emotions and seek how He would lead to you to process them aright. Now ask Him to reveal to you how Jesus and the Father see your parents. Write down what you see. Also, seek the Lord for a word specifically for your heart.

SEVEN

Knowing the Holy Spirit

We have discussed the significance of our relationship with the Father and the Son. Now we shift our attention to the crucial role of the Holy Spirit. He is not merely a dove showing up occasionally, nor is He an outlet to plug into when we are running low on power. He is not simply an influence; He is an actual *Person*. The Holy Spirit makes the love of the Father and the Son experientially real. We must not sequester Him, relegate Him to a corner, or treat Him with a cavalier attitude. He is not a vending machine from which we select a "gift" according to our perceived need. The Holy Spirit calls us to have a relationship with Him.

> But you will receive power when the Holy Spirit comes on you; and you will be my witnesses in Jerusalem, and in all Judea and Samaria, and to the ends of the earth.
>
> – Acts 1:8

The importance of the Holy Spirit cannot be overstated. The Greek word for "power" in the verse above is *dunamis*, meaning the ability to perform anything. It is the root word for "dynamite." To walk as men and women of integrity, we cannot rely on our willpower, no matter how determined we may be. Depending on our strength centers us in the false self, through fleshly control. We may walk in obedience for a time, but eventually, we will fail. We need power from outside of us, enabling us to obey.

Jesus walked in obedience, thus demonstrating His love for the Father. His obedience stemmed not from a sense of duty but a core of love. Obedience motivated by a sense of duty emphasizes the actions themselves. Not centered in the heart reduces actions to performance-based acceptance: "I do what's right because it's what I'm supposed to do. I perform so I'll be noticed, liked, or accepted." The drive to meet a standard of performance negates a connection with the heart. Jesus, by contrast, chose to align His will with the will of the Father through the affections of His heart. Love motivated Him.

We find our obedience and perfection in and through Jesus, who is our center and life. The obedience of Jesus unto death met the requirements of the Law. He fulfilled the Law's demands for us. The Law was to expose our human inability to meet it, thereby exposing our need for God. The result of Jesus' obedience frees us from striving—working in our strength—to gain the impossibility of perfection. When we strive through our efforts, we are placing ourselves back under the Law. Through the working of the Holy Spirit within us, however, He encourages and enables us to enter into a place of obedience.

What motivates your obedience to Jesus and the Father?

Jesus accomplished the will of the Father and then sent the Holy Spirit to us. Here again is a manifestation of the Trinity, revealing a significant connection with Jesus, the Father, and the Holy Spirit. According to W. E. Vine, "The Father acts in and through the Son, the Son acts as in the Father, and the Spirit acts in perfect unison of being and action with the Father and the Son."[31]

My Story

Early in my process, I often battled temptation and sin out of my strength. Taking what Paul writes in Romans 12:9—"Love must be sincere. Hate what is evil; cling to what is good"—I made the erroneous choice to focus on hating evil. In my flesh, I tried to drum up this hatred. Whenever a particular sin came to mind, I would try to hate it. I focused on hating evil emotionally instead of "[clinging] to what is good." Then the Holy Spirit began speaking to me gently: *Bob, if you fall in love with Me, you won't be so focused on sin.* I embraced a shift in my thinking.

Previously, motivated by duty, I would think, *A good Christian man wouldn't be thinking such*

[31]W. E. Vine, *John, His Record of Christ* (Oliphants, 1948), p. 132.

thoughts or doing such actions. Now I chose to pursue deeper intimacy with God, thinking about Him instead of trying to hate the sin. Doing so, I eventually experienced greater freedom from life-dominating sin. My motivation not to sin now rose from the growing love and intimacy I had for my Beloved. I did not want to grieve Him. I began to hate sin because it disrupted my intimacy with God.

When tempted, I focus on my relationship with God. Doing so draws my attention away from sin and the enemy's tactics. The Holy Spirit within compels me toward a loving relationship with the Father and away from my fleshly striving. Listening to Him and aligning my will with His results in obedience. I looked up and out of me, clinging to the Lord, who is good.

Who the Holy Spirit Is

> If you love me, keep my commands. And I will ask the Father, and he will give you another advocate to help you and be with you forever—the Spirit of truth. The world cannot accept him because it neither sees him nor knows him. But you know him, for he lives with you and will be in you. I will not leave you as orphans; I will come to you.
>
> – John 14:15–18

In the context of the previous section, note how Jesus starts these verses: "*If you love me.*" Jesus did not set any conditions for obedience other than *If you love me*. Implied in the Greek, this is an ongoing process. True obedience is rooted in love and relationship, not performance. Jesus knew the difficulties of walking in this world. Out of His love, centered in the Father's will, Jesus anticipated the release of the third Person of the Trinity. He knew that our relationship with the Holy Spirit would lead us into obedience.

Various Bible versions translate the Greek word *parakletos* as "advocate, helper, or comforter." This word has legal implications. In a court case, this is someone who comes in from the outside to offer support in time of need or trouble. This person is capable of providing a defense through either witness or expertise. Do you ever need such an individual? Like an advocate, the Holy Spirit comes to plead our cause.

The word *comforter* comes from the Latin *fortis*, which means "brave." The Holy Spirit enables us to be brave so that we can face our struggles. He wants us to live victoriously instead of in defeat. Through fellowship with the Holy Spirit, we receive encouragement, strength, and support. This expresses the heart of the Holy Spirit and His lovingkindness toward us.

What the Holy Spirit Does

In Romans 8:26–27, Paul addressed the reality of our day-to-day struggles:

> "In the same way, the Spirit helps us in our weakness. We do not know what we ought to pray for, but the Spirit himself intercedes for us through wordless groans. And he who searches our hearts knows the mind of the Spirit because the Spirit intercedes for God's people in accordance with the will of God."

In our weakness, we may not know what to pray, but the Holy Spirit does. He searches our hearts and, like Jesus, acts on our behalf.

Have you found yourself in a time of deep struggle when you were at a loss for words? I certainly have. These are the very moments when the Holy Spirit rises within us, enabling us to press through to endure the moment. He willingly meets us exactly at our place of brokenness, providing specifically for our present need.

The world cannot receive the Holy Spirit because it will not accept the truth. Devoid of moral responsibility and continually eliminating God, the world renders itself incapable of recognizing the conviction of the Holy Spirit. The prevalence of evil in our culture diminishes the human capacity to sense sin—which is now an archaic word. In failing to recognize Jesus, the world cannot recognize the Holy Spirit.

The Holy Spirit, on the other hand, speaks the truth and defends it. In John 16:5–11, Jesus addressed the capacity of God's Spirit to bring "sin and righteousness and judgment" (verse 8). He told them "unless I go away, the Advocate will not come to you; but if I go, I will send him to you" (verse 7). Jesus knew that the presence of the Holy Spirit would bring uninterrupted fellowship forever. Jesus was anxious for His friends and followers to walk in this spiritual reality. Jesus indicated that the Holy Spirit would bring conviction similar to a legal cross-examination. The cross-examination exposes the crime and the weakness of the defense against the conviction. In the same way, the Holy Spirit convicts us of any sins we have committed. He provides proof.

He exposes our unrighteousness in light of the righteousness of Jesus. The Holy Spirit does this exposure out of compassion and love for us. His goal is to evoke godly sorrow within us for our sins, which leads to confession and repentance. Then He brings us peace, reminding us of the work of the cross of Jesus, which wrought our salvation and forgiveness.

No matter what your condition, you can always come as you are to the foot of the cross of Jesus.

But, disappointed from the battles and struggles we face, we can become weary. It may appear as if the idols around us grow ever more powerful when we grow weaker. The abyss of despair sometimes feels as if it is right outside our door. Can you identify with me in having these feelings? Lacking a relationship with the Holy Spirit, we fail to seek His strength. This is especially so regarding the empowering of our wills. Instead of focusing on our defeats, we must welcome the Holy Spirit in to renew our atrophied wills.

There is no question that you receive the Holy Spirit when you make Jesus your Lord and Savior. How often, however, do you ignore, deflect, or defy Him? Even though He is present to you, are you present to Him? Ouch! Where do you quench His presence? I have pretended the Holy Spirit is not there, blocking my ears to His voice. When I say we must welcome the Holy Spirit in, it is, so we acknowledge Him. We permit Him to manifest Himself as He chooses. We need His assistance to be overcomers!

Our relationship with the Holy Spirit, the Comforter, helps us endure the struggle. He encourages us, guides us to the truth, and convicts us of disobedience. The result is obedience and a fuller experience of the life God created us to live.

To align our will with the will of the Father, however, we must allow the Holy Spirit to empower our wills.

The Empowering of the Will

"If I am a child of God, I realize not only that God is the source of my will, but that God is in me to will."[32]

I Kings 18–19 recounts Elijah's confrontation with Ahab and the priests of Baal, and then

[32]Oswald Chambers, *Our Brilliant Heritage* (Discovery House, 1998), p. 130.

his flight from Jezebel. Within the scope of these events, we see Elijah having two mountain top experiences, one at Mount Carmel and the other at Mount Horeb. In the first, we see his zeal and prophetic calling in full measure. In the second, we see a weary, broken man, humbling himself before the Lord.

Elijah had confronted King Ahab boldly: "You have abandoned the LORD's commands and have followed the Baals" (1 Kings 18:18). He challenged Ahab to assemble 450 priests of Baal at Mount Carmel to test them against the Lord's sovereignty. Two altars were assembled, one to Baal and one to the Lord, where portions of a bull were to be burned.

The priests of Baal spent many hours crying out to their god to send fire to burn up their sacrifice. They became frenzied, cutting themselves (as was customary) until their blood flowed. Nothing happened.

Then Elijah had the Lord's altar doused three times with water and called on the Lord to answer him. Fire from heaven consumed the offering completely. Elijah commanded the slaughtering of all 450 priests of Baal. Imagine being there and seeing the fire of the Lord come down from heaven with such power and might!

But when Jezebel, Ahab's wife, and queen, found out what had happened on Mount Carmel, she was furious and sent a messenger to Elijah promising to kill him. The prophet ran for his life, ending up in the desert. "I have had enough, LORD," he prayed. "Take my life; I am no better than my ancestors" (1 Kings 19:4).

The Lord sent an angel to feed and strengthen Elijah for his long journey ahead. The prophet traveled for forty days and nights to Mount Horeb, where he spent the night in a cave. Then the word of the Lord came to him: "What are you doing here, Elijah?" (verse 9). Elijah replied that he was zealous for the Lord, adding, "I am the only one left, and now they are trying to kill me too" (verse 10).

We know this was not true, for the Lord had hidden away "seven thousand in Israel—all whose knees have not bowed down to Baal" (1 Kings 19:18). Elijah, however, was a broken man who now ran in fear.

Years earlier, another great man of God stood on Mount Horeb. God met Moses there through the burning bush. He, like Elijah, was all too well acquainted with his inadequacy and past failures. Look up the story in Exodus 3.

Can you identify with Elijah or Moses? In your early process, did you walk with zeal and expectations? Did you have times of amazing victory and enthusiasm? I think many of us, like Elijah, know what it is like to see God manifest His presence powerfully in our lives. We have had mountain top experiences like Elijah's on Mount Carmel. Just like Elijah, however, we came down into the valley, where we experienced challenges that eventually wore us down. Faced with disappointment and disillusionment, we tend to turn inward and run from God.

In the valley, circumstances or people confront us, beckoning us to return to our false self. Like the Hebrews after crossing the Red Sea, the enemy taunts us with his lies, tempting us to take control: *Go back to Egypt. Wasn't it better there than where you are now?* Where or what is your Egypt? The enemy wants us to forget the power of Jesus' cross and the reality of who we are in Christ.

Zeal will not carry us through our long journey in the valley. Hope turns from the belief that it will turn out well for us and into the embrace of despair, believing it will turn out badly for us. We make vows not to sin, attempting in our flesh to overcome the life-dominating sins and behaviors that plague us.

I have been there and done that. Have you done so as well? We respond to the Sunday altar call, rededicate ourselves, and plan to be good once again. Nevertheless, these efforts ultimately end in failure, cycle after cycle. Repeated failure wears us down. Despair chokes our heart, resulting in bitterness and cynicism. Our wills wither until we, like Elijah, ask the Lord to let us die.

Did you realize you were in such good company?

Instead of turning inward with these vain attempts in the flesh, we need to turn up and out of ourselves. We need to seek and identify with, the One who is greater than we are. We need the manifest power of the Holy Spirit as we come into His presence to renew and awaken our atrophied wills. Like the "smoldering wick" of Isaiah 42:3, we may feel nearly burned out. However, just as Lord sent His angel to feed and strengthen Elijah, the Holy Spirit will come to us to renew our spirits and empower us to rise.

THE ENEMY WANTS US TO FORGET THE POWER OF HIS CROSS AND WHO WE ARE IN CHRIST.

In chapter 3, we learned that, through the cross of Jesus, each of us is a new creation and receives a new, established center. In chapter 6 we found that we have a Father responsive to our needs, who longs to bless us as His children. Now we see that the Holy Spirit comes to us with His *dunamis* presence and the power to do anything. The Holy Spirit as the *parakletos* comes alongside to defend and support us.

The Trinity manifested in fullness extends a mighty outpouring of love toward us. Once again, the Father's voice beckons us: Rise, My son! Rise, My daughter! The Holy Spirit enables us to escape whatever cycle of destructive behavior constrains us. Instead of operating out of the flesh—the false self—we embrace the obedience to walk in our true self with new strength and purpose. We may invite God's Spirit to come and empower our wills.

Prayer for Empowering of the Will

Father, I come before You struggling, broken, and in need. Thank You that my need does not make me needy, but simply reveals my humanity. I confess that I have walked in the false self, taking control of my process. In my zeal, I have battled in vain attempts to overcome. The results have been disappointment, fear, anger, bitterness, and cynicism. Like Elijah, I want to run and give up.

In my discouragement, how have I turned inward on myself? Where have I allowed my weakness, inadequacy, and behaviors to define my value and worth? I confess my performance-based acceptance, seeking to please You by what I do instead of who I am, as Your beloved daughter or son. I invite You specifically into those places where I experience shame and self-hatred, those places where I want to hide from You.

You are almighty God (*El Shaddai*), God my righteousness (*Jehovah Tsidkenu*). I need Your strength and empowering to call me forth, to enable me to rise again, standing in my true self. Father God, I long for Your will to inhabit my will. Lord Jesus, Your cross, and resurrection established my true self, making me one with You. I welcome You, Holy Spirit, as the Spirit of truth, as One who comes alongside with power. Holy Spirit, come and center me in the fullness of Your presence. Help me to love that which is good, motivated by love instead of duty. Guide me to walk in Your truth. Empower me to be the son or daughter the Father intended from the beginning of the world. I lay down my struggles, yielding my soul, and will to You.

Father, command what You will, then will what You command. May I know more and more what it is to be in-willed, empowered, and regenerated by You.

The Renunciation of Idols

As we mentioned earlier, the working of the Spirit in us will lead to repentance. Many of us find great vulnerability in the breaking of the first two commandments: "You shall have no other gods before me. You shall not make for yourself an image in the form of anything in heaven above or on the earth beneath or in the waters below" (Exodus 20:3–4). Through the work of the Holy Spirit, we choose not to bend the knee to the sexual and relational idols we have created and worshiped. He empowers us as sons and daughters to take a stand against that which the Father detests. The Lord wants us to make a decision regarding the idols we have contained within our hearts. He wants us to free us from any stronghold established in our thinking.

The Lord called His people uniquely unto Himself: "For you are a people holy to the LORD your God. The LORD, your God, has chosen you out of all the peoples on the face of the earth to be his people, his treasured possession" (Deuteronomy 7:6). "Therefore, 'Come out from them and be separate, says the Lord. Touch no unclean thing, and I will receive you.' And, 'I will be a Father to you, and you will be my sons and daughters, says the Lord Almighty'" (2 Corinthians 6:17–18) From the very beginning, the Father, knew what was best for His creation. He established the boundaries necessary for us to walk in wholeness and integrity.

Earlier, I talked about Elijah's encounter with the priests of Baal. Baal was a significant god of the Canaanites. He was the sun god of Phoenicia and called Lord Possessor. There were multiple variations of his name in ancient cultures. Asherah was his wife and called the queen of heaven. We see multiple references in Scripture to Baal's temples and altars, built upon the high places, capturing the rays of the rising and setting sun.

God's instructions to the Israelites, were whenever they encountered the Canaanites, to destroy them completely. He wanted to keep His people separate from the idol worship of Baal and Asherah. The worship ceremonies were rife with orgies and many expressions of sexual immorality. Male eunuchs dressed as women served as temple prostitutes. Asherah poles, part of the sexual worship mentioned in the Scriptures, were phallic images carved onto poles. Fields of these poles existed and were brought into the Lord's Holy Temple during times of apostasy.

Another prevalent god of the Canaanites and Ammonites was the god Molech, a fire god. Worship of Molech often consisted of the sacrificial burning of babies. These babies included those borne out of the sexual worship of Baal and Asherah. The worship of these three demonic gods involved death and all forms of sexual immorality.

They followed worthless idols and became worthless themselves.

– Jeremiah 2:5

But my people have exchanged their glorious God for worthless idols.

– Jeremiah 2:11

We become that on which our hearts are set. In my story, I indicated that my drive was to hate sin, focusing on it instead of on God. In these two Jeremiah passages, we see the same problem when we turn to idols: We become like them, worthless, exchanging the glory found in God for what is lifeless. What a contrast with Jesus' promise that He came so we can experience abundant life!

I often heard Leanne Payne share at her conferences that "we are wired to be worshipers. If we do not worship God, we will worship something or someone else." Today our culture worships both sex and the spirit of death. These are present in all forms of media. The world is increasingly desensitized to evil and more acclimated to darkness. Avoiding the pain of light, it prefers to remain in the shadows. The worship of Baal and Asherah, as in the ancient world, is rampant in the sexual brokenness all around us today.

Just as in the Temple of Jerusalem, many denominations now allow and even encourage sexual immorality in their churches. The worship of Molech takes place through acts of abortion. There is nothing new under the sun.

The spirit of death is "a spiritual influence, a shadow over our days that veils the way we view life, subverts our perceptions, and shapes a fatalistic mindset. It is…the spiritual essence and atmosphere of a fallen world emanating from 'the god of this world.'"[33] Its pervasive occurrence

[33]Jonathan Hunter, *Breaking Free from the Spirit of Death* (Xulon, 2008), p. 17. This booklet is a tremendous resource for addressing the unmasking of the spirit of death and breaking free from it.

is not limited to terminal illness. It is glorified through music and mutilation, from extremes of body piercings and cutting, and especially in violent video games and pornography. Besides through abortion, we see it manifested in acts of euthanasia and suicide. The thought life is a stronghold for its presence. It is all around us.

The Lord convicted me to stop watching multiple criminal investigative television programs. My eyes constantly took in images of bullets penetrating bodies or of corpses in varying degrees of decay as the result of a violent attack. The spirit of death flourished in those programs.

Where is the spirit of death influencing your life?

Choose Liberation

We find liberation from idol worship in ongoing and progressive choices. This liberation requires growing in the reality of Christ's authority in us and yielding our control. Abiding in, and then fostering, an intimate presence with the Holy Spirit is a necessity. We allow Him to search our hearts for where we are allowing idols to remain. The empowering of the Holy Spirit enables us to expel and renounce our ungodly idols. We must be intentional to nurture our relationship with the Lord. Finding true intimacy with God will aid us in preventing false intimacy from taking its place.

Liberation from idol worship involves choices:

> This day I call the heavens and the earth as witnesses against you that I have set before you life and death, blessings and curses. Now choose life, so that you and your children may live.
>
> – Deuteronomy 30:19

> But if serving the LORD seems undesirable to you, then choose for yourselves this day whom you will serve, whether the gods your ancestors served beyond the Euphrates or the gods of the Amorites, in whose land you are living. But as for me and my household, we will serve the LORD.
>
> – Joshua 24:15

Both of these verses reveal the urgency and obligation of choice. Are you willing to choose to renounce the idols that have taken residence in your heart, mind, or home?

We will focus on three areas that require renunciation in our hearts. These areas need the Lord's revelation and cleansing. I encourage you to pray the renunciation prayers at the end of this chapter with those you trust, but you can also pray them on your own. The Lord knows what He wants to reveal to you and release from you. Trust His presence to guide and direct your prayers.

Idols from Your Family Tree

The first area requiring renunciation is idols worshiped in your family tree. When Gideon argued with God about his call, making excuses, the Lord instructed the young man to tear down the altar and Asherah pole his father had built to Baal. After he had done so, "the Spirit of the LORD came on Gideon, and he blew a trumpet, summoning the Abiezrites to follow him" (Judges 6:34). Empowered and encouraged by the Lord, Gideon rose in his true self and calling. Once Gideon broke the generational attachment to his family line, he embraced the Lord's strength and purpose.

In your generational prayers, ask the Lord to go back individually through ten generations and expose any idol worship or predominant sin in your family line. Do not discount anything that comes to mind. It might be alcoholism, sexual immorality, abuse, pride, or greed, to name only a few. Confess any idols or sins to the Lord and ask Jesus to cleanse you from any connection passed down to you. Then invite Jesus to establish His authority between those idols or sins and yourself. Ask Him to place His cross as a holy boundary in the family tree to represent His Lordship over your life, and ask Him to break any existing strongholds.

Victimization through Sexual Abuse

The second area requiring renunciation in your heart involves victimization through sexual abuse. This may be especially challenging for some. Renunciation here focuses on the sin of another who forced his or her sexual idolatry on you. It includes renouncing any attempt of the evil one to hold you bound to the lust of another. Understandably, your emotions require time to process and heal; but this a starting place for severing connections made through inappropriate physical encounters. Later chapters will address the processing of abuse and the loosing of forgiveness. You are inviting Jesus to establish His cross between you and your abuser, establishing His holy boundary.

Personal "Designer" Idols

The third area needing attention is the renunciation of any personal "designer" idols. These idols were created to align with your brokenness specifically. Give the Lord permission to expose any strongholds you have established in your heart or through your actions. Seek Him to reveal any sexual and relational idols—anything you turn to for intimacy, security, or acceptance. In a time of quiet, invite the Holy Spirit to search your heart. As He exposes any idol, bring it to the cross of Jesus, confessing it, and surrendering it to Him.

In each of these areas discussed, ask Jesus to establish His cross and authority. Through the power of His blood, seek His cleansing, repentance, and restoration. Ask the Holy Spirit for future discernment and revelation whenever you resurrect or establish a new idol. This is the ongoing process of sanctification in becoming the man or woman you were intended to be. Any idol God exposes, He does so out of love for you. He longs to set you free so that you may continue to embrace His transformational work in you. God is jealous for you (see 2 Corinthians 11:2), meaning that He wants nothing to hinder your becoming and overcoming.

Wrapping Up

The good news of the Gospel of Jesus Christ is that His cross frees you from everything that binds or hinders your soul. The freedom and life Jesus offers you are for the here and now. He welcomes you to embrace Him as your way and the new life set before you. This is not just gaining head knowledge, not just another item on your checklist. It is building the bond between your renewed mind and your living heart.

Choose life this day, my friend! Choose life!

Prayers for Repentance and the Renunciation of Idols

Lord, I come before You just as I am. I admit my brokenness and my vain attempts to live a holy life through my strength and control. I have sinned in my weakness, and I confess my failures. I desire to know the reality of how my sin breaks Your heart. I want to be in that place where I can sense godly sorrow each time I turn to sin instead of turning to You.

I choose now, through the empowering of the Holy Spirit, to renounce these broken and sinful behaviors. I choose to acknowledge You alone as Lord of my life. I repent of my sin. I want nothing to hinder Your redeeming work in my soul. Through You, Father, Jesus, and Holy Spirit, I rise in my true self. I seek Your ever-increasing capacity to become who You have created me to be. Regenerate in me the capacity to rise out of my darkness and come into Your marvelous light. Lead me on this path through the wilderness.

I bring before you the idols I have created and established in my life. I confess I have bowed the knee before them. I have engaged in sexual and relational sin. I have attached my security, significance, and well-being to these idols. My sin is worshipping these idols instead of worshiping You, the one true God. I have allowed these behaviors to create walls to create barriers from Your leading and guidance.

By the empowering of the Holy Spirit, standing in my true self, in the name of the Lord Jesus Christ, I choose to renounce these idols. I renounce every false god I have embraced. I renounce the worship of Baal, Asherah, and Molech. I renounce any presence of these idols and any sexual immorality in my family tree on both sides going back ten generations. I renounce and rebuke any sin committed against me through the sexual lust of another. With the sword of the Spirit, I cut any created soul-ties. I renounce the presence of the spirit of death in my life. Holy Spirit, expose any ways through which I engage with the spirit of death in thought, word, or deed.

I affirm that I am God's child. I affirm that I am redeemed through the precious blood shed on the cross of Jesus of Nazareth. My price has been paid through the sacrifice of Jesus, and now I belong to the family of God. I renounce any claim on my life by the evil one. Lord Jesus, come now and inhabit those places which are now renounced and severed. Fill that which has been emptied. Restore that which was robbed from me. Renew a right spirit within me.

Thank You, Lord, for this redeeming work in me. Thank You for not abandoning me when I turned my face and heart away from You. Thank You for Your faithfulness and lovingkindness, which You grant me. May I continue to become more and more Your true image-bearer. By Your aid, may I continue to walk in righteousness on Your path of holiness.

Soul Work

1. How have you resisted the Holy Spirit in your life? How can you become more relationally engaged with Him?

2. Corresponding to Jeremiah 2:5, quoted earlier in this chapter—"They followed worthless idols and became worthless themselves"—how has the presence of idols brought any sense or feelings of worthlessness into your life?

3. Where have you engaged with the spirit of death through thoughts, words, or actions?

4. Why doesn't having an understanding of root issues or our past broken relationships bring true victory or the ability to overcome?

Journaling Moment

We often define ourselves through our failures, wounds, or sins. This becomes a shroud we drape over ourselves. Ask the Holy Spirit to reveal how you have identified yourself through your past sins. Then ask Him to give you the vision to see yourself as a whole man or woman. This vision may be an image or even just words that come to you. Can you receive what the Lord wants to show you? Can you allow the Father to show you how He truly sees you? If you cannot receive this vision, ask the Lord what is blocking you from seeing it.

SECTION 2

LOVING OURSELVES ARIGHT

Examining that which keeps us bound to our brokenness

Loving Ourselves Aright

In this section, we will explore the things that hinder or even prevent us from being present to God and others in community. The focus is on those areas which prevent us from knowing we have value and are lovable. We will explore how the impact of our past hinders us in the present.

We will also address the diseased introspection, faulty belief systems, and misbeliefs or lies that keep us bound to our brokenness.

Chapters 8 and 9 examine our deep need for true intimacy and the reality of how we have either responded or reacted to desire. These chapters reveal that our deepest God-given need is for true intimacy. That desire influences how we relate to the people and the world around us. It will lay the foundation for section 3, which explores how we live and connect in community.

This section may be difficult due to focusing on the sin(s) that may have been committed against you. It is especially crucial to pray before reading each chapter, asking the Holy Spirit to help you to remain present to the content. Allow adequate time to read, reflect, and do the Soul Work assignments. Press through any hesitation or procrastination, which may be rooted in an emotional reluctance to address some of your deeper woundings.

Chapter 13 on forgiveness may be the most important in this section. The capacity to forgive and receive forgiveness is critical for our becoming and maintenance of healthy relationships with God, others, and ourselves. Any blockage to forgiveness will prevent you from embracing the abundant life God has for you here and now, and from becoming the man or woman God has created you to be.

So stay alert as you begin this section. Ask the Holy Spirit for discernment regarding spiritual warfare and any attempts of the enemy to distract you from your becoming process. Remember, the enemy is afraid of who you are becoming. We are not to fear him, but we need to be wise and attentive. “You, dear children, are from God and have overcome [false spirits] because the one who is in you is greater than the one who is in the world” (1 John 4:4).

EIGHT

The Disciplines of Process

BUT SEEK FIRST HIS KINGDOM AND HIS RIGHTEOUSNESS, AND ALL THESE THINGS WILL BE GIVEN TO YOU AS WELL.

– MATTHEW 6:33

In our brokenness, we seek answers, support, and direction. We understand that something is amiss in our lives. This awareness has existed for a long time. For some, it has dominated their thinking and vision. This diseased self-awareness often obscures our capacity to see beyond our brokenness.

The verse above directs our focus into correct alignment. Your process is not merely about overcoming a particular sin or struggle. That focus is far too limited and earthbound. It is centered on the immediate and temporal.

My experience has shown that those who move beyond their struggles have done so by shifting their focus. Instead of focusing on their struggles, they primarily focused on increasing their pursuit of true intimacy with God Himself. The freedom they sought was to increase their relationship with God. How more could they love Jesus?

God desires for you to pursue Him, and in turn, He also pursues you. The Song of Songs contains the remarkable reality of this pursuit, especially in chapter 2, verse 16, "My lover is mine, and I am his." I find this to be so amazing!

The verses preceding Matthew 6:33 (above) address our preoccupation with and anxiety about practical needs such as food and clothes. Jesus says, however, that there is a concern of greater importance. This focus, which must be the highest priority in our lives, is seeking God's righteousness and His Kingdom.

Here, the righteousness of God refers to His sovereignty over everything. As we read in chapter 3, Jesus' life was one of obedience. This is righteous living—fulfilling the will of the Father and the total of what God requires of us. Living our lives in and through Jesus, in His strength, is the only way we can achieve this.

Embracing God's Kingdom is the big picture, which we accomplish through choosing to center our lives in God. He extends to us His leading, purpose, vision, and will. The Father, being a good Father, will always provide for what He calls us to do and to be. We respond with inspired choices, knowing we cannot accomplish righteous living by our merit or by any other condition. Right action results from trust and from placing our faith in Jesus alone. Within the Body of Christ, your calling and higher purpose are made known and shaped by the Father's plan for your life.

Embracing the Process

Recognizing our higher purpose helps us to focus less on our brokenness. We must shift from focusing on our failings to focusing on the continual love God extends to us. "There is no fear in love. But perfect love drives out fear because fear has to do with punishment. The one who fears is not made perfect in love" (1 John 4:18). The inspirational love of the Father, and of our beloved Jesus, and of the Holy Spirit will diminish the dominance of fear, anxiety, and worry in our lives. Isn't this the abundant life Jesus promised? Isn't this what you have been desperately searching and hoping?

I am by no means trying to minimize your pain or suffering. I do not want you to compartmentalize or suppress anxiety or fear. Nor is it my purpose to say, "Just get over it." What I hope to advocate is a balance in your life—the capacity to acknowledge the reality of your struggles without their obscuring the presence of your greater calling. Do you doubt that God has a calling on your life? Have you asked Him to reveal your higher calling?

I come before God just as I am, expressing my pain and emotions to Him. I seek His presence, helping me to apprehend and receive His love amid my struggle. I desire to focus on what He is doing at this moment. By faith, I trust that He will enable me to endure and to become. Often during times of ministry, I ask the Holy Spirit to grant others the gift of faith to believe: to believe that God is capable and willing to meet us in our place of need. We must align our will and passions with those choices that produce life in us.

This is the reality of process: "a series of actions directed toward a specific aim."[34]

The specific aim, the goal, is not your definition of healing. No, the goal is growing in greater intimacy with Jesus, so that the Kingdom of God may be made manifest in your life. This does not happen overnight but through patient endurance, as you make consistent choices to see Him and to do His will. Change within you is the byproduct of your growing intimacy with God. It is essential, at this point in our journey, that we embrace the process of what God is doing in our lives rather than focusing on some specific form of healing. Process focuses not just on the destination ahead but also the day-by-day journey, living in the "what is." The big picture is not just stopping one particular behavior, but multiple behaviors—who you are becoming in your entirety. Do you have tunnel vision, focusing on only one area? It was eye-opening for me to recognize that my one area of concern was not unto itself but intricately connected with others. I needed to expand my vision.

There are many aspects and nuances of process. Embracing process is seeing it as a journey to our true home. You are on a pilgrimage.

The Lord gave me this verse as an inspiration for my first sabbatical:

> This is what the LORD says: "Stand at the crossroads and look; ask for the ancient paths, ask where the good way is, and walk in it, and you will find rest for your souls. But you said, 'We will not walk in it.'"
>
> – Jeremiah 6:16

The "ancient path" I took was to spend ten days in a monastery. I was seeking the Lord in that particular setting, which many have done before me. From the many Christians who have walked the path ahead of us, we can learn invaluable tools for walking out our process. I want to share with you some spiritual disciplines that are of great benefit in our journey home.

[34]"process." *Merriam-Webster.com*. 2016. http://www.merriam-webster.com (15 November 2016).

A SPIRITUAL DISCIPLINE IS AN ACTIVITY WITH THE GOAL OF HELPING US DEVELOP GREATER INTIMACY WITH GOD.

A spiritual discipline is an activity to help us develop greater intimacy with God. It is not an activity on a checklist based on Christian performance. It is a spiritually nurturing action with the intent of ushering us into God's presence that He may transform us.[35] It encourages authenticity on our journeys by promoting spiritual growth. We make a deliberate choice, interrupting our routine, to shift our focus from the finite to the infinite.

In the rest of this chapter, we will look at some of these ancient disciplines. Let the Lord guide you as to how to incorporate these disciplines as part of your pilgrimage home. Do not strive to fit them in, but seek the Holy Spirit's aid in how He will integrate them.

The Discipline of Obedience

Embracing process starts with being committed to God. Within that commitment, I am seeking the primacy of God in my journey. I am allowing the Holy Spirit to convert my life, over time, into the image of Jesus. His active presence converts my self-will to that of the Father's divinely inspired will.

As I walk in obedience, a holy, dynamic tension exists as I die to self and embrace the life God has for me. I die to any choices, ways, and thoughts that hinder my process of becoming. This holy tension is the evidence of the Holy Spirit working in your life. If His presence were not with you, you likely would not be wrestling with the choice to sin. This tension reveals the Lord's pursuit of your heart and His desire for you to become so much more. Once again, I state what a marvelous thing it is that our Creator pursues us because He loves us so deeply.

[35]I highly recommend *Celebration of Discipline* by Richard J. Foster, an in-depth exploration of spiritual disciplines used by many who have gone before us.

Have you experienced that tension in your own life? Perhaps up to this point, you have despised this tension and even prayed for God to remove it. Why not pause here and praise Him for the conflict, since it is evidence of His pursuit? Its presence is the explicit indication of God's deeper work in you.

For me, conversion made possible through making Jesus Savior of my life was only the beginning. Conversion is a daily ongoing process, making Jesus Lord over every aspect of my life. The conviction of the Holy Spirit opens the way for confession, leading to repentance, which results in restoration. I embrace repentance, which enables me to make choices of right thinking and right living. To remain faithful to my process is remaining open to the continuing work of the Holy Spirit.

Making the Father's will my priority is to embrace obedience. "Son though he was, he learned obedience from what he suffered and, once made perfect, he became the source of eternal salvation for all who obey him" (Hebrews 5:8–9). Our acts of obedience help to instruct and shape us. They affect change occurring from the inside out. Lasting change on the outside originates first in our obedient hearts. Jesus became perfect through obedience and suffering (chapter 20 contains an in-depth discussion about suffering). So do we, by following in His footsteps of obedience.

Embracing the discipline of obedience is embracing the discipline of freedom. Dying to my demands and control, I yield myself to the One who is greater than I. Disobedience, which has the illusion of freedom (that is, I get to choose what I want), actually, limits the freedom and change my heart desires. Yielding, on the other hand, allows God to search my heart for those places where I resist Him. "Obedience to the will of God, then, is choosing to do what is asked of us, knowing that God wants us to be fulfilled and free, for we can be sure that God knows better than we do what we need."[36]

The Discipline of Quiet Time

My preferred pursuit of quiet time is through journaling. I have known many Christians, however, who have bought that "special journal" which, after a few attempts, is now covered with dust on a shelf. The danger about quiet time is that, rather than seeking God personally for a way that opens us to Him, we try to adapt it to what has worked for others. It is for you to discover

[36]Brian C. Taylor, *Spirituality for Everyday Living* (Liturgical Press, 1989), p. 28.

with the Lord, how your quiet time is to be structured. Although there are aspects of quite times which overlap, I do not want to mimic what has worked for others. I need to ascertain where and when I am most receptive to the voice of the Lord.

What is the goal of having a quiet time? To pursue a quiet time is to seek an action or setting through which we open our hearts to God and, in turn, receive something back from Him. It is a time to have a dialogue with Him. (Yes, I did say dialogue.)

Some require a sequestered area with minimal noise or distractions. Others find quiet time in the middle of a crowd (i.e., a coffee shop), with activity occurring all around. The goal is finding a setting where your heart can be fully open to the Lord, and you are receptive to whatever way He would manifest Himself to you.

It may be helpful to reflect on how it is that you extend love to and receive love back from God. Gary Chapman describes in *The 5 Love Languages* the five basic ways we express and receive love in healthy relationships. They are words of affirmation, quality time, receiving gifts, acts of service, and physical touch. How does God directly communicate His love to you? When do you feel the closest to Him? When are you most open to His revelation? Pursue Him however, and whenever you can truly enter His presence.

Individuals often talk about their faithfulness in seeking God in the early hours of the morning. They indicate that they rise before the crack of dawn, to earnestly pursue God. At times, I have heard people share this with almost a prideful tone, as they draw attention to their sacrifice. Yes, for some, early morning quiet time may be a valuable exercise in discipline and hearing God. For others, however, it becomes a self-defeating battle because this choice conflicts with their body clock and capacity to be present in the morning.

I have had deep, quiet times in the middle of the night, the early morning, mid-afternoon, and early evening. Do you speak to your close friends only at one specific time during the day? We must not make an idol of when we have a quiet time. Be sensitive to when God is calling you to come away with Him. It can be especially beneficial for those who have struggled with addictions to establish a disciplined pattern. The bottom line, though, is that it is not as important *when* you have a quiet time as *that* you have one.

The goal of quiet time is a one-to-one dialogue with God. It can be a time when I can express whatever situations or emotions are dominating my life now. Quiet times may contain thanksgiving, praise, prayer, intercession, and worship. However, I have seen individuals who use

THE GOAL OF A **QUIET TIME** IS ONE-TO-ONE **DIALOGUE WITH GOD.**

this time as a file dump on God, regurgitating their pain, frustration, anger, or disappointment. When they have purged themselves emotionally, they get up and walk away, neglecting to wait on the Lord for His healing word. God is waiting to minister to their needs, but they have signed off with Him.

Often in my own quiet time with the Lord, I have expressed various emotions encountered in my process. This was especially so in the early years when recovering from living eleven years as a gay-identified man and addicted to pornography. I waited on the Lord to speak to my heart, either to what I had just written or into a very different area. The Lord—Father, Son, and Holy Spirit—knew the exact words of healing that my soul needed in those moments.

A common question is how we know we are truly hearing from God. Words arising from our brokenness and diseased introspection often contain shaming words like *You should know better*, or *You are such a fool.* God does confront and convict us, but He never shames us. His words, grounded in love, draw us toward Him. If what we hear makes us feel like running from God, they are words of condemnation. When the Holy Spirit convicts us, He will draw us in the same moment to the Father and Jesus. This is why it is so important for us to know God's true nature and character, free from any transference issues (as we have covered in earlier chapters). Another way to discern if we are truly hearing from God is whether what we hear agrees with His Word, the Bible. If what we hear is contrary to the Word of God, the enemy is trying to divert us.

In my quiet times, I am honest and transparent; expressing whatever is present in my heart. Why would I not be, since He already knows what lurks there? A significant portion of my healing has resulted from the words God has spoken to me in these times. How often do we seek the voice of others—whether through books, conferences, or audio downloads—but fail to go to God directly? Does our reading of Scripture result in our knowing facts *about* God but failing to grow in intimacy and the relational *knowing* Him? The goal of the quiet time is to help us grow relationally closer to God.

Doug's Story

I have found that the challenges I encounter related to the discipline of Quiet Time can be broken down into four categories:

Doing. Reading more, writing/journaling more, basically filling my time without allowing God to speak to me. I find my inner over-achiever kicking in as I want to accomplish one more 'thing.' I want to read another chapter in my bible reading, or pick up and read another devotional, or journal for a few more pages. All of these things are valuable to my quiet time, but when it becomes all about doing, there's no room for me to receive anything from God. I'm reading, journaling, or otherwise doing I discover that I'm not dialoguing…I'm monologuing.

Dashing. Rushing through the reading and firing off a short prayer before running off into my day. It's a "fire and forget" mentality where I'm trying to check the box quickly and move on to the 'more important' things in my day ahead. Of course, I don't think of the other things as more important in my mind – if asked, I would say my devotions are most important, but my actions say differently when I'm dashing.

Distractions. This is when my quiet time is interrupted by trivial and not-so-trivial worries. Whether I paid a certain bill, what emails I've not responded to, wondering what might be on Facebook or LinkedIn, or if so-and-so ever responded to the text message I sent. Some of these silly timewasters, others are valid concerns – but none have a place in my thoughts during quiet time. For the important ones, I will usually try to keep a post-it note close by so I can write them down and purge them from my mind. This helps me return my focus to quiet time with God.

Deflections. Sometimes, I'll read a verse like Galatians 6:1 "Brethren, if anyone is caught in any transgression, you who are spiritual should restore him in a spirit of gentleness" and I'll start thinking about people who didn't live out this verse in my past experience. This is similar to when we hear a sermon and spend our time wishing someone else was there to hear it rather than focusing on how it applies to our self. When deflections come, I have to remind myself that the passage before me is intended for me at this moment, not for others (no matter how much my inner voice insists they need to hear/read/heed it).

The Discipline of Scripture Meditation

Your word is a lamp for my feet, a light on my path. – Psalm 119:105

This verse distinguishes between God's Word, the Bible, as a lamp and light. A lamp is an object that serves a specific purpose. It has one task to accomplish—to produce light. Light is the outward manifestation of the lamp's purpose. In the same way, God's Word provides light for us something He created that meets needs and serves His purposes—in this case, for feet to find their way in the dark. God's Word results in illumination, guiding us safely through the dark. His Word also provides a foundation on which we stand, with the boundaries and standards we need to live lives of wholeness and integrity.

The goal of reading Scripture is at least twofold: first, we invite God to write His Word on our hearts; and second, we come to know whom He is, knowing Him not just intellectually but relationally.

One of the ancient paths practiced by those who have gone before us is reading God's Word through the practice of *lectio divina*, or divine reading. *Lectio divina* is composed of four components: *lectio*, reading; *meditatio*, meditation; *oratio*, prayer; and *contemplatio*, contemplation. A vital key to this practice is not rushing the process.

Lectio, reading is self-explanatory. We find a place and time that best suits our capacity to attend to and concentrate on God's Word. It is not reading for reading's sake, not meeting an obligation. We must take the time to digest, receiving the words inwardly. Read the words aloud (recommended) or in silence. You may read a verse several times or focus on one or more specific words. It is a *listening* reading. Linger to allow the words to draw you to God.

During my first sabbatical at a monastery, God asked me to read the book of Isaiah. Every afternoon, I read portions of the book in the chapel. He asked me to read them aloud. It was a blessing to hear God's spoken words echo back to my hearing.

Meditatio or meditation is the practice of integrating, pondering, or ruminating over the words. Stop to allow your heart to respond to the words. Which ones stand out to you, and why do they do so? Does the reading evoke emotions? How do those words relate to your life—past, present, or future? Is God implying the initiation of any action on your part? This is not to be a time of diseased introspection, but taking the words, consuming them, and offering them back up to God for His revelation.

Oratio is turning the meditation of God's Word into prayer. Take the revelation and pray for its application in your life or the lives of others. Does the meditation bring about the need for confession? Do you have prayers of thankfulness, praise, or intercession? Seek the Holy Spirit to give form and structure to produce fruit from your meditation. Move in God's understanding, not your own.

Contemplatio is contemplating who God is because of what you have just experienced. How did the previous exercises take you into the very throne room of God? You have responded to God's Word. How does He now respond to you? When you use this exercise for your quiet time, contemplation is waiting for God's healing word back to you.

This discipline of Scripture reading is not for checking a box off your to-do list. This is a very different practice than trying to read the Bible through in a year, which can become simply goal-oriented. Rather, through the practice of *lectio divina*, we seek to make God's Word alive in us through specific verses. Reading His Word in this fashion enables the renewing of your mind, for you to have the mind of Christ. That renewal eventually results in an outward change.

The Discipline of Praise and Worship

> Therefore, I urge you, brothers and sisters, in view of God's mercy, to offer your bodies as a living sacrifice, holy and pleasing to God—this is your true and proper worship. Do not conform to the pattern of this world, but be transformed by the renewing of your mind. Then you will be able to test and approve what God's will is—his good, pleasing and perfect will.
>
> – Romans 12:1–2

IN AN ACT OF TRUE WORSHIP, WE EXPERIENCE THE CHANGING POWER OF GOD.

Praise and worship are a significant part of our becoming process. As I have indicated in earlier chapters, we are created to be worshippers. When we enter into acts of true worship, we are focused on God and not our brokenness, struggles, or circumstances. We are acknowledging who God is in relation to who we are. It comes from a place of gratitude and love for that which He has done for us in our lives. Everything becomes a shadow in the light of God's presence.

Often we use the words *praise* and *worship* together, sometimes synonymously. What is the difference between the two? Although the Bible uses several words for *praise* and *worship*, certain words occur with greater regularity.

Common words for praise:

Hebrew: *halal*, which means to make a show, to boast, to be clamorously foolish, to rave, to celebrate.

Hebrew: *yadah*, of which the root word means to hold out the hand or to throw at or away; connected with the extension of the hands, casting out praise.

Greek: *epaineo* or *epainos*, reflecting activity: to applaud, commend, laud, praise, and ascribe glory to God.

Common words for worship:

Hebrew: *shachah*, for which the primary root word means to depress, indicating to bow, pressing or lying down; to prostrate oneself, fall down, and humbly beseech; doing all these before someone who is superior.

Greek: *proskuneo*, for which the root words are *pros*, meaning toward, and *kuneo*, meaning to kiss, indicating acts of homage or reverence and implying a level of intimacy.

We have already discussed how the design of the Temple in ancient Jerusalem reflects our design as body, soul, and spirit. Praise occurs, in a certain sense, in the outer court, and the Holy Place. When we praise, we celebrate God's mighty deeds and acclaim what He has done. Worship, however, takes us into the Holy of Holies. The act of worship highlights who God is: His true character and nature. Our acts of worship are reverence, and homage offered to a holy God. As noted with the word *proskuneo*, worship suggests a level of intimacy through which we come to know God on a deeper level; we kiss the face of God.

Worship arises from an inward condition associated with the attitude of one's heart. Praise is the outward expression of that inward condition. Worship occurs when we open up our hearts to the reality of God's presence and Person. Worship happens deep within our hearts, connecting us with the core of our being, our very identity. During worship, we embrace God's design for who we are as His son or daughter. In the act of true worship, we experience the changing power of God. It is a fundamental and necessary part of our process. "Yet a time is coming and has now come when the true worshipers will worship the Father in the Spirit and truth, for they are the kind of worshipers the Father seeks" (John 4:23).

There are several ways that we can come into an attitude of praise and worship. Observing the beauty of God's creation around us can make us aware of the power of His majesty and glory. Early in my process, I would often seclude myself in a room to listen to worship music. Some songs were more contemplative, taking me into a deeper place of quiet intimacy. Others were more praise songs which lifted my spirit, making me want to dance. How can you incorporate worship music into your daily schedule?

Because of my past addiction to masturbation, taking a shower could remind me of my past sin and vulnerability. I needed to re-symbolize my bathroom. To do so, each time I took a shower, I played praise and worship music. My bathroom now became a place of joy and peace. How can you bring worship music into places or situations where you feel vulnerable to temptation?

The Scriptures record two especially powerful personal worship experiences: Isaiah's encounter with God (Isaiah 6:1–13) and the Apostle John's encounter with Jesus (Revelation 1:9–20). Read these two passages and reflect on them. They may help you understand how powerful worship can be in revealing the presence and Person of God.

In my past, I abandoned myself to the sinful worship of God's creation, worshiping the bodies of others rather than worshiping the Creator. But, it was through praise and worship, early in my process, that God began to cleanse me of the idols I had established in my heart.

The Discipline of Fasting

Choosing to fast is to deny the body. Fasting is choosing to delay satisfaction. In fasting, I deny myself something which is not evil or destructive. I, mentally, and with my will, decide to wait and temper my desire for the immediate. That delay is so to gain something of the infinite. Fasting, therefore, is a powerful discipline for those who struggle with addictions.

Fasting is not commanded, nor is it a legalistic punishment of the body. In the Scriptures, we see it exampled by Jesus and others. It is humbling of one's self for a greater purpose. In a designated time of abstinence, we learn to quiet the desires of our physical and emotional being. In so doing, it allows for a more profound, spiritual desire to surface. It is a hope that we may enhance our becoming. It is a choice to glorify God with our bodies. It is a means to increase our devotion to God.

There are many ways in which we can fast. The most common approach is to abstain from food, but it can take on many forms of denial such as caffeine, television, social media, entertainment, or for married couples, sexual intimacy (see I Corinthians 7:5). However, the focus is not to benefit in some physical or monetary way, but to benefit spiritually (i.e., fasting is not done to lose weight.)

When we fast, we shift our focus off of the world and our physical desires. We increase our pursuit of true intimacy with God. It is seeking to have a greater alignment of our will with that of God's will. As I addressed in chapter 6, we seek the Holy Spirit's empowering of our wills. Through fasting, we can strengthen our capacity to choose life when death is knocking at our door. It is empowering us to deny false intimacy.

Fasting is a personal and private choice. It is not done as a demonstration to others of our spirituality. There are seasons where Christians corporately do a chosen fast, so all know you are fasting for a designated purpose. However, when we choose to fast individually, as Matthew 6:17-18 indicates, "But when you fast, put oil on your head and wash your face, so that it will not be obvious to men that you are fasting, but only to your Father, who is unseen." However, wisdom is needed as in some cases, to let designated individuals know about your fast (e.g., family members, a spouse, or pastor). The bottom line is not to boast when you fast.

Fasting may also take on the form of fasting from time. Individuals choose to fast through the sacrificial offering of their time to serve others. This denial of self can be volunteering at a food bank, soup kitchen, or church outreach. Here we see that fasting can become a ministerial lifestyle. Instead of a short designated time, it can become a longer season of devotion.

I have often seen how the sacrifice of time has a spiritual impact on those who struggle with addictions. In the proper season, those who have received much in their healing process, with wisdom and discernment, now choose to be a gift to others who are wounded. In so doing, their experience of true intimacy and depth of spiritual growth increases. " Then I heard the voice of the Lord saying, "Whom shall I send? And who will go for us?" And I said, "Here am I. Send me!" (Isaiah 6:8).

Although fasting can be a time of activity, it also is a form of resting. It is not an act of restless activism, but a seeking of greater devotion to God. Instead of being driven by our desires, our desires come under the sovereignty of God. We create greater opportunity and space for us to be present to God. We decrease our devotion to earthly passions to increase our devotion to knowing him.

The Discipline of Confession

> Therefore confess your sins to each other and pray for each other so that you may be healed. The prayer of a righteous person is powerful and effective.
>
> – James 5:16

Confession (in Greek, *homologeó*) means to assent, to agree with, to confess, declare, or admit. Note that it is an act of speaking, openly declaring something. It involves agreeing with the Holy Spirit's conviction. We adhere to the Holy Spirit's truth and our violation of it. Confession is a vital part of our process, enabling us to come out of the shadows and take a stand for truth.

Forgiveness for every sin—past, present, and future—occurs once we have truly made Jesus Lord and Savior of our life. Must we make a complete tally of every sin we have ever committed? No. Do we have to confess every sin by name to be clean? No. Do any of my sins remain unforgiven if we forget one or have sinned unknowingly in the moment? No. Does God's forgiveness give us a license to live immorally? Absolutely not!

Through the work of the cross of Jesus, we are fully cleansed and fully forgiven due to our original confession, but we live our lives with integrity and wholeness. So why do we confess our sins if we know they are forgiven? We do so because it acknowledges the wrong we have done and releases us from shame. We appropriate His grace at the moment for that which was done for us so long ago. We also do it because it is relational. I have grieved the One who loves me more than I can fathom. If I grieve someone who deeply loves me, I ask for their forgiveness because of our relationship and not as an act of duty. It is the same with my Beloved.

> Blessed is the one whose sin the Lord will never count against them.
>
> – Romans 4:8

> Blessed is the one whose transgressions are forgiven, whose sins are covered. Blessed is the one whose sin the Lord does not count against them and in whose spirit is no deceit.
>
> – Psalm 32:1–2

Confession requires our surrender to God. Surrendering to God is an act of the will, made perfect in community. Confession requires us to recognize our need of God and the futility of our vain attempts at perfection. We yield control to the One who created us and knows us best. We come out of isolation, beginning to trust others to come alongside us. We come out of passivity to rise up. We take a risk by yielding our self-protective mechanisms, pride, and perfectionism. The result: We are continually transformed into overcomers.

About the discipline of confession, Dietrich Bonhoeffer writes,

> In confession, there occurs a breakthrough to assurance. Why is it often easier for us to confess our sins to God than to a brother? Why should we not find it easier to go to a brother than to the holy God? But if we do, we must ask ourselves whether we often have not been deceiving ourselves with our confession of sin to God, whether we have not rather been confessing our sins to ourselves, granting ourselves absolution.[37]

Confession requires us to remove our masks of perfection with each other. Confession requires the dropping of any fig leaves or façades, thereby becoming real and known with one

[37]Dietrich Bonheoffer, *Life Together* (Harper & Row, 1954), p. 110.

another. We experience healing as a byproduct of entering into true community.

Confession is a choice that opens up our hearts to God. It is necessary and results in our benefit. It allows us to obtain the support of others, thereby creating relational intimacy within the Body of Christ. Confession helps us cast off our garments of shame, enabling us to receive God's mercy and grace. Confession calls us out of isolation and loneliness.

Confession of sin is a form of praise to God. Genuine confession of sin results in giving glory to Him. In our confession, we acknowledge God's sovereignty. Our act of contrition then becomes an act of praise, which brings glory to God. We can rise, knowing we have been cleansed and forgiven.

"If sin within the soul is not named," writes Leanne Payne, "and is seen merely as psychological and emotional imbalance and illness, then there is an understanding of man and of his predicament that reconciles good and evil at the core of man's being."[38] But sexual and relational brokenness is *not* merely an illness or psychological condition; they are because of sin. The roots of brokenness are due to sin. So Payne addresses our awareness of sin in our lives and our reluctance to name it as sin, and she stresses that only the cross of Jesus brings reconciliation.

Below are five key steps to confession, ideally done in the presence of others:

1. We seek the Holy Spirit to search our hearts and expose any sin. We may be aware of a particular sin needing confession, but we allow God to identify the presence of any other sin.

2. We specifically name the sin(s) revealed, confessing it (them) verbally.

3. An individual hearing our confession speaks out, binding the confessed sin to the cross of Jesus. This individual makes clear that the broken body of Jesus bore all our sins. It is also of great benefit to bind away any garments of shame associated with the sin. Allow a moment for the Holy Spirit to minister through the presence of any godly sorrow.

4. The individual hearing our confession speaks words of truth that the death of Jesus has wrought our forgiveness and salvation and that we no longer carry this sin. There is a full release of the confessed sin and cleansing of it. During this time, the application of water may be beneficial as a physical symbol of the deeper spiritual reality of cleansing: "Let us draw near to God with a

[38]Payne, *Healing Presence*, p. 238.

sincere heart and with the full assurance that faith brings, having our hearts sprinkled to cleanse us from a guilty conscience and having our bodies washed with pure water" (Hebrews 10:22).

5. Others in attendance now pray words of affirmation and blessing. This crucial step reminds us of our true self. The enemy would prefer that we turn inward with diseased introspection and accusations. We may be anointed with oil as a reminder of whom we belong to—a reminder of who we are in Christ and who He is in us.

Ongoing confession is not an option but a necessity. Confession enables us to enter into community. It calls us to renounce our sins and rise, standing as the Father's sons and daughters.

The Discipline of Repentance

The word repentance (Greek, *metanoia*) means an afterthought, a perception afterward, a change of mind, to think again. It includes the presence of action. A change in thinking that does not include a change in behavior reveals that repentance is incomplete. I am by no means indicating that when we fall in our becoming process that our repentance is not genuine. However, if we arbitrarily dismiss our behaviors without embracing the necessary life-choices ahead of us, then our repentance may lack divine inspiration. Repentance is an inner work of the Holy Spirit, empowering us to make godly life choices. It is change from the inside out.

When there are strongholds and periods of life-dominating sin, our responsiveness to repentance can be lacking. Through repeated vain attempts to break our cycles of sin and the recurrence of disappointment, we become cynical and close ourselves off to the Holy Spirit. To break this barrier to repentance requires the acknowledgment of our powerlessness to overcome on our own. Our admission of defeat allows God to be strong in our weakness. We will begin once again to feel sorrow for our sin, which opens the way for our restoration and freedom.

"Godly sorrow brings repentance that leads to salvation and leaves no regret, but worldly sorrow brings death" (2 Corinthians 7:10). The fruit of the Holy Spirit's conviction results in godly sorrow. Its presence conveys our openness to Him. We are receptive to His conviction. We are responsive to God for the continuation of our process.

Godly sorrow carries a realization that I have embraced control through living in my false self. I have turned my back on the Lord who loves me completely and longs for my freedom, joy, and peace. I realize how holy and majestic God is and how small I am. Godly sorrow is not my attempt to drum up my emotions, but the deeper work of the Holy Spirit within me. It is an interior sadness, a grieving, which reflects that I have broken fellowship with my Beloved. I have broken His heart. I have allowed an action to create a barrier in *my capacity* to stay present to God. Godly sorrow will result in my learning from my sin. I gain wisdom and understanding so that, when faced with it again, I am better able to say no.

Repentance is a work of God that enables me to receive divine revelation, which then influences my behavior. It needs to be Holy Spirit–led and not evoked through striving or restless activism. I relinquish my vain attempts to "get it right this time." I also need God's help not to descend into diseased introspection.

Repentance allows for the following:

- The renewing of your mind
- Less influence from worldly patterns
- You're being conformed to the Father's perfect will for you

Confession and repentance have a deep connection. Without repentance, confession becomes merely reciting a list of offenses. It lacks gravitas. It diminishes the importance of grace and mercy. It leads to a cavalier attitude about the sacrifice of Jesus on the Cross. "*Jesus took care of all my sin, so all my future sin is covered, and I can relax. No problem.*" Repentance is coming before God to seek His deeper work in me, so I will not sin again.

An important aspect associated with repentance is knowing the difference between condemnation and conviction. The accuser wants you to experience condemnation, as does the world, and to run from God. Therein is the plumb line for differentiating between the two. The Holy Spirit brings conviction with the goal of drawing you to God. In the moment of question—is this condemnation or conviction? —ask yourself if you want to run from or run to God. Then, if you realize you are being condemned, renounce the enemy and turn toward the Lord.

Conviction speaks truth into our broken choices for false intimacy and unhealthy attachments. Conviction confronts our issues of being in control, resisting God's sovereignty. It will challenge any choice we make to stand in the false self. It impacts every aspect of how we live in thought, word, and deed.

An aspect of repentance, which is extremely helpful to understand, is when self-hatred enters the picture. In times of vulnerability, the conviction of sin would turn me inward accessing my self-hatred. I would turn the conviction into condemnation, listening to my diseased self-talk: *See, you've failed again. You are such a fool.* But in my quiet time, the Lord reminded me of Romans 8:28: "And we know that in all things God works for the good of those who love him, who have been called according to his purpose." *All things* include when I sin.

Now my sin has become an opportunity for God to work it for my good, turning it to my advantage. Every challenge I face in life is an opportunity for God to manifest His presence within me. He is teaching me through every experience in my life. Conviction exposes part of my heart, which I control and now have the opportunity to turn over to Him. In so doing, I become more the man He has created me to be.

Seek the Lord to expose where you resist embracing repentance. Where are you shut down to His conviction and evoking of godly sorrow? Ask for His wisdom to incorporate the fullest expression of repentance in your life.

Wrapping Up

These disciplines may sound daunting. Never forget that your process is one made up of daily choices. It is letting go of your control, the definition of healing, and any imposed timeline. God knows you completely. I intend that statement to evoke peace and not shame. Peace comes from knowing God's sovereignty over your life and from confidence "that he who began a good work in you will carry it on to completion until the day of Christ Jesus" (Philippians 1:6). He is committed to your process of overcoming and becoming.

Obedience, quiet time, Scripture meditation, praise and worship, fasting, and repentance are aspects of process practiced individually with regularity. Confession, however, has a greater spiritual impact when experienced with others. When incorporating each of these disciplines into your schedule, the fruit of this adaptation expresses itself in the community around you.

Begin slowly, but with intention. There is a difference between being motivated and being intentional. Motivation focuses on thinking, knowing that these disciplines are good and will benefit you. Intentionality is how you plan to put these disciplines into action. It may be of great benefit for you to write out your plan for the next few days or the next week. Schedule these disciplines on your calendar.

Start with small changes. Don't plan, for example, on a two-hour quiet or meditation time; perhaps start with ten minutes. Seek obedience in one small area. Listen to favorite praise or worship songs in your car, or play them at home in the background while doing chores. Seek the Lord's wisdom as to who to approach for confession. Adapt in small increments, expanding them as they occur with greater regularity in your life. Resist the temptation to turn the process into a checklist or system. Allow this process to be relational as you listen to the heart of God, guiding you forward.

Prayer

Lord, You know what I need to continue on the amazing path You have laid out before me. I do not want to lag behind You or run ahead of You. I desire to walk in step with You. I need Your wisdom and discernment for that which is most beneficial for me.

Holy Spirit, please help me not to strive or to embrace restless activism. I want to be open for your leading as to which of the Christian disciplines need greater focus in my life. Please show me how to incorporate aspects of these disciplines as part of my devotion to You. Whom may I approach to come alongside me for the discipline of confession? Teach me about the various aspects of repentance, but help me not to get sidetracked with behavior modification or place myself under the Law.

Jesus, You learned obedience through what You suffered. Thank You for Your example. Please help me learn to walk in obedience, especially in those difficult times, especially in those times when I am suffering. I am forever grateful that I am not alone in my pain, but You are present, walking with me through those challenging times.

Lord, once again, I release to You every aspect of my process. I choose to place my trust in You. Jesus, You are my way, You are my truth, and You are my life. May I continue to abide and remain in You as You abide in me.

Soul Work

1. Which of the disciplines in this chapter are most difficult for you, and why? What is the challenge preventing you from incorporating them more in your walk?

2. What prevents you from walking in the discipline of obedience? What is your motivation for walking in obedience? How is your motivation centered in performance-based acceptance? What needs to change, so your motivation for obedience is inspired by love rather than duty?

3. Reflect on a recent situation that resulted in your choosing sin. After reviewing the section on repentance in this chapter, in what aspects can you embrace repentance for your choice?

4. How is the discipline of confession present in your walk? What level of transparency do you embrace when confessing your sin(s) to another? What holds you back from confession with another individual if you do not have an accountability partner or someone to whom you can confess your sin(s)?

Journaling Moment

Reflect on where you have been reluctant to be brutally honest and transparent with others. Ask the Holy Spirit to reveal how you practice the presence of the false self by not letting others see your areas of brokenness and shame. Ask Him to reveal how this reluctance limits you from standing in your true self. Also, seek the Holy Spirit to show you what your false self and true self look like in comparison to one another.

NINE

True Intimacy and Inspired Sexuality

WE LIVE IN A CULTURE SATED WITH SEX,

BUT WE REMAIN STARVED FOR LOVE.

– CHRISTOPHER WEST[39]

Many books focus on intimacy and sexuality. Numerous authors and experts discuss these areas in detail. Indeed, these topics dominate the attention of our culture. Nevertheless, many of these books miss a deeper core. The question is, what do human beings hunger for in our innermost beings? The prolific attention placed on sex and sexuality suggests a connection with that hunger. Something deeper causes humankind to seek out sexual expressions and relationships. The continual pursuit of sex and its diverse expressions indicates a presence of this hunger that never seems to be satisfied.

I believe the answer to what drives us is a hunger for true intimacy. The reason for the lack of satisfaction (does a Mick Jagger song come to mind?) is that we turn to sources that provide only false intimacy.

False intimacy seeks satisfaction at the expense of others and me. I no longer look up to God but take control in my own hands to meet my needs the way I feel I am best served. The search for immediate gratification focuses me on the finite, supplanting at the depths of my

[39]Christopher West, *Fill These Hearts* (Image, 2013), p. xii.

being the desire for the infinite.

What is the origin of this innate and ever-present drive for true intimacy?

The sexual revolution in the mid-twentieth century furthered the split of love from sex. Sex devoid of commitment and whole relationship ruptured its purpose intended by God. Also, when humankind brings disorder to God's design, the result is never satisfying or sound.

To understand God's purpose for intimacy and sex, we must go back to its origin in Genesis. Here we discover that the drive for true intimacy originates in God Himself.

At the Beginning

The Pharisees asked Jesus about divorce. "'Haven't you read,' he replied, 'that at the beginning the Creator "made them male and female"'...?" (Matthew 19:4). Jesus was making a definitive statement regarding God's intent. He wanted to draw their attention to the significance of what occurred in the Garden of Eden.

God's existence in the Trinity, as we have seen in earlier chapters, is an expression of relationship. It is love revealed in the Person of God, who is love itself. Note how the Lord uses a plural pronoun in Genesis 1:26: "Let us make mankind in our image, in our likeness." God introduces Himself as the Creator who exists in relationship.

Our existence, then, originated in the heart of God, who desires that we share in His love and goodness. God extends to humankind the ecstasy He experiences within the Trinity. Stop for a moment and ponder that spiritual reality. The One who has created you, named you, desires for you to experience a spiritual ecstasy that no earthbound experience comes remotely close to duplicating.

God is not a sexual being, yet there is significance in how He created those biologically who would bear His image. Since God is Spirit, how can His image be reflected in the flesh He created? It is important to consider the Hebrew word *likeness* (*demut*). "Man is not just an image but a likeness-image. He is not simply representative but representational. Man is the visible, corporeal representative of the invisible, bodiless God. *Demut* guarantees that man is the adequate and faithful representative of God on earth."[40] The breath God breathed into the nostrils of Adam

[40]R. Laird Harris, *Theological Wordbook of the Old Testament* (Moody Press, 1980), p. 192

(Genesis 2:7), was more than just air. It was *zoe*, God- life. The life of God became part of Adam. Within you, then, is the very breath of God! Once again, reflect on this for a moment.

God did not need Adam. Need or loneliness on His part was not why He created Adam. No, Adam's creation stemmed from love. By the outpouring of God's love, which is relational, Adam now existed. Adam was different from the rest of creation. Apart from Adam, God spoke all of creation into being. However, He formed Adam out of creation itself (i.e., the dust of the earth). The breath of God occurred in no other part of creation. Adam was unique, the pinnacle of God's handiwork.

God commented in Genesis 2:18, "It is not good for the man to be alone." I have often asked individuals what the next thing God did after making that statement. The frequent answer is, God created Eve. That is not so. The next thing God did was assign Adam a task: to name the animals. Adam was in direct relationship with God and lived in the Garden of Eden amidst the rest of creation. So how was Adam alone?

God brought all the animals and birds before Adam with the task of naming them. I assume that the animals came to Adam as male and female. What do you suppose Adam felt as he saw pair after pair of animals come before him? How did he feel when he looked into the eyes of the animals? Augustine wrote that our heart's desire is to see another and to be seen by that other, in a loving glance, in return. In the 2009 movie *Avatar*, the Na'vi people greet each other with the phrase *I see you*. This greeting indicated that the Na'vi saw beyond the surface and acknowledged the personhood of one another.

The animals saw Adam physically, but they could not see his personhood. Adam did not receive a knowing glance in return. We want others to see us in a way that goes deeper than our exterior. Did Adam wonder if there was another "body person," a human being, like him somewhere? Adam was the only body person in all creation. He lacked being in relationship with one who was like himself. We have been surrounded by body persons all our lives. We cannot imagine what it was like for Adam.

After completing his task, God caused Adam to sleep. While he slept, God removed one of Adam's ribs and created Eve. Let us stop here for a moment. God formed Eve out of a living portion of Adam's body—not like the way He formed the rest of creation, which He created out of dust. Eve, therefore, not spoken into being, differed from the rest of creation. This is significant. God used bone and living cells out of Adam's body to form Eve.

WE WANT OTHERS TO SEE US IN A WAY THAT GOES DEEPER THAN OUR EXTERIOR.

Adam exclaimed, upon first seeing Eve, "This is now bone of my bones and flesh of my flesh; she shall be called 'woman,' for she was taken out of man" (Genesis 2:23). Yes, Eve was different physically from Adam; but for the first time, Adam saw one which was another body person, a human body—another part of God's creation but one who uniquely shared *his humanity*. Adam saw someone with whom he could equally share life and relationship. As I ponder this incredible miracle, the word *joy* comes to mind. Adam's unique solitude was gone forever.

In the Garden of Eden, the nakedness of Adam and Eve was both exterior and interior. Their seeing each other transcended mere outward appearance. Not only were they physically naked; they were also interiorly naked. Nothing remained hidden. They were wonderfully aware of each other's humanity. They saw not only each other's physical body but someone who bore the image of God.

Adam and Eve's defenselessness enabled them to see each other without masks or façades. Adam, relating to Eve as another human being, experienced a level of intimacy he had not previously known. Intimacy was now occurring with God and with one another. Integration occurred not only with each other but also completely with God. There was no separation, no veil. Naked and defenseless, there was no shame about themselves or with each other.

It is challenging to imagine how Adam and Eve could relate to each other while being physically naked. They were innocent, lacking the later knowledge of sin that would turn them inward with shame. Upon first meeting, they were not married. They related to each other in wholeness, integrity, and purity. There was an innocence in the way related to each other and reflected God's image as man and woman. This all had occurred before they experienced their nuptial joining in the Garden. Their biological sex, specifically designed by God, was divinely inspired and part of how they represented the fullness of His image. The sacredness and purpose of our physical bodies, therefore, must not be diminished. God created them specifically to reflect Himself.

Genesis makes clear that being male or female, man or woman is reflective of God's nature in us. That reflection carries a significance beyond sexuality or marriage. Adam and Eve were able to relate beyond the physical dimension, seeing into the other's personhood, their inner being. They were secure in who they were as male and female. This is right relating between man and woman, apart from sexual union. They experienced true intimacy on multiple levels.

Eros, Agape, and Intimacy

In the Garden, *agape* and *eros* were one, joined together. God called that union good.

Agape love is a love that gives of itself—self-emptying and sacrificial. *Agape* focuses outside of itself, showing attention and concern for another. *Agape* evokes a longing in us to find the good of another.

Our culture associates *eros* love as merely having a sexual connotation. Does it sound a bit odd when I say, *eros love*? If *eros* is only sexual, it feels disconnected from love. *Eros*, however, has such a deeper meaning and purpose. Plato defines *eros* as our longing for all that is true, good, and beautiful. The longing of *eros* is a yearning for what is real—the real of God. *Eros* is passionate about beauty. It rises in us seeking expression in relation to beauty.

To embrace the wholeness of *eros* requires the infilling of *agape*. *Eros* and *agape* joined as one results in relational consummation and true intimacy. True passion takes into consideration those outside oneself. The good seen in another provokes a healthy, passionate response. We may experience this type of response when we see the beauty of God's creation. Limiting *eros* to the confines of eroticism diminishes the fullness for which God intended it.

We can pronounce the word *intimacy* as "in-to-me-see." Adam and Eve experienced *agape* and *eros* harmoniously together within the bounds of true intimacy. Intimacy occurred with

each other and with God. The only mirror that existed was that reflected in the eyes of the other. God surely took great joy in presenting Adam and Eve to each other.

Adam and Eve experienced true intimacy as designed by God. In all aspects of their lives, relationally and nuptually, they experienced and expressed intimacy. Their nuptial connection was not only physical but also sacramental, carrying a spiritual significance. They related to each other as man and woman, male and female, which was whole and reflected the image of God.

The Great Mystery

> For this reason, a man will leave his father and mother and be united to his wife, and the two will become one flesh. This is a profound mystery—but I am talking about Christ and the church.
>
> – Ephesians 5:31–32

The word *intimacy* in our culture, like the word *eros*, is typically associated with the sensual and sexual. Our culture has lost its wonderful nuances and breadth of meaning. In the Garden, as we have seen, oneness went beyond sexual union. It was a key part of life experienced mentally, emotionally, and spiritually. True intimacy, the hunger at the core of our existence, has been lost or buried through the endless pursuit and experience of false intimacy.

Jesus' response to the Pharisees' question on divorce carried a critical message about marriage and our relationship with the Lord. The marriage in the Garden, redeemed later as the result of a choice made in a different Garden (Gethsemane), ultimately culminates in a marriage feast in heaven, hinted at by Paul in Ephesians 5, above. These marriages are holy bookends of the Bible, with the Song of Songs in the middle.

"We exist because God wants to make a gift of Himself to us because God wants to share His infinite goodness and bliss with us." "In short, these heavenly nuptials are what we long for (desire); they're what we're created for (design), and they're what we're headed for (destiny)." [41] What began in the Garden of Eden will reach its zenith with the future marriage feast in heaven.

[41] West, p. 102.

Note that in heaven, there will be no marrying nor given in marriage as seen here on earth (a topic on which I rarely hear any teaching). Those walking in the state of singleness or celibacy enter the same future without being relegated to the sidelines. God did not forget about us who are single or celibate! Earthly marriage is not the ultimate goal but the pursuit of true intimacy with God. More on this topic will follow in later chapters.

God desires for us to experience His life and love. This is part of our deepest calling and desire. Our sexual desires, aligned with His boundaries, carry deep spiritual truths. This applies to all of us, single, celibate, or married. God designed and created our bodies as male and female, to relate in a healthy relationship. That design manifests the love of God and is, therefore, sacred. The prophetic words in the Old and New Testaments indicate what Jesus has planned for us since the beginning of time.

The expression of the sexual union between a man and a woman, as God intends only in marriage, is a holy, sacramental occasion. There is profound sacredness in our sexuality, which is lost in our culture. This holy nuptial union foreshadows what is to come when Jesus claims His Church as His bride. Therein lays the great mystery of which Paul wrote.

I shudder to think about how I profaned what God called holy through the actions I engaged in sexually, in my brokenness. I stand forgiven at the foot of the cross, however, because of the Lordship of Jesus in my life. Beginning to grasp the sacredness of our sexuality helps us better to guard and protect it. If we truly recognize this spiritual reality, we will not give our bodies indiscriminately away to another or before marriage with our future spouse.

Ponder this spiritual reality: God wants to marry you! He, who is so above us, so great in majesty and infinite, desires to become one with us. I can barely grasp the fullness of this mystery. Jesus took on a human body—He became fully human—to identify with His bride. The infinite met the finite. The divinity of God joined with our humanity. This joining is intimacy on a cosmic level. It is meeting the ache buried within us, inherited from Adam and Eve. The longing for fulfillment and completion is now satisfied. "'I have come that they may have life, and have it to the full'" (John 10:10). And, "The Spirit and the bride say, 'Come!'" (Revelation 22:17).

> God made us as relational beings, and he constructed a relational network within which we can flourish. This relational network exists not merely to keep us occupied, but is a place for each of us to belong, to live, to love, and to be loved from the day we were born

until the day we die. Indeed we are part of a network that encompasses the entire human race. Understanding our relational nature helps us comprehend who we are meant to be. Deep down we yearn to know others and ourselves.[42]

It is within the Body of Christ, His Church that our becoming process— recognizing who we are in Christ— is worked out. "To be loved but not known is comforting but superficial. To be known and not loved is our greatest fear. But to be fully known and truly loved is a lot like being loved by God. It is what we need more than anything."[43]

Wrapping Up

Before the creation of the universe, you were in the mind of God. Your physical story began in the Garden of Eden. Ponder this amazing truth. The bottom line is that at your core, created in His image, you yearn for the true intimacy Adam and Eve experienced in the Garden. This is the buried ache which drives all relational and sexual brokenness. We hunger for true intimacy but repeatedly settle for that which is false. The result: We remain hungry and driven. Chapter 10 will address the impact that the Fall had on desire, and its results found in our broken reactions.

It is my firm belief that if you can grasp the holiness and sacredness of your biological design and sexuality, it will better enable you to resist temptation. We need the Holy Spirit to bring His revelation and to awaken this spiritual reality at the core of our being. Every time we use or manipulate another human being to meet our needs, we profane his or her sacredness. We interfere with his or her image-bearing capacity. Anytime we choose any sexual activity outside the bonds of heterosexual marriage, we lose our perspective on the holiness of this gift from God.

Here is the big picture: Our sex and sexuality are of divine design and are, therefore, holy. Will you trample this precious gift from God in the mud?

Created in God's image, you express His image as male or female. Created in His image, you are relational, just as He is. Therefore, you will become who God intended you to be through engaging in healthy relationships in the Body of Christ. God has established a sturdy foundation

[42]Kuehne, pp. 131-132.
[43] Tim Keller, Facebook, July 21, 2015.

on which to stand. Will you presently join with Him in preparation for the nuptial union to come at the marriage feast of the Lamb?

Prayer

Jesus, help me recognize that at the core of my sexual and relational temptation is the real desire to know You and others. Please align my desires with Yours. Help me not settle for false intimacy but lead me to the life-giving sources of true intimacy. Fulfill my desire to know and be known, and not to settle for the finite! Meet me in this place and satisfy that which You have imparted in the core of my being.

Jesus, would You meet me when I am tempted to seek false intimacy? Holy Spirit, would You reveal where I have allowed the separation of sex from divine love? Where have I lost the sacredness of my body and sex? How have I agreed with the world's limitation of eros love to merely eroticism? Restore to me the reality of Your divine plan for my sexuality. Reveal where I have made either singleness or marriage an idol. Reveal any hatred I have regarding my singleness or marital state. Reveal where I have lost the holy symbolism of marriage.

I seek true intimacy with You, Lord Jesus, who knows me better than I know myself. I acknowledge Your deep desire to be in relationship with me. I acknowledge that You want me to be connected intimately with Yourself. Jesus, You desired this so much that You left the majesty of heaven, taking on a physical body. You did this so that one day I will experience the joy of being part of Your bride. I join with the bride and the Church in saying, "Come, Lord Jesus."

Soul Work

1. In your own words, how is our culture saturated with sex but starved for love?

2. How is eros expressed in your life, which centers you in your true self and centers you in your false self? How can you decrease the ways that center you in what is false but increase the ways that center you in what is true?

3. How have you pursued false intimacy in your life? What was your motivation for seeking false intimacy? What are some sources of true intimacy that you can incorporate into your life, and how will you do so?

Journaling Moment

Seek the Lord for His revelation of how He wants you to enjoy deeper levels of true intimacy with Him. Ask the Holy Spirit to reveal if there are any blocks within that prevent you from experiencing new depths of knowing God in this way. Jesus is our Beloved, and we are His beloved. Ask Jesus to show you how you can enter into knowing Him better as your Beloved.

TEN

Inspired Desire

"THE LORD GOD MADE ALL KINDS OF TREES GROW OUT OF THE GROUND—TREES THAT WERE PLEASING TO THE EYE AND GOOD FOR FOOD. IN THE MIDDLE OF THE GARDEN WERE THE TREE OF LIFE AND THE TREE OF THE KNOWLEDGE OF GOOD AND EVIL."

- GENESIS 2:9

Before the Fall, Adam and Eve experienced life without shame, fear, or self-hatred. They enjoyed a relationship with God without hindrance or barrier. Their relationship with one another was completely open, affirming, and whole. It was a utopia.

The Lord gave Adam and Eve dominion over the earth. They were to be fruitful and multiply, subduing God's creation. We shudder at times with our responsibilities, but can you imagine being responsible for the whole planet? God gave them everything. God did impose one restriction, however: not partaking of the fruit from one tree.

As Genesis, 2:9 indicates, and as we have already seen, there were two special trees in the Garden: the tree of life and the tree of the knowledge of good and evil. Both of these trees stood in the center of the Garden. Were they standing next to each other? They had to be nearby as they were both at the center. I assume that Adam and Eve ate from the tree of life, and when they did, was the other tree within their field of vision?

Is the tree of life at your center?

As we discussed in chapter 1, God wanted Adam and Eve to trust Him for whatever they needed. He wanted the tree of life to be part of their lineage. All of Adam and Eve's offspring were to have their generations linked with the tree of life, their consciousness, and self-awareness centered in God alone, like the centering of the tree in the Garden. Satan was at work in the Garden, however, and focused Eve on the other tree.

The temptation to eat of the fruit from the tree of the knowledge of good and evil appealed to Eve on two levels. First, the enemy planted doubt about God's true nature and character. Did He have her and Adam's best intentions at heart? The fruit would give her control of her security. Second, Eve saw that the fruit "was good for food and pleasing to the eye, and also desirable for gaining wisdom" (Genesis 3:6). The fruit was a visual temptation, appealing to Eve's appetite. It looked edible and pleasing, and so appealed to her desire. It also appealed to her—after Satan cast doubt—to gain that which would make her more like God.

Satan, the father of lies, tempted Adam and Eve that they could be equal to the Trinity. Here began the rumblings of lust—the lust for power and control. I put my happiness, security, and need above that of another. Lust also now affected the expression of love.

Consuming the fruit ultimately divided *agape* from *eros*. Love and passion became tainted and polluted by self-awareness and egocentricity. Adam and Eve's eyes turned inward, replacing other-awareness with a diseased awareness of self. They now became self-centered. *Agape* split from *eros*, creating a self-focus on what would gratify themselves. This opened the door for lust, a selfish taking rather than a selfless giving. They split from each other and God.

The consequences were staggering.

AT THE VERY CORE OF OUR EXISTENCE IS THE LONGING TO FIND FULFILLMENT AND JOY.

There was another birth, too, besides that of lust: the birth of separation anxiety. Becoming detached from a source of life or security creates anxiety and trauma. Banished from the Garden, Adam and Eve experienced separation, aloneness, and fear. God performed the first sacrifice of blood, making garments of skin for them (Genesis 3:21), which helped cover their feelings of shame. Not until centuries later would another sacrifice of blood bear their and our shame on the cross.

Our Inheritance

Adam and Eve's expulsion from the Garden left them longing for the true intimacy they had known. That loss of true intimacy is our inheritance: the brokenness of sin and an inner longing for true intimacy. Over time, our hearts have settled for what is finite. The infinite experienced in the Garden has become a forgotten memory. Just as when we walk into a dark room, and our eyes become accustomed to the darkness, so humankind has adjusted to the darkness it came to know, lowering its expectations, settling for less, settling for the finite. It now centered in itself.

Not focusing outwardly on God, many of us turn inward, internalizing our anxiety. We may assume that others have it better. Diseased self-awareness keeps us in a state of comparison, evaluating ourselves through the lens of self-hatred, shame, and inadequacy. Our hearts know there must be something more to life. We search, consciously or unconsciously, for real life and true intimacy. Experiencing disappointment, however, we battle not to lose hope or become numb.

Our hearts are full of desire. At the very core of our existence is the longing to find fulfillment and joy. Human desire has created an amazing world of art and culture around us. It is the echo of the true expression of *eros*, to look for beauty and to experience passion. The taste of true intimacy and beauty, which Adam and Eve knew, still lingers buried within us, bound to our deepest desire.

Human desire is a constant companion in our journey of becoming and our journey home. When each intense moment of joy fades, we anticipate and search for the next. When the season between these moments is long, some abandon desire, replacing it with despair. Others deny that those moments are lost, choosing instead to sustain an illusion of joy and contentment through varying forms of addiction.

We must not abandon our deepest desire, settling for something less. We must not cut off our hearts and choose despair.

Knowing desire links us with becoming the men and women God has created us to be. Desire existed in the Garden, and God called it good. Desire, expressed with the union of *agape* and *eros*, is part of whole relationships. Sex, as we saw in the last chapter, is not the sole expression of *eros*. Beauty and passion can be part of any friendship, within the parameters of integrity and wholeness.

> To desire something and not have it—is this not the source of nearly all our pain and sorrow?... Desire is the source of our most noble aspirations and our deepest sorrows. We cannot live without the yearning, and yet the yearning sets us up for disappointment—sometimes deep and devastating disappointment. Because of its vulnerable nature, desire begins to feel like our worst enemy.[44]

Allowing ourselves to feel desire opens us to potential pain and repeated disappointment. We often shut down our hearts but doing so kills the heart. The results can be anger, rage, or bitterness. We bury the pain and desire more deeply, but it eventually resurrects in another form.

Because of our reactions to desire, we remain confused as to what we really want. This reminds me of the 1996 Spice Girls song "Tell Me What You Want (What You Really, Really Want)." Can we tell others what we really want? We cut off our hearts because they have gotten us into so much trouble, or so we think. We need God's clarity to address this battle within and its outward expressions as well. We hunger and thirst but never seem to be satisfied.

Our Battle with Desire

> There is a desire within each of us, in the deep center of ourselves that we call our heart. We are born with it, it is never completely satisfied, and it never dies. We are often unaware of it, but it is always awake....Our true identity, our reason for being, is to be found in this desire.[45]

Jesus encountered many men and women familiar with disappointment who suffered for years. The man by the pool of Bethesda waited there for his healing for 38 years (John 5:5). How

[44]John Eldredge, *The Journey of Desire* (Thomas Nelson, 2000), pp. 15, 19.
[45]Gerald May, *The Awakened Heart* (HarperOne, 1993), quoted in Eldredge, *Journey of Desire*, p. 2.

long can we allow our hope to remain? How long before we begin to embrace despair, cynicism, or bitterness? How is alignment with God's will maintained when we take control, deciding how to fulfill our desires?

Christian life connects deeply with desire. God's invitation to us as well as to our desires is made plain in Isaiah 55:1–2:

> Come, all you who are thirsty, come to the waters; and you who have no money, come, buy and eat! Come, buy wine and milk without money and without cost. Why spend money on what is not bread, and your labor on what does not satisfy? Listen, listen to me, and eat what is good, and you will delight in the richest of fare.

Notice how God initially appeals to our desire for food and drink but then turns it heavenward. Isaiah suggests that we try to assuage our desire through physical resources, which will not meet our inward need.

Knowledge and performance have replaced relationship at its heart. Lacking in true intimacy with Jesus, our desire focuses us on striving to find satisfaction and adequacy. Striving becomes a religion of restless activism. This type of religion instructs us to *do* to be accepted, while the Bible says we *are* accepted; now do.

As we discovered in chapter 2, Jesus does not want us to settle for mere knowledge about God; He came to give us life in abundance and fullness. For the Pharisees, desire was irrelevant and knowledge supreme. This hardened their hearts. Many today search for outward behavior modification rather than engaging the heart and their deepest desires.

How have you pursued knowledge at the cost of your heart? Reading these words right now, are you searching for that magic pill that will somehow stop all your unwanted behaviors or remove your unwanted attractions?

Jesus appeals to our hearts and, therefore, to desire. If He truly has our heart, our behaviors will change as a result. Stop and ponder that sentence! Too often we equate the numbing of our heart, the suppression of desire, with living a life of integrity and holiness. The lie I believe is that I must kill desire and live by the rules, shifting the focus from living as a human "being" (centered in Jesus) to living as a human "doing" (centered in my control). Jesus appealed to desire because, to bring life, desire is essential.

In Reaction to Desire

Facing our desire can evoke three reactions: the stoic, the sensualist, or the sojourner.[46] Each of these reactions results from encountering the ache of our deep desires. That ache often expresses itself through pain: the pain of loneliness, isolation, or fear. The choice of response varies depending on our temperaments and experiences.

The Stoic

Stoics suppress and avoid the pain of desire. This reaction is rooted in fear: If I dare be in touch with my desire, I will lose control. So stoics suppress desire because allowing it to surface, in the past, took them down paths of darkness, getting them into trouble. Here we often see white-knuckling—burying desire as deeply as possible through fleshly control, utilizing their own strength.

Desire is associated with the question of morality. To live a moral life, the stoic says no to desire, suppressing all forms of it in their hearts. The choice I make, then, is to clamp down on desire, shutting down my heart. I focus all my energy on sobriety, trying to achieve a perfect record through fleshly control.

The stoic filters the Scriptures as a set of rules to control desire, and embraces "religion" instead. "Religion" is creating my standards and rules, which I feel makes me acceptable to God. Instead of seeing sex as something spiritual, a God-inspired gift, I see it as something secular, requiring suppression at all costs. Instead of entering into life-giving relationships, I resist letting others to become too close.

Have you gone this route? How long have you been white-knuckling it, living with the fear of experiencing desire? How has sobriety become your goal rather than becoming Christ-like? Are your relationships only superficial in nature?

The Sensualist

To avoid the pain of desire, sensualists feed on the finite. They embrace false intimacy. At least they can acknowledge desire. Instead of shutting down the heart, they open it to anything that will relieve or escape their pain.

Some believe since I am made in God's image, and I have these passions, it must be from

[46] I am indebted to the writings of Christopher West and John Eldredge for some of the content in this section.

FAULTY THINKING BELIEVES THAT HOLINESS RESULTS FROM THE KILLING OF DESIRE.

God and is totally acceptable. Others, unable to maintain rigid control, lose hope, and turn away from God, abandoning themselves to their passions.

The most common escape is through some form of addiction. Addictions can look acceptable and take on the appearance of "good" expressions, including religion, perfectionism, workaholism, and service. We all have some form of addiction, making attachments other than to God. We create and design our idols and gods. Settling for false intimacy and escape only further accentuates our inner pain because the longing for true intimacy remains unsatisfied. "Behind every false god, we discover our desire for the true God gone awry."[47]

The Sojourner

Sojourners learn to acknowledge that there are deeper desires within, but they choose not to suppress, avoid, or pacify the pain associated with that deeper desire. They choose God over self-protective mechanisms and escape. They choose to remain vulnerable before God. He is not far off but present to my needs and struggles. My sobriety or religious perfectionism does not form the basis for God's acceptance of me. I find my acceptance only through the redeeming sacrifice of the cross alone. I can do nothing to make God love me more.

Sojourners learn to do without certain pleasures which the world says are necessary. They learn to find joy and true intimacy with others without objectifying them for worship. Sojourners, transfixed by the deep love of God, focus their desire on a more intimate relationship with Jesus. They resist settling for mere gratification and find beauty, intimacy, or connection without idolatry. They live and enjoy life in the temporal with a divine reality. Living in that reality does not happen overnight but over time through intentional daily life choices.

In the Garden, Adam and Eve experienced the good of desire. God designed us to experience pleasure, both His and our own. Man's origin and end, thanks to the cross, are found

[47]West, *Fill These Hearts*, p. 131.

in paradise. To embrace God's life within, we must embrace the good of desire. Faulty thinking believes that holiness results from the killing of desire. The underlying belief is that the enemy of holiness is passion. The actual enemy, however, is apathy, emotional emptiness. God provides the tools we need to help us walk as men and women of integrity.

Christian disciplines, as we discussed in chapter 8, are tools to aid us in controlling the waywardness of our desire. The goal is not the enforcement of control, found in rigid rules, but the delight and bliss encountered in our walk with Jesus. How many individuals focus on what they have to give up before coming to Jesus rather than on what they will gain? Our initial thinking is so small! An intimate relationship with Jesus, however, will cause us to experience pleasure in life—pleasure lined up with God's desire and passion in our hearts.

Disowning Our Desire

Our hearts seek the One who will complete and fulfill us. We seek Jesus. Following God out of duty alone diminishes the expression of desire. The redemption of our desire occurs when we give over our passions to Him. To be alive in Jesus is to be present to desire. "Complacency is a deadly foe of all spiritual growth. Acute desire must be present, or there will be no manifestation of Christ to His people. He waits to be wanted. Too bad that with many of us He waits so long, so very long, in vain."[48]

This reality is amazing and sad at the same time, is it not? The Creator of the universe wants you to desire Him, and yet we focus our desires elsewhere. Desire is at the core of our relationship with God.

Our past, however, has often led us toward self-protective mechanisms. Experience has taught us that, by making ourselves vulnerable, we place our hearts at risk. However, to embrace the deep desires of our heart, we must choose to risk. Disowning our desires decreases our capacity to know what is real and true.

Is the fear of vulnerability resulting in the burying of your desire?

Misaligned desire embraces illusion in place of the real, settling for the finite. Numbing ourselves to any pain, we seek the easiest path to gratification, one that requires minimal sacrifice. We lose the capacity to wait for what is better, forgetting how true fulfillment feels. "We cannot

[48] A. W. Tozer, *The Pursuit of God*, (Martino Fine Books, 2009), pp. 17–18.

revert to killing our hearts. We must have life. The only problem is in our refusal to wait. That is why God must rescue us from the very things we thought would save us."[49]

When we embrace false intimacy, we create our own hell. The enemy allows us to experience lesser pleasures to distract our attention. Stimulation and sensuality tempt and divert us from the real. How prevalent is this in our culture? How many individuals, walking down a street, glued to their cellphones, are missing the experience of life surrounding them? We avoid the risk of a real relationship with God and others.

On a whale-watching trip in Hawaii, I, as well as many others, were videotaping the whales using their cell phones. Instead of viewing the whales in the expanse of nature, we were observing them through the minimized view on our cellphones. I decided to put my cellphone away so I could view what was happening in the vast ocean in front of me. How often do we view life through a minimized lens and therefore limit the experience which could be ours?

We often encounter a gap between the desires of the heart and the circumstances of life. We feel okay if our life lines up with our desires but experience suffering if it does not. To avoid suffering, we try to change our circumstances or detach our hearts. However, changing our circumstances only means we will have to face them again later. Squelching our desires can cause us to become cynical, hard-hearted. Neither choice yields life. Both disown our deepest desire.

We achieve freedom when we realize that our desires will find their completion only in God. In Gethsemane, Jesus did not squelch His desires or try to change His circumstances. He acknowledged His desires, redirecting and putting them into the Father's hands. Jesus did not avoid the suffering but obeyed, for the sake of the love of the Father, amid the suffering. He *loved into* the suffering.

Jesus helps us love through our suffering, too (more on this in chapter 20). We need to redirect our desires, taking and pouring out our heart's deepest desires to the Father.

My Story

> See! The winter is past; the rains are over and gone. Flowers appear on the earth; the season of singing has come.
>
> – Song of Songs 2:11–12

[49]Eldredge, *Journey of Desire*, pp. 86.

In C. S. Lewis' *The Lion, the Witch and the Wardrobe*, the White Witch keeps the land of Narnia frozen and under her control ("always winter but never Christmas"). The Witch seduces Edmund, a key character who is angry and embittered. He wants to rule and be in charge. The Witch offers Edmund Turkish delight, a sweet that distracts him and appeals to his immediate desire and gratification.

My exposure to gay pornography in 1969 opened the door to what would later become my nuclear winter, my frozen Narnia. Although Jesus came to my heart that same year, I walked away from Him in 1976 bewildered by my same-sex attractions. I metaphorically welcomed the White Witch to bring her winter, since I wanted to rule alone in my frozen, disappointed heart. I allowed the enemy to distract me with his Turkish Delight. I chose "sweets" to satisfy my desire. I will call my Turkish delight, "George."

George brought me to his kingdom and provided experiences I never knew. Freezing my true desire, I could no longer see aright. I abandoned myself to the delight that now filled my vision, obscuring what lay beneath in the depths of my heart.

However, you can consume Turkish delight for only so long before it becomes familiar, boring, and unappealing. Because that delight has no true substance, its sweetness eventually becomes bland. It lacks life. I started searching for my next "confectionary." After eleven years of sweets, my heart craved substance, for what was real!

When I looked into the eyes of my lovers, I saw only a mirror image of myself looking back. I looked to these men for something I lacked; however, they were looking to me for that very same thing. We were two empty vessels looking for the other to assuage that emptiness. The illusion on the outside made every man I slept with look as if he had the substance for which my heart hungered. When we became naked with each other, however, our nakedness only revealed the common emptiness of our souls. Neither of us could supply what the other lacked. Is this not the same story for any form of broken sexual union? Do we not partake of "sweets" which are slowly killing our hearts? Never satisfying us?

My heart had settled for *eros* without true *agape*. I looked into the eyes of my lovers to see what I could take. I believed the illusion I was giving myself *to them*, but the reality was that my motivation was *to take* from them. It was not sacrificial love but desire that was self-serving and egocentric—the ultimate expression of false intimacy.

Reclaiming the Good of Desire

> As we pursue the goal of constructing our own reality through the illusion of false intimacy, the further we move from the reality in which God has placed us and calls us to live, the more we create our own insanity.[50]

The depth of our desires connects with our capacity to hope and dream. Loss of that capacity within limits our potentiality. We forget our original design and purpose, not allowing our deep desires to penetrate the icy barriers we create.

But the faithful Lover of our souls does not abandon us; He pursues us relentlessly. He is jealous for us to discover what He originally meant for us to experience and to be. God created us for intimacy with Him. However, He wants our love given freely. Giving us the power to reject Him, He also empowered us to enter an incredibly deep love as His beloved.

As I discussed in chapter 9, the sacredness of marriage and its sexual intimacy reflect the mystery of the intimate relationship God desires with us. To enter this kind of relationship with Him, we must turn from possessions, power, and relationships with their many illusions. We need to stop running after temporary gratification, to yield our control, and to wait with holy anticipation. In healthy relationship, we must trust God to be our source of acceptance, security, and significance. Our desire and sexuality need to be God-inspired rather than earthbound.

In marriage, as ordained by God between a man and a woman, the two become one flesh. Their being and complementarity transcend into a holy oneness. The physical joins with the spiritual, which points to the future marriage feast awaiting us. Do we not crave that depth of intimacy and knowing? Regardless of whether we are single, celibate, or married, God intends each of us to come out of our aloneness and isolation. What we crave is not simply marriage but true intimacy. What we desire is oneness with our Creator—the great mystery we discussed in chapter 9.

The church often makes marriage an idol. It promotes marriage as the ultimate form of intimacy, and yet, the ultimate form of intimacy is *oneness with God*, not one another. When there is an indication that marriage is the ultimate form of intimacy, those who are single or celibate can feel they are left on outside looking in. They are in a holding pattern or are somehow

[50]Schaumburg, *False Intimacy*, p. 19.

incomplete. The lie believed is that I will never experience completeness unless I am married. The truth is that our completeness is found only in our *union with God*.

Marriage's true, higher purpose is to reflect a covenantal love. A man and woman make a covenant to remain committed to one another through good and difficult times. It is to reflect how God has made a covenant, a blood covenant, with us. He is fully committed to us and promises never to leave or abandon us. This is why God hates divorce. It is the tearing asunder of a covenantal love. He wants our deepest desire to become one with Him. Such unity returns us to the Garden, where healthy other-awareness existed, replacing our current egocentric self-awareness. This is a holy act of worship.

You may glimpse such unity momentarily in your quiet times or when you gather in community with other believers. That unity is what you were originally designed to experience and what you will eventually know. Jesus wants you to know Him as your Bridegroom. Stop for a moment and ponder this level of intimacy.

God is the wellspring, the life source of the deepest romance we can ever experience. He shows us glimpses of it in His creation and through our relationships. Our triune God invites us continually into the dance, into the symphony, into the communion of relationship with Him. He also calls us into healthy, holy knowing of each other in community.

Our hearts are of profound value to God. We, in turn, must realize this. They are truly our most precious possession. Our culture promotes "giving our hearts" based on personal pleasure rather than on a more profound knowing, exchanged within holy parameters. We cannot grasp the vision of beauty that our hearts are—whole and precious—when we cut them into pieces and give them away through illicit and random sexual encounters. How fractured is your heart due to the number of times you gave pieces of it away in either emotionally destructive relationships or sexual liaisons?

> Once we realize what a precious thing this is, our heart's desire, we must see that to guard it is worth our all. To neglect it is foolishness. To kill it is suicide. To allow it to wander aimlessly, to be trapped by the seductions of the evil one, is disaster. We must be serious about our happiness.[51]

[51]Eldredge, *Journey of Desire*, p. 174.

Inspired Desire

Losing God's perspective regarding our hearts means the loss of a bigger picture. True, holy, and good desire becomes a distorted, broken dream. We now believe that dream was only imaginary, a foolish child's wish. We need to awaken from this distortion and begin to face our deepest disappointments.

God promises to give us a new heart, a heart of flesh to replace a heart of stone. A heart without desire is a heart of stone, lifeless, and cold. The new heart our Creator gives us has God-inspired desires and is alive with holy passions. We discover these inspired desires by carving out the time to search for them. We seek them with spiritual sensitivity to God and in community. The Holy Spirit wants us to know our truest desires without the deception of counterfeits.

Augustine writes, "The whole life of the good Christian is a holy longing. What you desire ardently, as yet you do not see. [So] let us long because we are to be filled.... That is our life, to be exercised by longing."[52] Augustine is urging us to let go and allow these holy desires to be awakened in us. Paul learned the secret of being content when his longings were not met (Philippians 4:11–12). We find contentment by allowing the free flow of God-inspired longings to rise up and out of our hearts. God is capable of restoring that which we have carelessly given away, so our hearts are once again whole and not fragmented.

Wrapping Up

To be alive to our desires means we will still thirst, hunger, and long for completion. We will always experience the ache of desire within us. Does a married couple experience sexual knowing and intimacy with one another only once? Likewise, we seek our true Beloved repeatedly for the pleasure and oneness of His presence. We learn to respond to the invitation He is always extending to us.

The communion and union we desire occur within our deepest forms of worship. In the Holy of Holies, we abandon our being to His, allowing our desire for Him to be fully revealed and expressed. Intimacy with God is the deepest desire of our hearts. Adam and Eve experienced it with awesome abandon.

The loss of this perfect intimacy created our ache within, which drives us. We must battle with the "what is," looking with holy anticipation for the coming of the "not yet." We make the challenging

[52]Quoted in Eldredge, *Journey of Desire*, p. 181.

choice not to be anxious, which tempts us to take control. Taking control leads us eventually to false intimacy and embracing the haze of addiction. Yielding our control to Jesus leads us to life.

The Holy Spirit, at work within us, brings us up and out of dungeons of our making, our personal hells. He enables us to hold onto true hope and believe it will turn out well for us. Hearts abandoned in true worship allows the experience of true intimacy we desire. In this place of true worship, we release our grief, sorrows, aloneness, and despair. All things are brought into perspective in the true presence of Jesus. We lay down our losses at the foot of the cross.

There we discover our hearts' truest passion and deepest desire. In our surrender, we receive that which is true—not merely a resignation of self but a passionate desire, making the profound choice to choose Jesus above all.

Offering Him the precious gift of your heart changes everything. The more God reigns in your heart, the more you will experience change in your life. Change is not behavior modification on the outside but transformation on the inside, which eventually manifests itself on the outside. Interior change will result in a regeneration of the intimacy and desire that were lost. Your heart will once again become complete. It is discovering who you are in community, in the Body of Christ. "I am my beloved's and my beloved is mine" (Song of Songs 6:3).

Prayer

Father, I come before You with a heart full of desires. Some of these desires are for the good things of You, while others are for that which draws me away from You. But You have imparted to me the deepest desire of all—to know and be known by You. I ask for that desire to become my prime desire. May all the desires of my heart be aligned with the desires of Your heart.

Lord, I have wandered off the path on my journey home, the way, which You have made for me. At times I have been in reaction to my desires. At times I have shut down my desires—my heart—out of fear of where those desires would lead me. At other times, I have chosen not to listen to Your voice but abandoned myself to those desires. I need Your presence, Holy Spirit, as the Spirit of truth, the wise Counselor who is always present to me, and also as the Comforter, when I recognize my wandering heart. I long to bring joy to Your heart rather than cause You grief.

Inspired Desire

Jesus, help me surrender my heart to You at the foot of Your cross. Help me stay present to those places in my heart that need Your holy order to calm my chaos. Transform me from the inside out. I long to let go and allow You to be at the center of my heart. May I be empowered by You, Holy Spirit, to hold out for the infinite instead of settling for the finite which will never satisfy or fulfill my soul. May I come into a place of rest, knowing that my desire is for You as Your desire is for me.

Soul Work

1. How have you walked as a stoic, a sensualist, and a sojourner in your life?

2. What are the lesser, finite things you have settled for, experiencing immediate gratification, rather than genuine satisfaction or fulfillment?

3. How have you been in reaction to desire? How have you feared it? How have you avoided it?

4. How can you let go of control and begin to line up your desires with God's desires?

Journaling Moment

Ask the Lord to reveal how you have been in reaction to your heart. Ask Him to show you the ways you are either in reaction to or responsive to your heart. In a quiet moment, invite Him to align your heart's desires with His. Wait and ask for a healing word from Him for wherever your heart is unsettled or restless. Invite Jesus to enter there, that He may reveal Himself as your Beloved, and in so doing, reveal that you are His beloved.

ELEVEN

Processing Our Past

Walking in wholeness requires recognizing that our past influences our present. Although we are new creations in Christ, any unresolved emotion or wounding from our past still requires resolution. We cannot ignore the pain and hurt that remain within us. Indicating they are "under the Blood" does not resolve them! Denying our unresolved emotions only prolongs our struggles. We need the Lord's guidance to reveal what resides unhealed in our souls.

We either respond or react to our environment. When we respond, we can rightly discern and process the events and people around us. We engage personally in our setting. When we react to our surroundings, we wall off the events, emotions, or individual(s) involved. We turn inward, with heightened sensitivity, not being present to our setting. We must become more responsive, rather than reactive, to our surroundings.

The goal of this chapter is to provide understanding and insight into how the experiences of our past have shaped our present emotional and relational responses or reactions. It is crucial to identify where we are still carrying past wounds and unresolved, toxic emotions.

We are not to gloss over or diminish any sins committed against us, whether overt or covert, intentional or non-intentional. We must identify those sins and call them sins. However, those sins absolutely cannot be an excuse for my present choices to embrace sinful behaviors. The sin of another against me does not permit me to sin in return, in the moment or later.

As I have stated before, children are the greatest recorders of information but the poorest interpreters. We must identify any interpretations or lies believed that have laid a foundation of faulty beliefs. God will expose the distorted lens—formed by the people and events of our past—

through which we view our present lives and relationships.

Building Our Identity

The capacity of our parents to connect with, affirm, and bless us significantly affects how we see ourselves, others, and God. We all come from dysfunctional families to a certain degree. All of us have grown up with intimacy and relational deficits that influence our sense of identity. When we are in reaction, we compensate for those deficits apart from Christ.

As young children, we search for indications of who we are, where we belong, and our value. Our family and experiences within our environment establish the foundation for how we view life and relate to those around us. As children, we begin to form our relational patterns and identity on this foundation. When our legitimate needs go unmet, it weakens the foundation.

Imagine, if you will, the Parthenon in Greece. It has a lower level, upon which there are columns that support the surmounting pediment. Now apply this image to yourself. The lower level represents the foundation laid in your early years. Built upon that foundation are three pillars, which we will name belonging, worth, and competency. The pediment represents your identity, upheld by the strength of the three pillars laid on your foundation.

Belonging

The pillar of belonging stems from your core desire to connect relationally with God and others. Your sense of being and well-being influences the security of this pillar. As we discovered in previous chapters, you have a deep drive to fit in, to be part of something.

If you are not living out of your true center in Christ, however, you may have an elevated need to belong. This need can easily turn to control, resulting in your relationships becoming idolatrous. (You may manipulate others, for example, to form a connection with yourself.) The core of these relationships is your brokenness, which results in your taking from, rather than giving to, others.

Worth

The pillar of worth rises from your desire to know that you have importance and value and are lovable. Lacking an inner sense of worth, not knowing the price paid for you by Jesus, you turn to outward means to confirm your worth. You may look to others to define you and tell you that you are worthy. But these false sources of worth will eventually fail. Only can God truly affirm your incalculable worth.

Competency

The pillar of competency connects with your desire to be capable, adequate, and proficient. Knowing your God-given worth allows competency to center you in Christ. He strengthens and enables you to do all things. When the pillar of worth is weak, the pillar of competency shifts your focus from "being" (resting) to "doing" (restless activism).

When there are deficits or weaknesses in one pillar, it results in the stressing of the other two. The foundation for your emotional development and sense of identity arises from your reactions and responses to life. How did you respond or react to any shame, rejection, or lack of love in your past? Who or what became your source of security, peace, or fulfillment? What are your current attempts to repair your past wounds? Behavior modification does not address underlying drives and emotions. You need God's clarity to see your life aright.

Addressing Our Families of Origin

The greater the presence of dysfunction in our families, the greater the instability of what supports the structure of our identity. Where there are cracks and deficit areas in our foundation, we may cope by choosing protective mechanisms, attempting unconsciously to repair our fragmented foundations. If the three pillars are unsteady, we will experience insecurity in our identity or sense of being a man or woman.

Our faulty foundation and weakened pillars create conflict between walking in the true or false self. When walking in my true self, I can embrace my weakness as an opportunity to experience the love and mercy of God further. By inviting Jesus to meet me where I am, in the present moment, I am free to acknowledge my deficits without shame or accusation. I practice His presence, reminding myself of the oneness I enjoy with Him.

The false self chooses to be in reaction to weakness and sin. Through self-hatred and shame, I view my weakness as unacceptable. Instead of practicing the presence of Jesus, I turn inward and practice the presence of the diseased self. The enemy relishes this condition, bringing his accusations; and my voice condemns me as well. I spiral downward, lost in introspection. I split into two, creating an outer façade of appearing okay but inwardly experiencing the prison of self-recrimination.

Family Rules and the Battle Within

To address our foundations, we must take a closer look at our family environments. We already know the four unspoken rules of dysfunctional families: *Do not speak, think, feel, or trust*. These can expand, however, into additional rules:

– Do not discuss problems, so be blind.
– Do not express your feelings, so be quiet.
– Do not question your experiences, so be numb.
– Do not be honest in communicating, so be careful.
– Do not rock the boat, so be good or perfect.

When these rules surround us, we incorporate them, consciously or unconsciously, into our lives. We become adept at wearing masks to hide our true feelings and disappointments. We take on role-playing (for example, becoming a peacemaker or a clown), behaving in certain ways to avoid further pain or to diffuse difficult situations.[53]

What mask did you wear, or how did you react when your home suddenly became tense or unsafe?

We bury and imprison our legitimate needs when they are unmet. This encourages the creation of a distorted view of self, which becomes the foundation for our false self. There begins the tendency to avoid transparency, to self-protect, or to isolate. We experience a decreased capacity to respond to our environment, limiting our capacity to receive what is good. We are in reaction.

Before going further, stop and reflect on the previous paragraph. The broken behaviors in our lives are the result of trying to meet legitimate needs in illegitimate ways. As we discussed in chapter 9, we have a legitimate need and desire for true intimacy and connection. Being in reaction when these needs remain unfulfilled, we take control, trying to meet them through our own means.

Being in reaction, the false self becomes preoccupied with investing in the non-real, fantasy, and escape. We create illusion and façades because reality is too difficult to accept. We cope and retreat. We seek false life sources because we have a diminished capacity to identify

[53]For an in-depth discussion of the masks worn and the role-playing occurring within dysfunctional families, I highly recommend *Love Is a Choice: The Definitive Book on Letting Go of Unhealthy Relationships* by Robert Hemfelt, Frank Minirth, and Paul Meier (Thomas Nelson, rev. ed. 2003) and the accompanying workbook.

true and genuine sources for life. Doing so leads to the creation of relational idols due to our heightened drive for security, happiness, and love.

Because we are not truly addressing our legitimate unmet needs, they become an ache that drives us. This results in repeated choosing of illegitimate ways, going after false intimacy, to meet them. The result of our broken patterns always fails to assuage the ache of our emptiness.

Habitual patterns develop due to reactionary thinking and feeling. These habits become life for us. We believe the lie that we will fall apart or die without them. Practicing these patterns for years, we are blind to our broken relational behaviors and habits. These patterns and diseased thinking can eventually become the basis for significant personality disorders.

Split off from God, the false self focuses on the created rather than the Creator. Our false life attachments influence, shape, and define our knowledge of love and acceptance. Not anchored in the Father's love, we settle for counterfeits and the finite. Not centered in Jesus, we turn either into ourselves or others for our security. Our reactions can flow between extremes. Some hyperactive reactions include these:

- The false self becoming relationally reactive to community
- The abdication of self results in emotional/codependency with others who become idols who define me
- The absorption of self (narcissism), with me becoming the one to be worshiped

Although our spirits are one with Christ, we are still on the path of spiritual development and becoming. Our will, the power of choice, wrestles with the Lordship of Jesus. We need healing in our capacity to be in relationship so we can enter into healthy community and deeper intimacy with God.

Results of Family Dynamics

The Holy Spirit reveals the underlying foundation of our sexual and relational brokenness. Our past relationships influenced the development of our identity. We become broken through dysfunctional relationships, so restoration occurs only through entering into healthy, whole relationships.

The framework for our emotional and relational development was impacted by our parents (as we saw in section 1). Mother is typically the first female we come to know and love. She is the first face and example of woman we experience. Father is usually the first male we come to know and love. He is the first face and example of man we experience. Parents model what it means to be a man or woman, and the way men and women relate.

How did your parents model what it is to be a man or a woman? How did they model relationship between men and women?

Parents also model how I am to relate to God. As a child, I look up and out to my parents (quite literally). Mom and Dad are bigger than I am; they know more than I do, and they provide for me. In learning to trust them, I also learn how to trust others. The trust we experience eventually becomes a trust we can experience with God. Parents, or other authority figures, provide the building blocks for how I will relate to community and God. Do you comprehend how their presence either helped or diminished how you relate to God? They influence how we see and know Him.

A child needs *consistent* nurture, boundaries, affirmation, clarity, and parental love. Where any of these are lacking, there will be gaps in our emotional and relational development. As children, we look to the adults around us for understanding, wisdom, and perspective. We need their direction to process our environment. Without wise and whole guidance, we turn to our own limited emotional and cognitive resources.

Our early experiences affect us mentally, emotionally, physically, and spiritually. These experiences and situations give rise to our sense of self. Our relationships influence our developing thinking and attitudes, which then help structure our identity and belief systems. Our beliefs influence our behaviors, which then affect all our relationships.

Did your childhood result in a healthy view of self, others, and God? Do you see how your childhood relationships created a foundation for how you presently approach life?

Our temperament and personality influence how we filter our surroundings. Those who are more sensitive often seem to internalize their environment to a greater degree, pondering and ruminating over it. The danger here is it can lead to a diseased self-awareness that turns egocentric. Focusing inward on ourselves, we can become lost in diseased introspection (a self-consuming inward focus).

Those who are less sensitive may have a decreased tendency to internalize. They may have difficulty in discerning or comprehending emotional cues. Instead of being overly self-aware, they can become oblivious to their inner emotions. Our stories are complex with nuances, which only God can bring into proper alignment.

As children, we may experience extremes in parental presence. Our parents may be too present or too absent, as we discussed in section 1. Many of us fall somewhere between these two extremes. But it is worth examining the effects children may experience in dysfunctional homes. As a gentle reminder, identifying the brokenness in our upbringing is not to identify the cause of our struggles. It is to help bring understanding of how faulty belief systems developed, which then affected our sense of self and identity. The difficulty with our parental relationships often reflects what we experienced as children. It all goes back to the Fall.

Parents can overrun a child's boundaries. They can restrict or control their children through dominance or use them to satisfy their own needs. Parents' behavior can also be rooted in fear or insecurity; they imagine that their children reflect their capacity as "acceptable" or "unacceptable" parents. Parental behavior may also stem from the need to be perfect or in absolute control. Whatever the reason, the child is limited in his or her expression and development.

In chapter 6, I spoke of the impact Father wounding can have on children. For further consideration, it is worth repeating how we, as children, can react to familial wounds. Below are some resulting reactions when Mother or Father is too present with their children:

- The child feels overwhelmed, crushed, devalued, helpless.
- The child is suppressed emotionally or manipulated; I have difficulty processing my emotions or engaging in community.
- A child robbed of the power to speak can feel the loss of his or her voice; my opinion is not valid.
- The child may turn to self-protection by creating walls, being guarded, and not trusting anyone.
- Often performance or perfection is valued, resulting in wearing masks and creating façades.

- The child may embrace the abdication of self; I have no self-worth and am here only to be controlled by others.

When Mother or Father is too absent, the following may result:

- The child feels lost, insecure, anxious, or unsettled because of a lack of covering or guidance in the development of healthy boundaries.
- The child is left with his or her emotions to figure out about life and relationships; I may have difficulty working through challenges or confrontation because I was never taught how to respond in a healthy way.
- The child may have a loss of voice because he or she was never asked to respond or have an opinion.
- The child has a growing ache for what was not received or blessed.

In either of these situations, children may detach defensively from their parents. This detachment is a self-protective mechanism in reaction to an unhealthy environment or individual. In reaction, they wall off the event, emotion, or individual(s) involved. They choose relational patterns that are self-protective. They create blocks to their parents, therefore blocking out both the bad and the good.

There can be dramatic consequences when we detach from our same-sex or opposite-sex parent; later, we may transfer these feelings onto all men or all women. Transference is reacting in the present when triggered by an unresolved memory or emotions of the past. The emotions resulting from past wounds surface toward whoever or whatever evoked them in the present. When a situation warrants an emotional response of two, on a scale of 1–10, but a reaction of a ten occurs, this is a good indication of the presence of transference.

Being in Reaction

This chain of events summarizes our previous discussion:

Experience > Emotional Reaction > Belief > Behavior

It all begins with an experience of some kind, which evokes an emotional response or reaction.

We have the choice to process rightly what just happened, or we can react, turning inward on ourselves. Instead of controlling our emotions, we allow our emotions to control us. When the experience is repeated, or if it is traumatic, it may create a foundation for our beliefs. When those beliefs are fully established, they guide our behavior and help lay the foundation for our identity.

Emotional reactions can vary based on our temperament, on the level of intensity of the event, and our relationship to those involved. Some individuals can let a situation roll off their backs; for others, it may result in agony. An experience of rejection may have a more serious effect if it comes from a parent rather than a stranger. It all comes down to how we individually process our life events.

Below are some examples of how we can react to a challenging event:

- Isolation or withdrawal: the event is too overwhelming to me, so I choose to turn inward.
- Self-protection: I look for the means to prevent further pain or struggle.
- Control: I take charge so as not to be vulnerable to other painful events.
- Self-hatred or self-rejection: I allow the event to define my worth or value.
- I develop a lack of confidence or security in being a man or a woman.
- Misogyny or misandry: My reaction in detaching defensively from Father or Mother turns into hatred for all men or all women (that is, transference).
- Vows: I make certain statements in reaction (consciously or subconsciously), such as "I will never let myself be vulnerable again" or "I will never express my opinions again" or "I will never let him [or her] be close to me again."

Over time, our life events come together to form our belief systems. If I encounter rejection repeatedly, my resulting belief may be that I am useless. If I hate my body or my inability to be what I feel a man or a woman should be, I may believe that I do not fit in with others of my sex. I may also feel inadequate in relating to the opposite sex. We establish these beliefs based on a faulty standard. Ultimately, they are lies and misinterpretations.

Our internalized attitudes become judgments through which we live. Whereas vows can be an immediate reaction, judgments involve a longer and deeper, and often subconscious, thought process. They become the labels we wear. *I am* statements typically reveal the presence of labels: "I am useless." "I am not a true man/woman." "I am tainted." Sometimes we allow others to place labels on us. Their words/statements become our labels. Judgments can also be placed on others: all men or all women are unworthy of my trust.

Over time, emotions rather than experiences can become a trigger for us, activating the established judgments. Loneliness, fear, or inadequacy may trigger us, resulting in our choosing some behavior to suppress, avoid, or pacify our pain. The death of a loved one, physical or mental illness, or unsolicited exposure to sexual sensuality may also trigger us. Our inability to identify our emotions prevents us from connecting with an underlying unmet need or faulty belief.

How does your past impact your current relationships with men and women? Do you seek men/women to provide what Father/Mother could not? Do you detach/avoid men or women? Are you seeking men/women to meet the unmet emotional needs of your past? Do you try to connect in a physical way to assuage your insecure feelings of being a man or a woman? So many questions and unresolved emotions can lie beneath.

Walking in Freedom

Our levels of brokenness developed over time. The healing from our past hurts and wounds will not happen overnight. God's timing is perfect, and He will provide our healing according to His time frame. It also requires a willingness to commit to and have endurance in our process. The length of our recovery, however, depends on our intentionality and commitment to the Lordship of Jesus. It is not about overcoming one sin, but many. It does not involve knowing every detail of healing our soul's need. It is about pursuing the Lover of our souls, Jesus.

Our process is not about a method but a Person, the personhood of Jesus. This may sound over-spiritual, but it is a reality. When my primary focus in on healing, my vision is inward, what Leanne Payne called "navel-gazing." When my focus is upward, on Jesus, who is my way (John 14:6), He lays the path before me in the wilderness. I am a follower of Jesus, not my healing. Jesus will cause me to connect with the right resources and community. Who is in control of your process, you or Jesus?

Below is a list of choices that have helped many in the process of overcoming. Previous chapters covered some of them, and future chapters will discuss others.

- Divine objectivity: Ask the Lord for the capacity to see your life and circumstances through His eyes rather than through the lens of dysfunction.
- Practicing the Presence of Jesus: Although Jesus abides in us, we do have places in our hearts that resist Him. Begin inviting Him regularly into your pain, emotions, and struggle. Relinquish control of your process into the hands of Jesus, walking according to His will and schedule.
- Be intentional about your quiet times!
- Confession: Invite others into your inner circle through confession. Part of being known is letting others know your weakness and failures. Confession is a vital part of our recovery process.
- Renunciation: Any time we worship the created again rather than the Creator, we need to renounce our idol worship and break these unions.
- Walking in forgiveness: Jesus gave us the command to forgive; it is not an option. Unforgiveness keeps us bound and in a prison of our making.
- The virtue of self-acceptance: Our battle with shame and self-hatred hinders our embracing of the virtue of healthy self-love; we must learn to accept our God-given lovableness and not let our behavior or sin define us.
- Counseling/support: Take advantage of the resources around you.
- Seek the Holy Spirit's counsel to resist restless activism, searching relentlessly for that "special source" of healing. Trust that Jesus, who is your path, has the way laid out before you.
- Community: The refining of our healing process takes place in community. Let God help you take off your mask and take down your walls to others. Dysfunctional relationships helped establish our broken foundations (as we saw earlier in this chapter), and whole, healthy relationships will be the venue for our healing.

Prayer

Lord, I thank You for knowing me and all that pertains to me. You know my past, present, and future. You have seen me since the moment I was conceived. You are fully aware of my unmet needs and where I need Your healing touch.

Lord, would You begin to replace any faulty foundation on which my identity is built? Would You reveal where there are weaknesses in the areas of belonging, worth, and competence? I need You as the divine architect to bring restoration to any areas that were not established according to Your design. Where are the areas of instability in my identity? I desire to stand upon Your sound foundation, which cannot be shaken.

I acknowledge that no family is perfect. My parents came from families of dysfunction. They did not have all their love needs met growing up. The healing I am now receiving is also the healing needed in their lives. Would You grant me divine objectivity to see my parents and my life as You see them? I need Your clarity to discern, where I am culpable of being in reaction. I also need Your wisdom to identify where there have been sins of intent in my family. Help me not be in denial or defensively detached. I am willing for You to show me how to release the burden of my past.

Holy Spirit, I welcome You to reveal any lies or misconceptions which originated from being in reaction to my parents or trusted authority figures. Expose any faulty beliefs I have developed through the observation of dysfunctional relationships. Expose any vows or judgments I have made in my past. I bring these lies, misconceptions, vows, and judgments to you that I may renounce them. In so doing, Lord, please speak Your truth and release me from these things, which I have allowed to limit and name me.

I long to love You and others aright. Seek out the memories that have tainted my view of men, women, and You. Bring Your truth to any distorted thinking that prevents me from entering into whole relationships. Please meet my unmet needs such that I can love others aright by Your will.

Lord, what needs to be addressed in my life so I can walk in freedom? In the place of any shame and self-hatred, may I begin to embrace the virtue of healthy self-love? Please help me accept my God-given lovableness. Help me renounce any way I let my behaviors or sin define me. How do You name me? How do You see me? This is the spiritual reality I yearn to walk in, allowing only You, my Creator, and my God, to determine who I am. You are a good Father, and all good things come from You.

Soul Work

Write a letter to your mother and father (two separate letters). Note that it is not the intention to mail these letters to your parents. These letters, with the Lord's guidance, are to be an exercise helping you to go deeper in reflection about your parental relationship. Before you begin, ask the Holy Spirit to center you and use this time for revelation.

In these letters, express your feelings regarding your upbringing. Give voice to how each parental relationship modeled what it meant to be a man or woman and to be in a healthy opposite-sex relationship. Ponder the unspoken rules of dysfunctional families and how they may have been present in your family. What personal beliefs have you formed due to unmet needs in your emotional development?

The goal of these letters is not to attack each parent's inadequacies but to express how things were and how they affected you. Resist the urge to make a laundry list of offenses. This is also not to be an exercise in diseased introspection, so keep each letter to one page only (two-sided okay, with readable font size!).

After you have written both letters, allow God to write you a letter! Ask the Holy Spirit to enable you to hear the voice of Father God responding to your letters. Ask Him to speak to your heart and allow Him to give you His perspective on your life. Let Him tell you how He sees you now.

This is a daunting assignment. I often see a reluctance or defiance to do this exercise. It is not my intent to shame or bring condemnation for not doing this exercise. However, ask the Lord to expose why you are hesitant. What is preventing you from doing writing these letters? Seek revelation rather than deflection. Press in instead of escaping. Grace is extended for those who feel overwhelmed even to attempt such a letter. But I hope that you will be able to write these letters eventually.

Receiving a letter from God can be just as challenging! Write down whatever comes to mind. Show it to those you trust and know you. Ask them if it rings true. Let God show you if it is His voice which is speaking to you, or are they the words of the enemy or your areas self-hatred. God will provide a way for you right where you are at this moment. Ask for the gift of faith to believe He will meet you.

Journaling Moment

Ask the Lord to expose the personal beliefs that you formed due to the unmet needs in your emotional development. What is the "stinking thinking" that resulted from your family of origin? How are you still in emotional reactivity or defensive detachment in your heart? Wait on

TWELVE

Broken Boundaries

BY BOB PERDUE

THE LORD IS CLOSE TO THE BROKENHEARTED AND SAVES THOSE WHO ARE CRUSHED IN SPIRIT.

- PSALM 34:18

I was present for the birth of my children and cannot begin to describe the miracle of birth. Watching a little person emerge from the mother's womb—still connected to the mother, still dependent—and then actually being the one to cut the umbilical cord and witness the infant's first moments as a unique independent individual, is amazing!

Each of us is born with the gift of individual personhood. We were each "knit together" in our mother's womb (Psalm 139:13) by a loving heavenly Father. Our unique genetic makeup and DNA set us apart from all others. We have boundaries that help us know where we stop and where others start. Inside these boundaries, and within the context of our personhood, we are free to grow, to question, to risk, to explore, and to experience life in our unique way.

We learn to relate to others while still maintaining our clear sense of being. We allow others to respond and react to us without owning their responses. We are free to relate without walls. If allowed to continue and encouraged by those closest to us, we become comfortable in our skin (within our boundaries) and develop a positive identity. This positive identity was part of the original creation;

and when it is redeemed by faith in the finished work of Christ, it blossoms, giving us a good sense of our value (Genesis 1:31); a sense of belonging and community (Genesis 2:18), a sense of power that frees the will to choose (Genesis 2:15–17); and freedom to embrace our personhood in healthy ways (Genesis 1:27). See chapter 2 for a fuller explanation of positive identity.

The safety and freedom created by the boundaries of individual personhood work together and encourage us to live the life God intended for us. This is the goal. This is right in the eyes of God.

Abuse Defined

Abuse is an invasion of those boundaries, an attack on our personhood. Abuse happens when someone stronger than we are overpowers us, either emotionally, physically, verbally, or sexually. Abuse is such a harsh word that many never even consider the possibility that they have experienced broken boundaries, simply because they do not identify with the word. But consider the following forms of broken boundaries:

Physical: Someone older and stronger harming your body, using his or her superior power. Hitting, biting, burning, excessive force, shaking, shoving, strangling, scalding, and depriving you of proper nutrition are some examples of physical abuse.

Verbal: Someone older using words to tear down your positive identity. Belittling, humiliating, embarrassing, cursing, screaming, name-calling, and manipulation are some examples of verbal abuse.

Emotional: Someone older using his or her power to manipulate your feelings. Withholding love, not allowing you to feel, exposing you to emotions that are out of control, excessive verbalization of fear, and excessive exposure to anger are some examples of emotional abuse.

Sexual: Someone older forcing sexual thoughts, visuals, or actions upon you. Fondling, genital contact, exposing you to pornography or graphic sexual images, inappropriate sexual talk, inappropriate kissing, oral sex, and intercourse are some examples of sexual abuse.

Boundaries can also be be broken by neglect, abandonment, spiritual manipulation, and more.

Take a few moments and review the above list one more time. Ask the Lord to reveal any evidence of broken boundaries in your life. The Lord promises that if we call on Him, He will answer us (Jeremiah 33:3). You don't necessarily have to go digging in your past; just open your heart to the possibility that a boundary was broken and then ask the Lord to reveal it.

The Effects of Abuse

There is no authoritative way to measure the severity of abuse. The age of the victim, the relationship with the abuser, the frequency of the abuse, and the reaction of others who knew about the abuse—all can be factors in how severely the broken boundaries affect a person. The impact of abuse is measured more, however, by how the victim processes it. Most of the time, the shame of the abuse or the threat of the abuser causes the broken boundary to remain hidden. With no one else to help him or her process, the young victim is left to interpret the situation with immature and limited knowledge. The conclusions reached in that young mind contain lies, labels, self-imposed rules for living, and feelings of intense shame and guilt. Robbed of safety and freedom, he or she falls into bondage to a protective system of living.

Abuse comes from outside of us and breaks down the boundaries of our personhood. The boundaries between the perpetrator and us become blurred. In spite of the reality that the abuse comes from outside, we tend to own some or all of the blame for the abuse and thus take on what rightfully belongs to the invader. With our personhood invaded and our boundaries destroyed, we are left vulnerable to the world around us and confused about who we are.

Even if the abuse is not "severe" in comparison to what others have experienced, the impact on our identity can be severe. Consider some of the following possible effects on our positive identity:

Value

Self-hatred: Part of me is bad. It must be rejected.

Shutdown of emotions: It's too painful to feel.

Lies about my identity: I'm no good. I am damaged goods. I am worthless.

Community

Isolation: I cannot trust others.

Fear of intimacy: I cannot allow anyone to get close.

Codependency: I have no value, so I must get my value in connection with another.

Self-sabotaging of relationships: I want community, but I fear it.

Power

Victimization: I have no power.

Control: I must have power so that no one ever overpowers me again.

Fear: I feel powerless because it might happen again.

Overly responsible: I cannot count on anyone. I must do it all myself.

Man/Woman

Insecurity: I'm confused about my sex.

Same sex attraction: I long for sexual connection to my same sex.

Eroticization of intimacy: All closeness leads to desire for a sexual connection.

Rejection of being male or female: I'm a "tomboy" or "effeminate."

Along with the damage to our positive identity, the invasion of our boundaries destroys our feeling of safety. Unholy offerings are deposited into our personhood. Shame, anger, fear, confusion, insecurity, and the spirit of death are some of the struggles that arise out of this brokenness.

It can be helpful as we move toward healing to "connect the dots" between the struggles we experience in our behavior and relationships and pain from our past. Read back through the list of some of the effects of abuse in the paragraphs above. Do you see some of these effects in your own life? Can you trace them back to a wound in your past?

Coping with Abuse

The presence of all this brokenness is the source of much inner pain. We can either allow the pain to drive us to seek healing or we can try to manage the pain through our coping mechanisms (flesh patterns). Followers of Jesus Christ always have the choice to live out of their spirits, empowered by God Himself, or to live out of their flesh, empowered by self. Galatians

5:16–17 tells us that these two ways of living are opposite. Responding to abuse in the flesh involves striving, denying, medicating, vowing, or yielding. Responding in the spirit involves confessing, forgiving, surrendering, and empowering.

The fear of exposure and secrecy of abuse provide the perfect environment for trying to cope on our own. Coping mechanisms (flesh patterns) usually develop quickly after abuse happens. Consider the following ways we attempt to cope with the brokenness or pain:

> Striving: I can do this. I can be better (altruism), stronger (exercise), wiser (academic pursuits), more beautiful (fashion), more spiritual (religious performance), or more successful (rich, famous, or in charge). I can create a sense of value, community, power, and security in being a man or woman by my efforts.
>
> Denying: I'm fine. The incident was no big deal and has had little to no effect on me. I choose not to allow the feelings to rise up (emotional shutdown) or else I dissociate completely from the experience.
>
> Medicating: I'm going to cover up the pain with something that feels good. The pain will trigger an attachment to the form of pleasure. This becomes an addiction, splits my will and eats up my desire. I can medicate with food, alcohol, drugs, sex, pornography, fantasy, watching TV, shopping, gambling, etc.
>
> Vowing: I'm going to will myself into healing. I vow never to speak of the incident, not to be like my abuser, not to feel the feelings, not to let anyone close, and more.
>
> Yielding: I am just damaged goods and worthless. I accept my status and learn to exist.

These are all flesh patterns, but over time they become embodied sin. They move past the mere choice of our wills and affect our minds and emotions. We begin to feel and believe that this is the right course of action, and it becomes almost automatic. It begins to seem normal.

My Story: Bob Perdue

I was abused verbally, physically, and sexually starting around the age of ten. Belittling, name-calling, being humiliated, being hit, and being held down and forced to perform sexual acts all had a profound effect on me. The conclusions I came to in my young mind provided the framework under which I would live for most of my life. I felt like a pervert and hated my body, so I became driven to prove my worth through accomplishments.

I vowed that no one would ever control me again, and I became a control freak in my family and on the job. I became a pastor and had many relationships, but kept everyone at a safe distance—including my family. I did not feel like a man, shied away from expressions of being a man, and fantasized about sexual relationships with other men. I formed a whole system of beliefs, rules, and behaviors as a result of the abuse. This system of striving drove me to exhaustion, depression, and despair. Becoming suicidal, I finally ended up in a psychiatric hospital where, after 25 years of silence, I began to process the system I had developed. I turned from coping to healing. I turned from my flesh patterns to the power of the Spirit of God in me.

Take a few moments and be honest with God about the flesh patterns you see in your own life. Sometimes these flesh patterns are blind spots and require open conversations with a trusted friend or counselor. Are there particular coping mechanisms the Father is urging you to surrender?

Healing from Abuse

When we allow the pain to drive us to seek healing, we choose (as we said) to live out of our spirits, empowered by God Himself. Responding in the spirit involves confession, forgiveness, surrender, and empowerment.

Confession

Healing begins with confession. Confession is not about asking for forgiveness; it is about naming the reality of our sin and wound in the presence of a loving Father. Confession is breaking the silence about our broken boundaries. Sitting with God, and perhaps a trusted counselor, and speaking out loud the reality of what happened to us is painful, but healing. As we acknowledge our pain in the presence of God, we also acknowledge the many ways we have tried to deal with our pain on our own. We confess our flesh. We confess our sin and wound. We stand before God naked and exposed.

Through confession, we invite Jesus into our wound. Jesus knows abuse, having been stripped, beaten, ridiculed, and crucified for us. He became subject to abuse and can absorb the pain of our abuse. We press our wound into His as He hangs on the cross. He endures the pain, pays for the offense, and then invites us to participate in the life of His resurrection without the pain. We identify with Him in His suffering and death and then in His resurrection and life (Philippians 3:10–11).

Through confession, we also invite Jesus into the memory of our wound. Yes, He was present at the time our boundaries were invaded. This can be a difficult reality to process. Faith in the goodness of God allows us to reconcile the harmful effects of His having given humankind free will. Men and women have the power to choose, to make choices that hurt others. The Father's love for us and His desire for love from us preclude His choosing for us. God allows but does not cause the poor choices, and He grieves them. He was grieving with us at the offense, and He began His loving pursuit of us toward the healing that we are just now beginning to access. We must allow ourselves time to grieve with Him and allow His Spirit, the Comforter, to bring us the needed comfort in our pain and lead us to a deeper faith in His love and goodness.

Forgiveness

Our healing moves forward past confession to forgiveness. Having brought the memory into the presence of God, we now name the abuse and the abuser in His presence. Holding the offense against him or her as a debt keeps us connected not only to the offense but also to the feelings and lies associated with the offense. The entire system we built in our minds to cope with life is connected to our hatred, anger, resentment, and unforgiveness toward the one who abused us. The power of this system cannot be overcome until this connection is broken. We are not powerful enough to break the connection. Neither our abuser nor we can pay the debt that was created by the abuse—but Jesus can and did.

In the parable Jesus told about forgiveness (Matthew 18:21–35), the king counted up the full debt of his servant and then totally released the debt. God decided to allow the death of His Son, Jesus, to fully pay the price for the debt our abuse created. We release the debt to Him, letting Him exact the judgment. If the abuser trusts in the finished work of Christ, then his or her sins were judged completely at the cross, as were ours. If the abuser does not trust in the finished work of Christ, then his or her sins—all of them together—will be judged by eternal damnation. Our forgiveness simply releases that person to God and sets us free from the damaging connection.

We must also appropriate God's forgiveness for our fleshly responses to the abuse. Having disconnected from the source that fueled the fleshly system we created in our minds and lived out in our behaviors, we must now bring that system into His presence and appropriate the forgiveness He has already given us (1 John 1:9). We owe nothing to Him in payment for our fleshly response. That debt was paid in full by the incalculable price of Jesus' blood. His blood washes away all sin. We are released not only from the penalty of that response but also the corresponding shame and guilt (Psalm 32:5).

Surrender and Empowerment

Having now disconnected from our abuser and from the fleshly system we developed out of the abuse, it is time to surrender all our flesh patterns to Him. We now identify the lies we have believed because of the abuse. We denounce the rules we have placed on our lives and the vows we have made. We surrender to the new identity He has given us (2 Corinthians 5:17) and begin to choose by His power to live out of that identity. We begin to believe that it is God who works in us and urges us to let His work move from the inside out (Philippians 2:12–13; Romans 12:1–2). We embrace the wonderful truth that, in our new identity, we can participate with God, doing His work in the world (2 Peter 1:3–4). This combination of surrender and empowerment is exactly what Paul meant when He urged us to "be filled with the Spirit" (Ephesians 5:18).

Our new identity and relationship with God through His Spirit begins to rebuild the walls that were broken down by the abuse. We begin to experience freedom and safety again in the security of His constant presence in our lives. We surrender to Him the unholy offerings that no longer have a place. Fear, anger, confusion, insecurity, and even the spirit of death are swallowed up in His love and grace, which creates hope that moves us forward.

The Father's loving desire is to meet you where you are in your pain and move you forward in the healing process. Ask the Father to help you locate where you are and then trust Him to lead you to the next step. Do you need to make some confession? Extend forgiveness? Appropriate forgiveness? Surrender flesh patterns? Lean into the power of the Spirit of God in you for life? Healing does not always happen in a moment in time; it often happens moment by moment.

Prayer

Lord, I come before You with the areas of abuse, known and unknown, that I have experienced in my life. Your Word says that You are close to the brokenhearted and that You save those who are crushed in spirit. I am choosing to trust that You are true to Your Word and that You are truly present to my pain. Thank You.

Soul Work

1. How has abuse affected you in the areas of value, community, power, and security in being a man or woman?

2 How have you coped with any abuse that has occurred in your life?

3. What are some of the boundaries you have created in certain areas in your life in reaction to your past—physical (actions/activities to protect you physically); emotional (things you do to isolate your heart); mental (how you react mentally to painful challenges, past and present); and spiritual (ways you perceive God or use religion as a barrier to keep others at a distance)?

Journaling Moment

Meditate on Revelation 3:20: "Here I am! I stand at the door and knock. If anyone hears my voice and opens the door, I will come in and eat with that person, and they with me." Ask the Lord to identify those areas of woundedness in your heart He would like to come into; talk with you about; dine with you, and help you experience His healing presence. Meditate on Proverbs 4:23: "Above all else, guard your heart, for everything you do flows from it." Ask the Lord to show you what new healthy boundaries you can incorporate (for example, not being in reaction) to guard your heart.

THIRTEEN

Forgiveness

THERE ARE THREE BLOCKS TO DISCOVERING OUR TRUE CENTER. THE FIRST TWO HAVE TO DO WITH THE FORGIVENESS OF SIN: EITHER OUR FAILURE TO FORGIVE OTHERS OR OUR FAILURE TO RECEIVE FORGIVENESS FROM GOD. THE THIRD HAS TO DO WITH ONE'S OWN INNER VISION OF ONESELF AND THE FAILURE TO ACQUIRE THE VIRTUE OF SELF-ACCEPTANCE.[54]

I had the blessing of attending eight of Leanne Payne's Pastoral Care Ministry conferences, the last three serving on her personal team. I can remember her speaking the above words. Although one often hears about forgiveness, the depth of its significance early on eluded me. However, I came to realize that forgiveness must be a fundamental part of our lives if we desire to become who God created us to be.

To live out of our true center is to embrace Jesus as our life. It requires continual dying to self and to the things that limit our becoming. By dying to self, we discover more who we are in Jesus. We begin to embrace the greater potentiality of our intimacy with God and walking in whole relationships. Forgiveness is a necessity to walk in whole relationships. Growing in our

[54]Payne, *Healing Presence*, p. 72.

true selves is to grow in greater dependency on Jesus.

Subconsciously I used to believe that as I matured spiritually, I would grow less dependent on God. I discovered, however, that my dependence on Him grew rather than lessened as I faced the challenges of my life. To live the life of Jesus in His fullness required my absolute yielding and dependency on Him. This was especially true in the area of forgiveness.

The cross of Christ is forgiveness personified. Through the death of Jesus, the sin that separates us from God is forgiven. "But now he has reconciled you by Christ's physical body through death to present you holy in his sight, without blemish and free from accusation" (Colossians 1:22). Jesus' commitment to the Father's will result in our forgiveness and reconciliation to the Father. Jesus made the way for us as believers to freely approach the Father.

Living from Our True Center

For us to live out of our true center, being image-bearers of Jesus is to embrace the ministry of reconciliation. Just as Jesus modeled it, so we must personify it in our daily lives. "All this is from God, who reconciled us to himself through Christ and gave us the ministry of reconciliation" (2 Corinthians 5:18). This means:

- Being reconciled to me: accepting my weaknesses and failures without self-hatred or condemnation
- Being reconciled to others: walking without judgment, bitterness, or revenge due to wrongs committed against me
- Being reconciled to God: releasing my anger, disappointment, and expectations toward God

Could you accomplish the above list apart from Jesus being your core identity? Forgiveness is a command, not an option. Jesus commands that we "love [our] enemies and pray for those who persecute [us]" (Matthew 5:44).

I heard Corrie ten Boom, a survivor of the Nazi Holocaust camps and a noted Christian author, share a personal story of forgiveness. After she had shared at a conference, a man approached to speak with her. She recognized the man: He had been a prison guard at her camp.

Now he had become a believer in Jesus and was asking her for forgiveness. In that challenging moment, Corrie ten Boom faced the impossible choice to extend her hand of forgiveness to the man who had been so cruel to her and her beloved sister. Could she have truly done so out of her own strength alone? No, she extended forgiveness to him by choosing to remain centered in Jesus and to be His image-bearer to this former Nazi guard.

Knowing the command to forgive, we may try to do so out of the sheer enforcement of our wills. Unless we also forgive from the heart, however, our forgiveness is incomplete. We may know the principle of forgiveness cognitively, yet remain walled off from those who hurt us. Forgiveness involves the mind, the heart, and the will. By acknowledging the mercy, we received from the cross of Jesus and standing in our true selves, we will be able to forgive. We must embrace the fullness of this knowledge in both head and heart. It must be the core out of which live. "Be kind and compassionate to one another, forgiving each other, just as in Christ God forgave you" (Ephesians 4:32).

Whenever you choose not to forgive, you rebel against God. You are choosing to remain in control. You then retreat into your prison of pain and shut the door, blocking God's entry. You also shut yourself off from community. Although God extends grace to us in this process, I believe we reach the point where the Lord reveals it is time to embrace the challenge of forgiveness. We need the Holy Spirit to help us yield our control so we may release forgiveness.

Pain and Forgiveness

> Many people in our lives who love us also hurt us because their own needs and unresolved conflicts prevent them from loving us in the way we want to be loved. But when we radically claim God's unconditional love for us, we can forgive those who have wounded us and set them free by our forgiveness.[55]

To be capable of extending forgiveness, we must grasp the reality of the cross. When we are amid our painful wounds, the pain, and suffering, Jesus endured provides a focal point. By remaining present to both our wounds and to Jesus, we can invite Him into our pain. At the cross,

[55]Henri Nouwen, *Love, Henri: Letters on the Spiritual Life*, (Convergent Books, 2016), p. 333.

Jesus meets us in our places of bitterness, cynicism, and vengeful hearts. Here we wrestle with God, allowing our emotions to rise, yet not letting those emotions justify our broken reactions. Jesus shared our humanity, therefore, can fully relate when we battle with the choice to forgive. As He hung dying on the cross, amid agonizing pain and the taunts of those around Him, Jesus said, "Father, forgive them, for they do not know what they are doing" (Luke 23:34). Here was a Man, totally innocent, who nevertheless showed compassion and forgiveness to His tormentors. Here I can identify with Jesus as the Son of Man. Here is where I let go of my emotions, lifting my troubled heart to the Father. Here is where I let Jesus absorb the pain and hurt, so that, through His strength, I can extend forgiveness. He reclaimed what was lost, restoring God's intent and purpose in my life. This is what we call redemptive suffering—allowing Jesus to enter into our pain and then letting Him bear it with us. As we stay present to both our pain and to Jesus, the pain can rise up and out of us into His holy wounds.

This all sounds spiritually wonderful, but how do we put this practice into reality? Here are five steps to assist us in processing our pain to extend forgiveness:

1. Seek the Holy Spirit's guidance in identifying the emotions and pain within you. It is important to express our feelings without turning them into accusations and demands: "God, I did this for You. You owe me! God, this is Your fault! Why didn't You come through for me?" Know how to change your statements from accusations to expressions of pain: "God, I feel as if this is Your fault, that You didn't come through for me."
2. Be real with God, able to express the pain. We hide nothing but become brutally honest, exposing what is in our heart. He already knows what is buried within, so why not speak it out? It goes up and out of us to Him.
3. Be willing to ask for His presence to come into the pain. Even though Jesus has not left us, we often block His presence in the walled-off areas of our heart where the pain and hurt reside.
4. Become still and let God manifest Himself to you in whatever way He knows you will be able to receive from Him. This is very personal. God wants to abide with you in your wounding. Once we invite Him in, then we quiet our minds and hearts, being open vessels to His revelation and healing.

AT THE CROSS, JESUS MEETS US IN OUR PLACES OF BITTERNESS, CYNICISM, AND VENGEFUL HEARTS.

5. Be willing to do what He asks of you. This may be challenging. Do you believe God knows what is best for you? Is the experience of greater freedom worth the cost of doing what He is asking? Will you trust Jesus?

Forgiveness is a crucial part of our becoming process. By not extending forgiveness to others, I am the one who suffers. Unforgiveness keeps me consumed with my wounds and pain and imprisoned by my thoughts. Not forgiving increases my vulnerability to diseased introspection or outward perfectionism (striving to hide my hurt). Instead of resting in my true self, I am practicing the false self.

To live Jesus' admonition in Mark 12:29–31—to love God, others, and ourselves with all our heart, soul, mind, and strength—forgiving is relationally foundational. Through the grace extended to us, we can walk in the state of forgiveness, which allows us to enter more deeply into whole community. Doing so causes change to happen within us.

Did you grasp this truth? It is not having some heady new understanding of your brokenness. Forgiving others brings us out of isolation and from behind our defensive walls. Walking in the true self will bring about the liberating changes your soul desires.

When we walk in our true selves and the state of forgiveness, we can name our specific wounds and acknowledge those who have hurt us. Our true self releases and calls us to name what is killing us. We can name our wounders rather than running from them, closing ourselves off from them, hating them, or pretending they are not there. In so doing, we release control over these wounds, the urge to self-protect, and living in a reactive condition. We can also release a victim mentality usually connected with diseased introspection, which has been reinforcing destructive, self-centered inner dialogues, statements like "I am damaged goods" or "I need to make sure they suffer for what they have done."

In Reaction to Others

Inherent in being in relationship is the need, at some point, to extend forgiveness. It is a reality that we will experience some form of hurt in any friendship. That hurt may be the result of intentional or unintentional wounding. It may be the result of misinterpretation on my part or the other person's part. But whatever the situation, I am the one choosing to react brokenly or respond aright.

The reality is, community is messy. It is crucial to recognize how the experience of past or present hurt gives rise to practicing the presence of unforgiveness. We may not be able to remember the exact hurt we experienced years ago, but our reactive emotions give evidence of its presence. Our hurt evokes emotions within us. We practice the presence of our pain over and over again instead of the Presence of Jesus.

A very common emotional reaction is the development of anger. Anger is a covering emotion. Other emotions remain buried beneath anger. With the help of the Holy Spirit, we can identify these emotions. Underneath anger can lay feelings of rejection, fear, anxiety, abandonment, or others. These emotions may connect to our faulty thinking or lies, we have believed. A friend who does not return an important call, for example, may trigger my feelings of low self-worth or abandonment. I believe the lie that I am not worthy of a return call. This lie may harken back to something that happened long ago.

Unforgiveness indicates a turning inward rather than to the cross to process our hurt. A present hurt may trigger a past wound, resulting in the transference of the past pain into the present. Our wounder then becomes the recipient of our projected pain. We become stuck and reactive. Our reaction can lead to vows and judgments. The false self becomes stuck emotionally and lacking in objectivity regarding the situation.

The result is we turn to self-protective coping mechanisms such as the following:

– We detach defensively, creating barriers to the person who wounded us.
– We take control of wanting to hurt or get even with our wounder.
– We turn to addictive behaviors to escape the pain we are experiencing.
– We disassociate mentally/emotionally if we experienced trauma.

The fruit resulting from unforgiveness may be the transformation into the one who hurt us. Consumed in our thinking, we focus continually on that other person. Even though I may make vows not to be like him or her, especially if the wounder was our mother or father, I do eventually become just like that person. "To hate a parent is, in the end, to hate oneself."[56]

We become whatever we worship. Over time, when we fixate on someone else's broken behavior, that behavior slowly develops in us. Focusing on the brokenness of our parents, we cannot see the good in them. Blocking out the bad, we also block out the good we could have received.

Practicing the presence of unforgiveness makes us more sensitive to the current events in our lives. Unforgiveness can cloud our capacity to discern rightly. Practicing unforgiveness makes us prone to internalize another offense by our wounder, whether real or imagined. We often lack objectivity and misinterpret the further actions or words of the other. An ever-growing reservoir of resentment occurs, blocking our relational capacity to see that person apart from our unresolved emotions. Our jaded heart can make us more, rather than less, sensitive to others and create attitudes that make us even more unwilling to forgive. It becomes a vicious cycle.

When a betrayed wife refuses to forgive, she often demands perfect behavior from her husband in her effort to avoid further wounding. Her expectations of legalistic control of her husband are self-defeating for both individuals. A husband must be committed to his recovery process and accountability for his actions and schedule. It takes time for trust to be reestablished with his wounded wife.

A woman cannot derive her security from the performance of her husband. Her security can only be found in Jesus. She must allow the Holy Spirit to search her heart to expose where she remains in a state of reaction. When she can release control and come to a place of forgiveness, it will allow Jesus to minister to her deep wounds. Through forgiveness and her husband's commitment to his healing process, their broken marriage will begin to heal.

The below sequence diagrams the fruit of unforgiveness:

Hurt > Anger > Unforgiveness/Vows > Self-Protection/Coping

It is helpful to recognize where we are in this flow when we have recently experienced hurt in a relationship or reminded of a past-unresolved wound.

[56]Ibid, p. 62.

Extending Forgiveness Further

In the previous section, I discussed extending forgiveness to others. We must also learn to extend forgiveness elsewhere. To love others like ourselves, we must explore where we harbor unforgiveness toward *ourselves*.

In our striving for perfection, we can create standards independent of God. Remember the stoic I discussed in chapter 10? By shutting down desire and ultimately the heart, my goal becomes perfect behavior. But when I fail to meet my imposed standard, I turn inward, shaming myself: *What's wrong with you? How could you fail like that again? What kind of Christian are you?* I may be able to forgive others, but not extend mercy or forgiveness to myself.

If God can forgive me, why can't I forgive myself? Do you see how pride can be part of this crippling thinking? My skewed thinking indicates I know better than God does. My sin is too heinous to forgive myself. It is my shame and self-hatred, preventing me from seeing aright.

I need to release myself from any self-imposed standard. To do so is to come into acceptance of my weaknesses. That acceptance is not to make allowance for sin. The faulty thinking is that if God accepts my weakness, then He is okay with my choice to keep sinning. God forbid! No, by accepting our weakness, I am saying that we learn to accept our humanity and human frailty. I am in process, running the race, and will not achieve perfection this side of heaven. When I fall into sin, I seek the Lord and confess it. Because God does accept my humanity, I can freely seek His throne. I am turning upward and not inward—not practicing the presence of the false self and shame. Receiving His mercy, I can release mercy toward myself.

Another area where we may need to extend forgiveness is toward God. This sounds rather controversial. After all, God is good and perfect. How could He wrongly hurt me? He is God, so whatever happens to me must be due to His perfect will, right?

It is not questioning the sovereignty of God to which I want to draw attention, but to what hides within our hearts. We need to discern, looking deep into our hearts if we harbor any places of unforgiveness or resentment *toward Him*.

How am I holding God accountable for the pain I have experienced?

When I have experienced trauma or abuse, something within may raise these questions: *Why did God let that happen to me? Why did He allow me to experience sexual abuse? Why did He let me marry an unfaithful spouse? Why did He allow me to have unwanted same-sex attractions?*

These types of questions do come across our minds due to our human frailty—and sometimes, these questions linger. For some, they linger just below the surface. Others bury them because a "good" Christian would not ask such questions. Ignoring them, however, creates levels of distrust with God.

Tom's Story

Tom, a friend of mine, asked me if I would join a few others to pray for him. When Tom was a young boy, he experienced abuse from a male family member. When Tom's son became the age at which Tom was abused, Tom's suppressed memories of sexual abuse flooded his mind. He wrestled with anger toward the Lord.

As we prayed, I encouraged Tom to express what he was feeling toward God vocally. His first prayer was, "God, I am mad at you."

"I think the word mad doesn't line up with the emotions you're carrying," I said.

So Tom said, "God, I am angry with you."

Once again, I challenged Tom.

But he replied, "I'm scared to express what I'm feeling outwardly. I have the feeling God will strike me with a lightning bolt."

"God already knows what you're harboring inside. Why not release it to Him?"

There was a pause. Finally, Tom exclaimed, "God damn You for allowing this to happen to me as a boy!"

At that moment, Tom became completely real with God. He allowed the depth of his emotions to surface—emotions that were toxic to him.

I prayed for God to meet Tom in his pain and suffering. As he opened his heart to the Lord, He purged Tom of those feelings.

In my closing prayer, I asked the Lord to come and fill the place where those toxic emotions had resided. As I laid hands on Tom's heart, the Lord replaced those intense emotions with His healing peace.

Extending forgiveness toward God is acknowledging the bitterness, cynicism, or anger in our hearts that block us from Him. It is not that God has erred toward me but that I am releasing my unresolved emotions toward him. By being real with God, releasing my emotions, and seeking His healing presence, I process or prevent the building of emotional, reactionary walls with Him.

Forgiveness:
Putting the Attitude into Practice

> In the Presence, there is the power to forgive others, even the "unforgivable." There is power to receive forgiveness from God and to stop identifying ourselves by the sin from which we have been delivered.[57]

Taking control and choosing not to forgive reveals that we are walking in the false self. The false self is egocentric and prone, therefore, to self-protection and defensive detachment. With divided hearts, our hurt and pain consume us. Here I am referring to those who choose not to process their emotions but who are allowing their emotions to build relational walls and isolate them.

Standing in the true self, being one with Christ, I will be able to forgive that which at one time seemed impossible. I truly "can do all things through Christ who strengthens me" (Philippians 4:13, NKJV).

The following form, obtained from Grace Ministries, Inc., provides a structured approach, based on scriptural principles, for extending forgiveness.[58] It is challenging because it will expose any misconceptions regarding forgiveness and any unresolved emotions. I know of individuals who have used many copies of this form to address the trauma in their lives. One individual used this form more than eighty times to resolve past hurts.

Walking through the form creates a memory that you have forgiven and canceled the debt owed to you. If you begin to doubt that you have forgiven, or when the enemy accuses you, bring to mind that you used this form and had forgiven the one(s) who wounded you. You may also use this form for forgiving yourself or God. It is helpful after using it to make a visual memory with it. For example, you can tear it up, shred it, or burn it, as I have known some to do.

It may be helpful to visualize in your mind the individual you are forgiving. It was helpful for me to face an empty chair and imagine the person sitting there. It is important to use this form verbally, speaking out each step. I have added comments in between the steps to provide additional understanding.

Pray before using this form, asking the Holy Spirit to identify a specific event He desires for you to process.

[57]Leanne Payne, *The Healing Presence* (Baker Books, 1989, 1995), p. 62
[58]Form used by permission from Grace Ministries, Inc.

1. "[Name of person], it hurt me when you ________."

    Be specific. Do not use generic terms here (e.g., "It hurt me for the years of abuse you inflicted on me"). Ask the Lord to bring up specific events that happened. Remember that you can use multiple copies of this form to address traumas. Some events stand out more to us or had an increased level of significance when they happened.

2. "[Name of person], as a result of this hurt, I felt ________."

    Multiple emotions can result from a wound. There is never just one. See appendix one for an emotional checklist. Mark all the emotions which seem to match what you are feeling. In situations where many emotions are identified, select the top three for this form.

3. "[Name of person], because I am by nature a forgiving person in Christ, I now choose to forgive you. You are forgiven! I release you from the debt you owe me. You never have to make it up to me or pay me back. Even though it would be nice if you came to me and asked my forgiveness, you never have to admit what you have done to me or be sorry for it. You are free."

    The first sentence reminds us of our true self and identity in Christ. Because I am a new creation in Jesus, I have His nature within me. Because Jesus walked in forgiveness, so do I. Step 3 nails that forgiveness with no strings attached.

4. "[Name of person], I accept you unconditionally, which means that my love and acceptance of you do not depend on you or your past, present, or future performance. I accept you just the way you are, even if you never change. Even if you get worse."

    This step is truly challenging. It will test whether we are basing our forgiveness on how those who wounded us behave. My choice to forgive is not contingent on the actions of another. Forgiveness involves only one person: me. This step may be particularly challenging when we have to be in regular contact with our wounder (for example, a spouse, family member, or coworker.). Wise counsel is necessary when processing these types of relationships. This form addresses individual hurts, not reconciliation.

5. "[Name of person], I give up the right to be the judge, jury, and prosecuting attorney in these matters. That is God's job. You are not responsible to me for meeting my standards of whether

you were 'right' or 'wrong' in what you did. I choose to let God be God, and I acknowledge that you and your behavior are His responsibility. You now answer to Him, not me."

Here we focus on releasing control. I must release my feelings of justification or revenge. I must let go of my judgment that this person must suffer for what he or she did to me. I accept God's sovereignty and place my heart and well-being into His hands.

6. "[Name of person], I release you from the responsibility to meet my needs for (a) _______, (b) _______, and (c) _______. I choose to trust the Lord, however He chooses, to meet my needs, especially my needs for (a) _______, (b) _______, and (c) _______."

   It is important to connect the emotions you are feeling with specific needs you feel that the wounding did not recognize. If the wound resulted in your feeling abandoned, then the need triggered may be the desire to be welcomed and loved. If the wound resulted in your feeling like damaged goods, the need triggered might be to know that you have value. If you feel inadequate, the need triggered may be to know that you have potential. We often look to others, believing that they perceive our needs and can perfectly meet them. Without healthy communication, however, the one who hurt us can be clueless that we were hurt. Only God can perfectly meet our needs.

7. "[Name of person], I recognize that choosing to forgive you is different from being in relationship with you. Because I am in Christ and am already safe, secure, and accepted, I am willing to trust Him alone as my wisdom about you and the nature of our relationship in the future. I will trust Christ in His mercy and grace should you hurt me again."

   Forgiveness involves one person and reconciliation involves more than one person. As stated earlier, we need to seek wise counsel for dysfunctional relationships and walk in the "state of forgiveness." Forgiveness needs to be at the forefront of our minds when we are hurt. We are not to rush to forgive as a reaction to suppress our hurt emotions. However, when a wound happens, I choose by an act of my will to begin the forgiveness process. I release those around me from the burden of being perfect. I accept the reality that hurt feelings occur in the best of relationships. Processing those hurts helps us effectively maintain healthy boundaries and true intimacy with one another. We learn the skill of being real with each other without accusation or judgment. This step does not mean you are to be a doormat for future abuse. Seek wise counsel regarding any abusive relationship.

8. “God, I give up the right to have my feelings change according to my schedule. Thank You that I don’t have to look to my feelings as the indicator of whether or not I have forgiven. Thank You that anger and fear no longer have to motivate me in this relationship.”

    Trauma results in deep emotions. Those emotions do not vanish overnight. It is an ongoing process of acknowledging and naming my emotions and seeking the Lord’s counsel regarding them. Emotions get triggered, and when they do, we know what to do. We do not let them stagnate and become toxic. Knowing we are to forgive and allowing the Holy Spirit to assist us in processing our hurts, we can forgive through a choice of the will. That choice includes a choice from the heart, believing that God will guide our emotions.

We cannot forgive if we are in denial about what remains buried in the heart. I have found that, for some, using this form helps them align their hearts in the forgiveness process.

An Undivided Heart

We need divine objectivity, seeing every aspect of our lives through God’s perspective. With His vision, we are better able to comprehend the world around us. Jesus will enable us to make the choices necessary to continue our growth in Him.

Forgiveness forces us to see our unsettled hearts. The choice comes down to managing pain our self or yielding our control to Jesus. Standing in the true self with Jesus’ resurrection power enables me to forgive. I can release my troubled emotions, which keep me bound to those who wound me. No one has the power to limit the true self but for me. My choices turn me inward, detaching defensively, or outward, attaching to God and reflecting His image.

Ask God for an undivided heart. Will you allow Him to search your soul and reveal any toxic emotions? When you feel your strength waning, lean on Jesus. He will meet you where you are and lead you in His way everlasting.

If you truly forgive an individual, then it is a completed and closed task. If you were to return to the wound and decide to “unforgive” the individual, then you did not forgive him or her in the first place. Those who wound us are released completely from their debt when we truly forgive. We move on with life. If any lingering emotions arise later, we remind ourselves that the debt is paid, and we remind our hearts, *I have forgiven that person.* Then I bring those emotions before the Lord, seek His guidance in processing them, and do not allow them to become toxic to me.

Wrapping Up

Forgiveness is a vital and necessary part of our Christian walk. Whenever we hold unforgiveness toward someone, we are preventing our continued growth in our becoming process. The act of forgiveness unites the head and the heart. Forgiveness is not merely a doctrine, but an act of choosing life. Living in unforgiveness keeps us imprisoned, with our hearts descending into diseased introspection. Forgiving causes me to stand in my true self, which then causes me to rise as the man or woman God created me to be. Forgiveness enables me to be a true image-bearer of Jesus.

Prayer

Lord, I carry the wounds of my past within me. Some I have buried so deeply that I can barely remember them, yet the pain they originally caused me is still real. Other wounds are so present that they obscure my vision in seeing others aright and keep me emotionally in a reactive state. Too often, I focus on how I have suffered and the debt I am owed. Only by Your divine intervention am I healed of these wounds, and my emotions brought into a place of resolution. I need Your presence, Lord.

Holy Spirit, I welcome You to come now and search my heart. You know which wounds in my heart need to be brought to the surface and healed. I seek Your divine aid in assisting me to be willing to face these wounds and then strengthening me to walk through the process of forgiveness. I also admit that I may first need to be willing to be willing to begin this process. However, I know, Holy Spirit, that You are the One who comes alongside me, to support me in this time of need.

Lord, I need Your divine objectivity to see my wounds, those who have wounded me, and how to embrace forgiveness. Please help me to forgive, not only from my head but also from the depths of my heart. I ask that You help bring my emotions to the surface and give me the capacity to name them. Reveal where I am holding onto vengeance. Show me where I have placed expectations on those around me, expectations they are not capable of meeting. How have I refused to extend to them the very grace and mercy You have granted me? Empower me to release the debt I am owed. I call to mind how You, dear Jesus, released and forgave from the cross those who abused and treated You so brutally.

As I go through this process of forgiveness, may Your presence surround and fill me. As I release those who have wounded me, I invite You to inhabit the place in my heart where I harbored unforgiveness. Cleanse me of any toxic residue from the emotions that so consumed me. I want Your mind, Lord Jesus, where I was plagued by the thoughts that replayed those wounds over and over. I now invite Your cross and presence, to be established where those memories resided.

Thank You for freeing me from the prison of unforgiveness and for restoring my soul. Thank You for Your cleansing blood and sacrifice, which made a way for me to be free. Through Your obedience, Lord Jesus, I can now stand in my true self and become who the Father intended for me to be from the beginning of time.

Soul Work

1. Read and meditate on the parable of the unforgiving servant recorded in Matthew 18:21–35. List four important aspects regarding forgiveness that Jesus demonstrated in this parable. Write down how you struggle with any of these aspects.

2. What are the things that hold you back from extending forgiveness?

3. Review the "Forgiveness: Putting the Attitude into Practice" form. What parts of this form are most challenging for you, and why?

Journaling Moment

After completing Soul Work question #1, ask the Holy Spirit to reveal a time from your past when you chose not to forgive an individual. Ask Him to reveal the specific hurt you felt. Seek revelation for what ways you reacted to that hurt through self-protection or any coping mechanisms. Have those reactions become a pattern in your life for when you are hurt? Ask the Lord to show you how to break any of these reactive patterns.

FOURTEEN

Broken Worship, Broken Relationships

BY KYLE BOWMAN

HE HIMSELF GIVES EVERYONE LIFE AND BREATH AND EVERYTHING ELSE.

– ACTS 17:25

When you think about the difficulties you experience in relationships, your thoughts may turn first to the idea that other people are the problem. But if the Holy Spirit is working in your heart, you will get around to examining your own actions and motives to see how you may be a contributing factor in your relationship woes. As Jesus put it, you may need to "first take the plank out of your eye, and then you will see clearly to remove the speck from your brother's eye" (Luke 6:42).

Relationships can be difficult. Because we want our interactions with others to be comfortable, we can manipulate or lean into others so that our relationships follow the path of least resistance.

When the devil tried to tempt Jesus, he offered Him the kingdoms of the world if He would just worship him. Jesus reminded Satan that worship belongs to God alone.

You might be thinking, Yeah, I know that already. So what's your point? My point is, Have you ever considered that relationship problems might lie with your worship? If you begin to think differently about your relationships, you may see that worship affects your ability to relate to others in a healthy way.

Let me explain.

The Impact of Sin

Any conversation on how relating to others can go so wrong has to start with sin. Sin, as we learned in chapter 2, separated us from our true Source. This separation left us to interpret the world around us and make decisions based on limited knowledge. Why is our knowledge limited? Because human beings did not create the world; God did. He is the only one who knows all things. He knows the true motivation for our actions.

But from the time we enter this world, we begin to make decisions based on environment, personality, socioeconomic background, ethnicity, and culture. We take the information we receive from each of these sources—information that is flawed—and set into motion the actions we believe are necessary to respond to any situation we find ourselves in. Bob Hamp says it this way: "The human being is the only creature that can lie to itself and believe its own lie."[59]

So, for example, let's say you were raised by a parent who yelled a lot and was prone to send objects into orbit when angered. Maybe you had the ability to calm your mom or dad down by running to their side and begging them not to yell anymore. Or maybe you got them to stop yelling because you yelled back. Regardless of your response, you made a decision from that point forward as to how to handle people who yell. You treat everyone who yells the same way. It does not occur to you that some people get excited when they talk and it sounds like yelling, or that a person can have a momentary outburst because of a bad day (like the kind you have when someone cuts you off on the freeway).

Sin also causes an internal battle within us. We know that our relationships should and could be better because God has designed us to be relational. Deep in our hearts we know we should love others as Christ loves us. But sin creeps in and tells us we can get life from our relationships, instead of turning to our heavenly Father who sustains us.

And here's where worship comes in. Our struggle in experiencing healthy human

[59]Bob Hamp, *Think Differently, Live Differently: Keys to a Life of Freedom* (Thinking Differently Press, 2010), p. 60.

DEEP IN OUR HEARTS WE KNOW WE SHOULD LOVE OTHERS AS CHRIST LOVES US.

interactions generally centers around the WIIFM principle—that little voice inside that says, *What's in it for me? What is it about relating to this individual that will meet my needs?*

For some this means that others make them the center of attention. They experience fulfillment when they get compliments, when they are sought out for their opinions, when they are chosen as the leader among their friends. These people become addicted to the love they receive from others. Whether they know it or not, they have set themselves up as an idol.

Some people give others godlike status because those others are the ones, instead of God, whom they rely on.

Or there may be someone to whom they feel inextricably connected. This person, they feel, is all they need in life.

In each of these scenarios, the worship that belongs to God has been misdirected. And this is how broken worship affects relationships.

Addicted to Love

Love addicts have a need for praise and adoration. They need others to affirm how awesome they are. Not having a voice within the family of origin can leave a person starved for attention. Being told to be quiet or to shut up gives a child the impression that what he or she has to say is not meaningful. Some children are made fun of when they speak, leading them to believe that their words are not significant. As these young people begin to mature, their desire to be heard overshadows everything else in life.

Think about the times someone affirmed what you said. It feels pretty good, doesn't it?

Susan

Susan grew up in what some might call the average American household. Her dad was the primary breadwinner and her mother worked part-time to be available to Susan and her brother. Even before she could talk, Susan was a babbler. When she looked into the faces of her parents, she began her attempt at talking. Her parents were thoroughly amused because they felt she really had something to say. When she began to string actual words together, she expressed whatever came to her little mind. It was the way God had wired her.

But the cuteness factor of the constant talking began to wear off for Mom and Dad. When she rushed to her parents, excited to share some important news, she was told that there was no time right now or that she should learn to be quiet. Eventually she came to the conclusion that no one was interested in what she had to say, and she became a timid and shy little girl.

When the time came for Susan to go off to college, a professor directed a question to her in class one day. Although she assumed that what she had to say was not important, she gave her answer anyway, and he was impressed, as were her classmates. She was excited the rest of the day.

That professor continued to call on her and offered a smile of approval whenever she answered. Her classmates began to comment on how articulate she was and that she had a great way with words. They asked her to read their papers and give her opinion because no one could put words together the way Susan could. When one of the guys on the debate team asked her to help with his upcoming oration, she thought she would burst with happiness. The praise kept coming and it filled her with joy.

Things were different at first when Susan entered the workforce. People cared less about her abilities and it caused her to sulk. She felt as if the life had been sucked out of her. But one day her boss needed someone to give a presentation. She jumped at the chance to show her talent. When her boss gave her the assignment, she blew the board of directors away. The office threw a big party to celebrate her success.

The next day she felt deflated again—until her boss decided to put her in charge of all company presentations. What a thrill! All presentations had to go through her for approval.

Jack was the first to bring her his idea. She toyed with him, giving him the impression that his idea needed a lot of work.

"Look, Susan," he said, "you're the best at this presentation thing. I know I can never be as good as you are."

Her heart soared. *They need me*, she thought.

But she refused to help her co-workers until they lavished her with compliments. She became hard to work with. Susan turned into the master manipulator to get filled. She was addicted to the perceived expressions of "love" that she was getting. And the more "love" she needed, the worse she became.

As you read this, you may be thinking that Susan is a horrible person. She is not. She just needed to have the gift God had given her nurtured in the right way. Because that did not happen—although that does not make her parents bad people either—she wanted to be God to everyone around her. She saw herself on the throne and others as loyal subjects to worship her and her wonderful abilities.

Anytime you or I get others to praise us for who we are, we are not honoring the One who has given us the ability to bless others with the gifts He has given us.

"You're All I Need"

Sometimes we look to others to tell us who we are. But allowing someone other than your heavenly Father to give you your identity will at some point make that person your god.

It starts innocently. You meet someone different from your other friends. You have great conversations and that person seems to understand you better than anyone else. You have things in common so you hang out often. You feel more alive with this individual than you have with anyone else.

Then the day comes when you call your friend to get together and he or she has another commitment. While you may tell your friend that you understand, inside you are fuming. You cannot believe he or she is not willing to put those plans aside in order to be with you. You spend the day wondering what your friend is doing, and if he or she is having fun without you, because there was no response to the text you sent just to say hi. You sulk or cry or spew angry words. Your day is ruined.

But when your friend calls the next day, you feel much better. You don't like having to share your friend. You cannot imagine life without this special person.

Why is he or she so important? Why does it feel as if you can hardly breathe when this individual is not around?

As we go from childhood to adulthood, we have our own means of interpreting everything around us, even if we are not fully equipped to do so.

Paul

This was Paul's challenge. His mother worked very hard to keep him away from pain. She would promise things like this: "I'll help you with whatever you need." "You never have to want for anything as long as I'm around." "Let me show you what to wear." "I'll pick out a nice girl for you." "I'm your mother, I know best."

After Paul moved out on his own, he never understood why women thought he was lazy and clingy. He loved his mother dearly and always looked to her for affirmation. In fact, he idolized every woman he met, and thrust them into the responsibility of telling him who he was. Women were better than men, he felt. He brooded for days if a girlfriend wanted a girls' night out. Why didn't she just want to spend time with him? He truly needed her. Didn't women want a guy who worshiped the ground she walked on? He did not hesitate to ask the women in his life their opinions when he had decisions to make. His male friends just did not see things the way women did.

Paul did not realize he had turned women into little gods. His heart was always bowing at their altar asking for affirmation and self-worth. He could not sustain a relationship very long because the women he met could not handle being smothered.

Paul is not a bad guy. He is just like you or me—a person who, at some point in life, directed worship horizontally instead of vertically.

Changing Your Perspective

After reading the stories about Susan and Paul, are you beginning to see that worship is what went wrong in their relationships? They both took God out of His rightful place in their lives. Susan decided she would be God to others; and the women in Paul's life became God to him.

Maybe one of these stories reminds you of times you have done something similar. Even if you think Susan and Paul's situations are extreme, it is important to understand that anytime you seek to get life from people around you, it is the perfect recipe for creating idolatrous relationships.

The good news is, we do not have to continue to be influenced by the things that cause us to have unhealthy relationships. Changing your perspective is the key to ensuring that your worship remains vertical instead of horizontal. A change in perspective starts with understanding the condition of your heart. The world we live in is affected by sin, which ultimately affects the heart.

In the Garden, Adam and Eve were fully connected to God and got their identities from Him. As strange as it may sound, we were made to be dependent. We were not designed for independence, as our world tells us every day. As God's image-bearers, we were formed to rely on the One with the ability to meet our every need. He knows us intimately. We were never created to live our lives apart from Him.

All that changed when Adam and Eve ate from the tree of the knowledge of good and evil. "The knowledge of good and evil leaves incomplete people in charge of their own solutions."[60] For many of us, the solution has been to use the people around us as our source. It is like never using the charger that came with your mobile phone, but instead asking everyone else if you can use theirs.

Knowing that your heart is vulnerable to idolatrous relationships, you can begin to evaluate your true motivations as you relate to those around you.

Look at the statements below and answer them honestly. Be aware that thoughts that bring feelings of shame and condemnation come directly from the enemy. Be prayerful as you work through this exercise.

- When I am the center of attention, I feel ______ [e.g., powerful, smart, etc.].
- When I allow others to validate me, I feel ______.
- When my friends are not able to spend time with me, I feel ______.
- If I am not seen as important in a group, I feel ______.
- When I am unable to see or talk with my closest friends for more than a day or two, I feel ______.
- I feel most loved by those around me when ______.

Do you find some consistent feelings surfacing as you work through this exercise? Do you have a desire to be heard? Do you experience a deep longing to know that you are valuable or needed? Maybe you need to know that you matter to someone. Whatever those feelings are, it is important to acknowledge what you are feeling to God. He is not afraid of what is in your heart. His desire is for you to trust Him with it.

Know that your heavenly Father will not shame or degrade you for what you feel. He will ask you lovingly to surrender those feelings to Him so He can replace them with His truth. Take the time to offer your feelings in prayer to God. Write down what you hear the Holy Spirit say, so you have a guidepost for God's activity in your life.

[60]Ibid., p. 59.

Free to Be You

The realization that you use the relationships in your life for affirmation and identity can leave you feeling empty. This may be the point at which you ask for the checklist to getting fixed. "There is no formula that leads to a transformed life. Lifelong tendencies toward dependent relationships cannot be changed by following 'ten easy steps.'"[61]

So what is required to begin the journey to healthy relationships? Faith. It takes faith to believe that God wants you to remove the many masks you have been wearing so that people can get to know the real you. It takes faith to trust that God will help you "do life" with others. It takes faith to know that God has gifted you to be a blessing as you live authentically before Him. He is the one working in and through you (Philippians 2:13).

Once the Holy Spirit has confirmed in your heart that you can be the person God has created you to be, you no longer have to draw your identity from your relationships. You are free to speak life and encouragement to others. You are no longer on the hook to be anyone's savior, and no one has to be a savior to you. If you are concerned about people liking the real you, there is a stronger possibility that they probably don't care too much for the fake you! How awesome is it to know you have been placed in this moment in time so you can walk in your true self and radiate the light of Jesus?

If you are able to let this truth sink deep into your soul, you cannot help but worship the God of the universe. When you can appreciate your God-given giftings and even your quirkiness, you know there is no one on earth who deserves to be worshiped but the great I AM. So when you begin to feel that your interactions with others are overtly challenging or no longer fulfilling, take the time to look deep within yourself to make sure God is still on the throne of your heart.

Wrapping Up

IT TAKES **FAITH** TO KNOW THAT GOD HAS GIFTED YOU **TO BE A BLESSING** AS YOU LIVE AUTHENTICALLY BEFORE HIM.

[61]Lori Rentzel, *Emotional Dependency* (InterVarsity, 1984, 1987, 1990), p. 21.

It is important to remember that God is our Source. Relationships can never fill the void in our hearts the way He can. Ask the Lord to help you to be sensitive to the times you want others to lean into you, or you desire to lean into others, so that you can redirect your worship to Him. Here are a few indicators that you want others to lean into you:

1. Obsession with likes, follows, shares, and retweets. You cannot get life from social media.
2. Inability to listen to others unless the conversation is focused on you.
3. Inability to handle criticism.
4. Putting others down so you look good.

When you have a tendency to lean into others, or when you exhibit what is known as emotional dependency, you may display the following behaviors:

1. Jealousy when those important to you spend time with others.
2. Liking or disliking only what your friend or significant other likes or dislikes.
3. Becoming extremely distressed if your friend or partner is not validated by others.
4. Relying for your self-worth on the affection and approval of your partner or friend.
5. Idolizing others and then becoming devastated when they do not live up to your expectations.

Prayer

In the following prayer breaking one-flesh unions, in the blank spaces provided, insert the names of those with whom you have had sexual unions outside of marriage, or those with whom you have had a relationship based on dependency on one another and not on God. Use as many names as the Lord brings to mind. You can also use this prayer at any time with a trusted friend in Christ.

Breaking One-Flesh Unions

Lord Jesus, I come to You weighed down by my sexual union and/or emotionally idolatrous connection with ______. I seek and come into Your presence, Lord Jesus, bringing ______ before Your cross. I place him/ her at Your feet and confess this relationship as sin and idolatry. I ask that the darkness contained in this relationship now be fully contained and cleansed by You.

By the power of Your name and blood, Lord Jesus, I break the power of this one-flesh/relationally dependent union. I invite You, Lord Jesus, to come in Your sovereignty and establish Your cross between us. Take Your rightful place as the Lord and center of this relationship.

I ask for Your strength and grace to objectively see ______, and to be able to turn to You to meet the need(s) for which I looked to him/her. I forgive him/her for not being able to meet my needs and for all the pain wrought by this relationship. I also receive Your forgiveness, Lord Jesus, for my idolatrous attempt to be made whole through my union with ______.

Make my eye and heart single, Lord! May I come to know and understand what it means for You alone to be the desire of my heart.

Soul Work

1. What difficulties do you have connecting broken relationships to broken worship?

2. List one or two of the feelings you experienced when you did the exercises in this chapter. What surprised you about what you felt? How did you process what you felt?

3. What parts of Susan's story did you identify with and why? How about Paul's story?

Journaling Moment

Before you start journaling, ask the Lord to fill you with His Holy Spirit in order to prepare your heart to hear from Him. This chapter references how our environment, personality, socioeconomic background, ethnicity, and culture have an impact on the way we relate to others. Write out how you have seen each one of these affect how you relate to others. Ask the Lord for forgiveness in the areas in which you have sinned against Him and others, and ask to be set free from any that have brought shame or condemnation. Initially, you may not have something to write for each one. Allow the Lord to show you what He wants you to see. Try not to rush though this, so that you have an opportunity to experience God's love for you.

SECTION 3
LOVING OTHERS ARIGHT

Examining relationships with one another as men and women

Loving Others Aright

This section expands on our relationships in community. Section 1 focused on our relationship with God and our identity in Christ. Section 2 addressed areas of brokenness that prevent us from embracing or walking in the true self. Now we will address our relationships with one another as men and women.

Chapter 15 reveals how ancient heresy and current culture have departed from God's divine design for us as His creation. The world has generated such confusion, having chosen to define who we are apart from God's wisdom. Renouncing God, the world lacks clarity and understanding. Identity is based on feelings and attractions, producing erroneous ideologies and often ignoring biological reality.

Chapters 16 and 17 explore how we can embrace God's vision for us as women and men. We must return to biblical truth and free ourselves from the confusion shaped by secular nomenclature. If we lack understanding of how we express God's image in us, our relationships in community will suffer. Chapters 18 and 19 will discuss friendships, singleness, and marriage.

Once again, it is vital to remain present to each chapter. All of us need clarity for walking in the state of singleness, celibacy, or marriage. Remaining present will help you embrace the bigger picture God has for humankind, as well as for yourself.

FIFTEEN

The Significance of Image Bearing

SO GOD CREATED MANKIND IN HIS OWN IMAGE, IN THE IMAGE OF GOD HE CREATED THEM; MALE AND FEMALE HE CREATED THEM.

- GENESIS 1:27

The question "Who am I?" has been asked for centuries. This question originates in our desire to know our identity—what defines us. When God is not at our center, we experience an identity void. We turn inward instead of outward towards a higher authority to define us. There's a lack of knowing a higher meaning or purpose. We believe we are here by fate or chance. But innate within us is the God-given desire to know who we are, and without the Creator, the created (that is, humankind) has to define itself through the creation (that is, the world).

As seen in chapter 3, we know our identity is found alone in Jesus Christ. Our goal is to become more Christ-like as His image-bearers. It is God who established the foundation for our design as men and women. God provides wisdom and understanding for who we are and how we engage in life-giving relationships. He knows what is best for His creation. It is God, therefore, who defines who I am.

We sense the reality of who we are through an intimate relationship with God. He affirms our worth, value, and acceptance. We do not try to derive identity from work, appearance, circumstances, attractions, or the labels of others. Our sense of self originates in our center in Jesus. That center grows in affirmation and strength through engagement with healthy community.

As His image-bearers, our biology is important. Being male or female matters. I, Bob, being a man, bear God's image as a male. This is how God designed me. God designed women, as females, to bear His image differently, but of equal importance and value with men.

We represent God's divine design as male and female, as indicated above in Genesis 1:27. Reflecting the image of God separates humanity from the rest of creation. The wonder of God is seen in the beauty of His diverse creation, but only we, as men and women, *bear His image*. God's image and design are reflected both on the exterior and interior.

Seeing and Knowing

> The eye is the lamp of the body. If your eyes are healthy, your whole body will be full of light.
>
> –Matthew 6:22

In chapter 9, I referenced Adam's naming of the animals. When Adam looked into their eyes, there was not an equal knowing glance returned. When we look into the eyes of others, there is a knowing that occurs. That visual connection is part of image-bearing.

We often speak about looking into the face of God. However, what is it we desire to see? Is it not a longing to see into His eyes? Only humankind has the capacity of seeing and knowing at the same time. It's reflective of how we bear God's image to one another. Once again, remembering what Augustine wrote, that our heart's desire is to see another and to be seen by that other, in a loving glance, in return.

As we know, our inner, deepest hunger is for true intimacy. That intimacy can only be satisfied through experiencing healthy relationship with God, others, and even ourselves. When you take God out of the picture, you have lost the core of your identity. You then must search for

something or someone else to define you. Without God at the center, the hunger for intimacy becomes the center. That hunger and ache are given preeminence to define me. Without Christ at my core, my personhood attaches to my feelings and attractions.

Our culture no longer recognizes our divine design. By rejecting His plan for humankind, the world finds definition apart from God. In our culture, feelings and attractions are what determines my identity. Without God, I bear the world's image. The human body has lost its significance but is seen objectively as something to customize in order to confirm that image.

The Influence of Gnostic Thinking

In the first and second century AD, a heresy existed called Gnosticism, which created a schism between the spirit and body. That heresy gained secular prominence in the twentieth century. Feelings and desires took precedence over the human body. The body became less significant, which is gnostic thinking. Gnostics believed that the body (matter) was evil, but the spirit was good.

Making contraception readily available in the twentieth century diminished sexual union's God-given higher purpose for procreation. Now sexual union's greater purpose was for personal pleasure. I can modify my body to suit my desires and diminish unwanted consequences. The legalization of abortion furthered this reality. It has reached its ultimate horror in the twenty-first century when an abortion can be performed right up to moments before a baby exits the birth canal.

The sexual revolution of the 1960s separated sexual union from having a relational connection giving rise to our hooking-up culture. The desire to be known is now reduced to only a "carnal knowing." I don't want to know you; I only want to know your body. The body, losing its sacred significance, is only an entity considered for my pleasure.

Our culture does place much attention on the body. However, it is a narcissistic focus on how I can change my body to adapt to my personal feelings. I can add, adjust, or remove whatever suits my ideal. The most profound example of this is *genital cosmetic surgery*. The commonly used terminology for this surgery is "sexual reassignment surgery." However, is it impossible to reassign one's biological sex (i.e., altering the body does not change the genetics which remains the same).

We must see transgender ideology through the eyes of compassion as it is a very difficult and painful struggle. Nevertheless, it represents how one's inner feelings and thinking, takes precedence over biology. It is not a physical issue but one that is psychologically and spiritually based.

The transgender condition is not about outward appearance, genetic determination, sexual attraction, or cosmetic surgery. The condition (i.e., gender dysphoria) focuses on one's inner state conflicting with their biological sex. It is the presence of thoughts and feelings which conflict with one being genetically male or female. Transgender ideology is wed to gnostic thinking, which indicates the body lacks physical and spiritual significance.

Disregarding the significance of our biology results in minimizing the value of the body. Adam was the complement for Eve, and Eve vice-versa. God designed our bodies. Therefore, our biological difference is intended to create an attraction toward that which is other than me—an attraction that is not solely sexual. Our biology is important!

> Our culture says: Your psychology is your sexual identity—let your body be conformed to it. The Bible says: Your body is your sexual identity—let your mind be conformed to it.[62]

Many categories for identity are found in social media, which reflects gnostic thinking. The core of who I am as a man or woman is subcategorized into a *sexual identity*. Diverse sexual attractions or the lack thereof, now define me. The body is split from the spirit. As Christians, to fully reflect the image of God, we must wrestle with any feelings of insecurity or confusion. We must seek the Lord's guidance and presence to help us make peace with our design as a biological male or female.

Pause for a moment. How have you experienced insecurity as a man or a woman? Where is there any confusion? Ask the Holy Spirit to bring deeper revelation as you continue to read this chapter.

The Turmoil of Terminology

"Words, words, words, I'm so sick of words!"
–Eliza Doolittle, My Fair Lady

For many centuries, only the words male, female, man, and woman classified humankind.

[62]Sam Allberry quoted in Vaughan Roberts, *Transgender* (Good Book Company, 2016), p. 43.

The words heterosexual and homosexual did not come into usage until the late 1800s. Since that time, our terminology has greatly expanded.

The word gender can be traced back to the Greek philosopher Protagoras, but its use was limited. Until the twentieth century, gender largely had linguistic application for masculine or feminine adjectives or pronouns. Gender was not associated with human identity.

John William Money, a psychologist, sexologist, and author, researched the biology of "gender" in the 1950s. Money's studies explored the idea of gender as being a societal construct which impacted sexual fluidity. The current usage of the word gender is rooted in secular thinking and not from a biblical perspective. As the fallen complexity of sexuality and identity developed, so did a new vocabulary.

The words masculine, masculinity, feminine, and femininity are regularly used today. However, the usage of these words often creates confusion. These words are interchangeably used for multiple applications. They can categorize feelings, appearance, and mannerisms. They also are applied to things like objects or design. Our updated vocabulary now includes words like cis, binary, trans, and intersex. Many new pronouns are being introduced. Do these new words bring greater clarity or create greater confusion?

The term "sexual orientation" is a relatively recent addition to our cultural lexicon. A quick Google search says that sexual orientation is "a person's sexual identity in relation to the gender to which they are attracted; the fact of being heterosexual, homosexual, or bisexual." This definition exemplifies the practice to box an individual into a category or particular identity. Since for some, attractions vary during different stages of their lives, how can you be one category one week and another the next?

I want to eliminate the term sexual orientation from our vocabulary because of its false implications. I resist anything that attempts to attach my identity or personhood to my sexuality. Attractions are an aspect of my life but not who I am. As Christians, we have one identity—who we are in Christ Jesus. It is my position in Christ alone that defines me. I am not a heterosexual Christian. I am not a gay Christian. I am not a bisexual Christian. I am not an alcoholic Christian. I am simply a Christian!

Personality, temperament, and biology all work together to contribute to the expression of being a man or woman. So, what is a man or a woman? If someone tells you to be more like a man or a woman, what does that mean? What parameters would you use for answering such a question?

What does our male or female physiology tell us about ourselves? Is it in agreement with who God says we are? Do I feel insecure around certain men or certain women? And if so, why?

Christ-centered men and women have an inner core of confidence—security in who they are—that does not need to be bolstered by a forced expression or façade. Their inner core and outer reflection are in agreement with their biological sex, grounding and securing them in who they are in Christ, in their true selves.

However, there are other factors which directly and indirectly impact how we feel about ourselves. Let's examine some of them.

Right and Left Brain Influences

Our mental concept of being male or female encompasses a bigger picture. Our biology is intricately connected with my sense of personhood. How do I, as a man or woman, uniquely bear God's image? How are my specific gifts and personality reflected uniquely in being a man or a woman?

I am not to be form-fitted into what the world says a man or woman is to be. I need to seek God and ask Him what does it mean *for me* to be a man. What does it mean *for me* to be a woman? Do you see there is a bigger picture? How can I, in the uniqueness of who I am in Christ, reflect God through my DNA, body, and temperament? Where in my thinking, do I feel that I do not measure up? Do I think I have to prove who I am because of a perceived weakness? Do I project an outer façade because I don't fit the image or standard that I've created in my head? We need the Holy Spirit to expose what limits my capacity to be the man or woman I was created to be by the Father.

Over the centuries, roles, jobs, and behaviors have become associated with being a man or woman. But what determines these role designations? Is it biological or genetic? Using secular terminology, what appears to be "masculine" in one culture may be called "feminine" in another. How does nurturing, environment, and culture create a standard which defines what activities or behaviors are "correct" for boys or girls?

We live in a broken world. How can we better understand the complexity of what it means to be a man or a woman? Security in that understanding not only involves how we feel but how we think.

Currently, there is much research focusing on the brain. Discoveries of the plasticity of the brain, neural connections, and functioning of various components of the brain offer us exciting understanding. How does the way we think and relate in community impact our security in who we are as men or women?

Our brain hemispheres interrelate and this interaction has an impact on our personalities and behavioral choices. In women and men there are differences in the level of neural connections made between the two hemispheres.

Recent reports have demonstrated that one hemisphere of the brain can be more dominant. Depending on which hemisphere is dominant, certain conceptual qualities can be expressed through our personalities. Often the expression of these qualities creates an erroneous standard used for determining what defines a man or a woman. These qualities also may impact our sense of security.

The qualities, as seen in the following chart, are ways to understand ourselves, but are not absolutes. Although we can express a number of these qualities, some are more present than others. The broken expressions of these qualities is indicative of a reactive state which may contribute to insecurity.

Some of these qualities are associated as being more prominent in men or women. It is not important to determine what has created or influenced that predominance. What is important is how do you connect and identify with these qualities. How do they impact your sense of security?

Take a moment and study this chart. Which qualities are more expressed in your personality and relationships? Do you associate them with being more of a man or woman? Do you assign the qualities listed in the two middle columns with a value system, making some more or less desirable?

The Right-Brain and Left-Brain[53]

BROKEN EXPRESSION	RIGHT-BRAIN	LEFT-BRAIN	BROKEN EXPRESSION
Passivity	Being	Doing	Controlling
Rejecting	Receiving	Penetrating	Dominating
Quitting (sour grapes)	Resting	Action-ing	Forcing
Manipulating	Responding	Initiating	Overpowering
	Brooding	Shaping	
	Pondering	Deciding	
	Intuiting	Reasoning	
Hysteria/ Catatonia	Feeling	Thinking	Hyper-analysis
	Following	Leading	
Victim Mentality	Vulnerability	Protectiveness	Patronizing/ Chauvinism

[53] Chart used by permission of Connally Gilliam.

Some of these qualities are somewhat reflective of our physical bodies. For example, the act of sexual intimacy reflects men as penetrating and women as receiving. Our capacity to initiate or receive does influence how we relationally connect. Can I initiate a connection with others? Am I capable of receiving from others? In the big picture, all of these qualities are found, to a degree, in each of us. However, brain physiology does influence which qualities may be more prominent.

It is important to state that we have *whole brains*! In other words, both hemispheres of the brain are active in our lives. One hemisphere is not dormant. Identifying yourself solely as right or left brain can be restrictive and limiting. However, to a certain degree, we may be more expressive, according to which hemisphere has a greater influence. The question we must ask ourselves is if we have a distorted view of these qualities.

Difficulty occurs when these qualities are placed on a value scale. It has been my observation that linear thinking is often more highly valued in our culture than being intuitive. If a woman is more intuitive, to fit into what she feels is a "man's world," she may suppress or even come to hate her intuitiveness. For a man, if he is more intuitive, he may see or think of himself as deficient or less of man. We must understand how cultural nonconformity can contribute to our insecurity.

My Story

As I was growing up, doubt and self-hatred were ever-present. My feelings of inadequacy and weakness opened the door for emotional dependency. I leaned into others to define and tell me who I was. Having limited value and worth in myself, I longed for others to like and approve of me. The result in me was to embrace the broken quality of manipulation. I orchestrated my relationships so I could get what I thought I needed from them.

The presence of self-hatred was the foundation for my passivity, another broken quality. I often second-guessed or doubted myself. It was easier to acquiesce to that which offered the least amount of conflict or challenge. Fear was also associated with these choices.

Intuitiveness is a prominent quality I possess. I initially viewed this as a deficit. Struggling with unwanted same-sex attraction, I already felt separated from other men. Since most men I knew were linear thinkers, my intuitiveness only increased my feelings of insecurity and being less than other men. I did not value my intuitiveness and felt I needed to be more linear.

To grow and mature, I needed to examine my qualities. I could address the broken qualities I expressed, but what was I to do about my intuitiveness? Intuitiveness is not a broken expression. I could not force myself to be more linear. I needed to see my intuitiveness as a positive gift.

My intuitiveness was an important aspect of my calling. That intuitiveness was part of God's design in me and the way I bore His image in ministry. Embracing this quality helped me to mature into the man God created me to be. Accepting my gifts enabled me to be present with other men, rather than feeling isolated, less than, or different.

Secure men and women have a balanced perspective in the expression of these qualities. Feelings of fear or ambiguity begin to dissipate. Insecurity occurs when those qualities are not equally blessed or affirmed. Our level of security impacts our capacity to perceive the "otherness" of the opposite sex.

Sexual and relational brokenness results in expressing the broken aspects of these qualities. If the capacity to do is tainted by the presence of restless activism, we can become controlling or even abusive. When the capacity to feel becomes trapped in diseased introspection, it can become either hysterical or catatonic.

Studying the expression of your qualities can help your overcoming process. How does the expression of a particular quality line up with your giftedness? Which broken qualities are present which limit your becoming? These qualities are not to become rigid labels or restrictive limitations. The Holy Spirit will guide how to be rightly centered and aligned according to your calling.

The healthy expression of these qualities will be aligned with God's intended design for you. They work together with your temperament and personality to enhance your sense of security. These qualities enhance your calling. They enrich your capacity to bear God's image as a woman or a man.

There can be a variance in the way a particular quality is expressed in us. Initiation can appear differently when expressed through a woman rather than a man. Responsiveness expressed in a man may likewise be dissimilar. These expressions do not diminish or increase their value. It is the reality of how our biology impacts the expression of our gifts and the way we bear God's image. We express Him uniquely in our gifts but also in being male or female.

God's image is reflected in how we, as men and women, walk in His divine design. Satan despises the image of God, and so despises our expression of it. Therefore, He wages war by specifically creating hatred of that expression.

Hatred of Woman: Misogyny

Lacking the presence of healthy woman diminishes the way God's image is seen in community. Without woman, man cannot experience his fullest potential. One of the results of the fall for woman was this: "Your desire will be for your husband, and he will rule over you" (Genesis 3:16). Woman's relational giftedness and sensitivity became a place of vulnerability for attack.

Misogyny is the low view, hatred, dishonoring, and devaluation of woman. This hatred focuses on the embodiment of anything that personifies, culturally associates, or identifies with woman. Some cultural beliefs have misogynistic roots. Certain Asian cultures have devalued the birth of daughters, abandoning them or leaving them to die.

Misogyny affects both men and women. Misogyny may be a present reaction to a woman out of the past, which caused disappointment or hurt. It may arise from family dysfunction or abuse. In dysfunctional families, one or both parents can model misogyny, thereby increasing the potential for its development in their children. Wounds beget fears, internalized feelings, and defensive reactions. The impact depends on the degree of misogynistic expression and our temperamental sensitivity.

The impact of misogyny in our upbringing can result in one or more of the following:

- Women are to be dominated or controlled.
- Women and emotions are weak.
- Women have no value or worth.
- Men who are "true" men will subjugate women.
- Women or men having a hatred for mother may generically transfer it onto all women

Daughters or sons may not become anchored in a father or mother's love when dysfunction is present. The extent of the dysfunction influences the depth of impact on our emotional and relational development. It lays the foundation for how we relate to men and women later in life. Misogyny may have deep generational roots.

Satan, knowing that his demise would come through the womb of a woman (Genesis 3:15), delights in misogyny. He relishes anything that brings a sword between the sexes. A woman's capacity for responsiveness becomes his target for assault which can become a significant vulnerability. Also, her capacity to ponder and brood can become a source of great wounding.

The Internal Struggles of Misogyny

Misogyny results in ambivalent feelings for men. He must control women but keep them at a safe distance. Although he desires intimacy and love, he fears emotional annihilation: "If I love a woman, I give her the power to hurt me. If I become vulnerable, she will destroy me." Terrified, he hates the women in his life. However, fearing they will leave, he tries to control them. Two predominant factors for a misogynist, then, are a great fear of abandonment and a deep-seated need to be in control.

Male misogynists are masters at manipulating relationships. He never feels secure because an underlying sense of anxiety drives him to be in a relationship. He experiences internalized shame since he feels weak and inadequate. He also feels shame for needing woman and fears exposure of his neediness.

Therefore, his focus is to undermine a woman's confidence. Through manipulation, he creates insecurity, doubt, and low self-esteem in her. The abuse causes her to depend emotionally on him; she becomes so insecure that her identity is bound to his. Even though she is deeply abused, she can't leave him.

Women respond to misogyny by internalizing a diminished view of woman. She is in reaction to her body, her appearance, or her expression of what she feels it is to be a woman. Any misogyny she experiences around her—be it a comment, joke, or abuse—drives her pain deeper within. Absorption of misogyny over the years creates a toxic reservoir fueled by self-loathing. Internalized misogyny can also surface through transference, as she transfers her pain onto the women around her. She despises the women around her, treating them with similar disdain as do male misogynists.

Hatred of Man: Misandry

Man reveals the male aspect of the image of God. One of the results of the fall for man was this:

> Cursed is the ground because of you; through painful toil you will eat food from it all the days of your life. It will produce thorns and thistles for you, and you will eat the plants of the field. By the sweat of your brow you will eat your food until you return to the ground.
> – Genesis 3:17–19

Man, created from the earth, now would painfully labor with it. He finds his identity in what he does, driven to prove his worth through success. How many television programs or movies portray men as dolts or completely immature? This portrayal is misandry—the low view, hatred, dishonoring, and devaluation of man. Undermine his identity or highlighting his inadequacy makes him appear foolish, which creates discouragement in him. His need to be respected is crushed.

The relationships around us, as with misogyny, contribute to the formation of misandry. Wounded wives can poison their children against their fathers. Abusive or misogynistic fathers can cause their children to hate them, which later results in transference-induced misandry toward men in general. Relationally, men who internalize misandry can become passive, complacent, or isolate. They are reluctant to initiate. Women who internalize misandry can fear men, try to control or dominate them, or build emotional walls. Men tend to turn inward, to internalize their feelings, and to shut down. However, women tend to turn outward, creating defensive and protective mechanisms.

Symptoms of Misogyny and Misandry

These two areas of brokenness bear similarities. Below is a list of symptoms that may reveal the presence of misogyny or misandry.

- Pretending to value the opinion or input of one sex over the other, but then dismissing it
- Seeking advice or support from only one sex
- Accusing or blaming one sex
- Fantasizing or viewing pornography abusive or violent toward one sex
- Viewing movies or television programs demeaning to either sex
- Making derogatory or abusive jokes at the expense of one sex
- Inability to thank or receive from one sex, not wanting to be indebted
- Misuse of Scriptures regarding submission

– Demeaning self-talk regarding one's biological sex
– Inability to bless or affirm one sex

The Good News

As overwhelming as these issues may be, God has a plan and is committed to your restoration and healing. To grow in our security as men and women, the following are helpful suggestions:

– Invite God into your fears and feelings of inadequacy
– Increase your intimacy with God, dialoguing with Him to seek His words of healing in any areas of insecurity
– Seek revelation for the presence of misogyny or misandry, confessing and renouncing it
– Seek the Holy Spirit's revelation for any misguided beliefs regarding the conceptual qualities identified in this chapter
– Seek revelation where you are in conflict with God's design and definition for what it means for you to be a man or woman
– Confess any areas of self-hatred, diseased introspection, and self-absorption
– Know that each day, God is transforming you into His image, whether you can detect it or not

The security I developed in being a man was incremental. Eventually, insecure feelings rarely surfaced. However, when they did, it was during times of vulnerability or spiritual warfare. In those moments, I remind myself of God's truth. I process my feelings in light of the spiritual reality who I am in Christ. Doing so is not to over-spiritualize and deflect, but the seeking of God's counsel and direction. I connect with my accountability partner and others in community. I rely on God's promise that all things—yes, all things—are working for my good (Romans 8:28).

God will call you out of any victim mentality, complacent passivity, or diseased introspection. He will help you to have a "thicker skin"—a decreased capacity to internalize negativity. Remain open to the way the Lord uses others in your life. It is vitally important to recognize the source of the voice to which you give credence. Am I hearing the voice of the Lord, the enemy, or self-condemnation? I rest assured that Jesus goes before me, laying out His path through my wilderness.

Closing Thoughts

Due to the confusion in our culture regarding sexuality, gaining clarity in this area is challenging. We must be mindful of how we allow worldly thinking to enter into our consciousness. Doing so is crucial in our pursuit of becoming men and women who rightly bear and reveal God's image. The enemy does not want us to walk in the full potential God has for us.

Being at peace with being a man or woman strengthens our relationships and calling. Scripture study and intentional quiet times allow for the Holy Spirit to keep us centered in the truth. We invite Him to search our hearts. We choose not to isolate but to become known in healthy communities.

There can be deep wounding associated with misogyny and misandry. The pain has often been accumulating for long periods. Seeking wise counsel for a season often helps to access and process this pain. Jesus can walk us through these deep valleys. I suggest reading Isaiah 61:1–7 and personalizing it. For example, in verse 3: "…To bestow on [your name] a crown of beauty instead of ashes, on [your name] the oil of joy instead of mourning." When God reveals your areas of need or brokenness, He does not abandon you. His timing is perfect. He will guide your steps and meet you where you are in your process of becoming.

Prayer

Lord, You have created my innermost being. You have created me in Your image. Father, You have a plan for my life as the man or woman You intend for me to become. You have established my life and calling, and in You, I place my trust.

Would You reveal where there is any insecurity in me? Expose those areas in my thinking that do not line up with Your truth. Where do I have any lies or misbeliefs regarding being a man or a woman? Where am I at odds with Your truth and plans for my life? How have I been in reaction or defensively detached? Please come and meet with me in my places of perceived weakness, inadequacy, or self-hatred. Holy Spirit, please enable me to lift these places to You and renounce any sinful, reactionary choices. How have I sinned in reaction to the men and women in my life?

Lord, expose where there is any misogyny or misandry within me. Expose where I have wounds in these areas. Where have I allowed the actions or words of others to enter my soul? How have I been treated in a demeaning manner regarding my biological sex? How have my experiences resulted in faulty thinking? How have I internalized my wounds and pain? Expose any toxic reservoir that holds bitterness, contempt, anger, self-hatred, and unforgiveness. Where have I become like my wounders and committed transgression through misogyny or misandry against those around me? I confess my sin to You!

Holy Spirit, please meet me at any point of resistance within my soul and empower me to remain present to You. Jesus, please help bind away these wounds, pain, and sin into Your cross. I invite You, to enter into my ancient ruins that have been long devastated (Isaiah 61:4). It is only through Your resurrection power that I can become restored and renewed.

I no longer choose to agree with those who have sinned against me. I choose to remove any labels that do not line up with who I am in You, Lord Jesus. I renounce any false images I have regarding my personhood. Through the power of Your Blood, I renounce any curses or lies spoken over me, declaring them null and void. With the sword of the Spirit, I cut any ties that bind me to misogyny or misandry. Cleanse me of all defilement and desecration imposed upon me. Father, only You have the authority to name and define me. Standing in my true self, I choose to release and forgive those who have sinned against me through misogyny or misandry.

Lord, would You meet me in this place of vulnerability? Would You help me hear aright the words of life, the healing word You have for me? I choose to rise as the man or woman You have created me to be. I choose to see the conceptual qualities within me as a holy gift from You. May I daily flow more in union with You regarding these qualities. Help me embrace them and walk in concert with them as part of the calling You have imparted to me. Enable me more and more to stand in my true self, united with You. May I stand more secure as the man or woman You have created me to be. May I receive from You, Holy Father, the full blessing bestowed on me as your daughter or son.

Soul Work

1. Which of the conceptual qualities in the chart line up with you and your personality?

2. Which of the false expressions are you more susceptible to practice, and why?

3. How have you assigned a higher or lesser value to any of these qualities?

4. Where do you find yourself suppressing, or resisting accepting, a particular quality, and why?

Journaling Moment

Most who come seeking the Path through the Wilderness lack security in being the men or women God created them to be. The concepts of what it means to be a man or woman are often unclear and distorted. After reading this chapter, ask the Holy Spirit to reveal where there is insecurity in you regarding these concepts as reflected in your identity and relationships. Ask if there are any faulty beliefs or lies you have believed that prevent you from becoming and being present to others or having whole relationships.

SIXTEEN

God's Design for Women

BY JOYCE SMITH

Before examining how God defines what it is to be a woman, it is helpful to review several key ideas.

First, place your body image and feelings about being a woman in the context of God's design and His ongoing redemption of us. God cares about our bodies; He is their Creator and Redeemer. God designed both male and female to equally reflect His image, and their unity and diversity are necessary to show God's relational nature. We can take heart that He is at work—for one day, all believers will stand before Jesus, the Bridegroom, as the Bride, the gathered Church, prepared for the best wedding of all.

Second, if we imagine anatomical sex as the expanse of human canvas on which we are born ("painted"), being male or female is the underlying color of that canvas. Subsequent layers of life's "paint" (experiences, wounds, messages) may cause us to express right/left-brain traits in various healthy and unhealthy ways. Both men and women are to express healthy examples of being a man or woman on our God-given canvases. Our fallen nature, our wounds, and the reality of evil make this reality an impossible dream without the Spirit of God transforming us.

Third, this chapter does not lay out concrete or stereotypical boxes that confine what it means to be a woman, because the expression of the qualities as shown in chapter 15 has often been suppressed in both males and females, to the detriment of both. The solution is not to create a new, false structure of "women are like X," but to say that because we are all made in God's image, we can and want to reflect His nature when expressing right/left-brain qualities—even as these ways vary with each person.

Clarifying God's Design for Woman

Women reflect God's image in humanity. They often reflect the trait to be, which is in response to God and those around them. Women have giftedness to create a relational connection and the building of community. Just as she can birth life, through her intimacy with God, she imparts life to those around her. Healthy relationships are nurtured both with other women and men.

Although the titles for God in the Bible are male nouns, and Jesus was incarnate as a man, God does not hold a lesser view of the divine image as carried by women. He frequently uses female or maternal imagery in Scripture to describe Himself. Language about pregnancy, labor, delivery, and raising children is dotted through the entire Bible. Stories of barrenness and widowhood and loss of children are equally poignant ground for God's redemptive work.

Here are some examples:

- Deuteronomy 32:11–12: God describes Himself as a mother eagle hovering and protecting her eaglets.
- Hosea 13:8: God describes His anger like that of a mother bear robbed of her cubs.
- Isaiah 42:14: God describes His distress over Israel as a woman in labor.
- Isaiah 49:15: In an intimate portrait of tenderness, God describes Himself as a nursing mother who cannot and will not forget her nursing child.
- Isaiah 66:13: God describes Himself as a mother comforting her children.
- Matthew 23:37: Jesus says that He longed to gather Jerusalem under His wings as a mother hen gathers her chickens.

These biblical metaphors relate to motherhood, however, a role that no men will have and not every woman will have. How do we make sense of this pattern? In short, carrying and raising young is one of the clearest pictures of women which can be expressed in three-dimensional reality. This reality evokes images of deep emotion, vulnerability, gentleness, and self-giving love.

Using the chart in chapter 15 of the right/left-brain qualities, we can follow a rough pattern of traits as reflected in women, from covenant commitment through raising children. These traits and this sequence are often why unwanted singleness, childlessness, loss of children, and widowhood are particularly painful for women.

These can be experienced as a visceral sense of being cut off from expressing something good and true about being female. This may be true despite solid theological grounding that makes it clear that God is present, at work, and taking particular care of His children in these seasons.

The bottom line, then: Being a woman is not simply about having children! Being married or being a mother is not a prerequisite; in fact, these may, in some cases, be a hindrance to seeing the spiritual truth underlying these earthly realities. Instead, it is essentially about these stages in their spiritual context—all of which God does for and through us.

The stages of becoming the woman God intended, in a spiritual context look like this:

Union with God > Life from God > Nurturing life > Kingdom fruitfulness

1. Union with God. Salvation by faith in God causes us to be united with God (1 Corinthians 6:17).
2. Receiving life from God. He plants spiritual seeds in our hearts and simply asks us to abide in His provision (James 1:21; John 14–15).
3. Nurturing life, often in hidden places and with pain. God's life in us requires responsive care, trust, and obedience—often in places no one will ever see. Life on earth implies pain and loss, and we labor against sin, the flesh, and evil.
4. Kingdom fruitfulness. God's glory is seen, and His Kingdom grows.

This pattern is seen even in the creation narrative (Genesis 1:1–31):

1. Union with God and receiving life: "In the beginning God created the heavens and the earth. Now the earth was formless and empty, darkness was over the surface of the deep" (verses 1–2).
2. Nurturing life, often in hidden places: "…formless and empty, darkness was over the surface

of the deep, and the Spirit of God was hovering over the waters" (verse 2).

3. Kingdom fruitfulness: The entire rest of Genesis 1 is the explosion of God's creative power in beauty, harmony, joy, and God-glorifying complexity.

The underlying pattern of union with God, nurturing life, and Kingdom fruitfulness is a picture of encouragement for believers. We are all called to this spiritual posture in our walks. In one sense, we all embrace the right-brain quality of receiving in relation to God, because He is always initiating towards us (a left-brain quality). In short, because we are the receivers of God's initiating work, we are all able and called to reflect a receptive posture.

The Marred and Broken Image

We know, however, that the jagged edges this fallen world do not yet match the fullness of God's intent.

Adam and Eve lived in God's creation in perfect unity with Him and one another: "Adam and his wife were both naked, and they felt no shame" (Genesis 2:25). Their relational partnership, openness, and lack of shame were rooted in perfect connection with God. But from the first sin of Adam and Eve in the Garden of Eden, the image bearing of men and women became twisted and broken. Eve's refusal to rest in God's provision, and her insistence on meeting her own needs in her way on her timetable, continue to reverberate throughout our fallen humanity. (Adam's silence in the face of the whole situation is an issue for the next chapter!)

When God spoke the curses after the Fall, a crack appeared in the foundation of all human relationships.

Here are His words to Eve (some of which we looked at in the last chapter):

> "I will make your pains in childbearing very severe; with painful labor you will give birth to children. Your desire will be for your husband, and he will rule over you."
>
> – Genesis 3:16

There are dozens of interpretations of these phrases, but two key points resonate across translations: First, bearing children will be full of pain—physical and otherwise. And second, the power dynamics between men and women, especially in marriage, will be permanently broken and distorted. The implication seems to be that the brokenness will have more cost to women ("He will rule over you").

Broken Expressions

Suddenly, in a post-Fall world, vulnerability is no longer a gift. Reliance on others is met with betrayal.

Tender responsiveness is not a blessing but a curse in a world of exploitation. Weakness is leveraged (emotionally, physically, or otherwise) for the benefit of those in power, at great cost to the soul of women. Children are the source of immense, sometimes life-threatening pain. Some of those called to provide, protect, and lead, choose instead to rob, exploit, or remain in passive silence.

Regardless of how or when it happens, many women learn quickly that expression of her gifted qualities becomes a source of shame, exposure, and pain; and that survival in a fallen world requires some adaptation.

These false structures of adaptation have many expressions, but they generally fall on a spectrum with the following extremes:

1. Formless emotional dependency (broken right-brain expression): becoming a relational "pretzel," consumed with preventing abandonment by molding herself into whatever her important relational partners desire; complete reliance on others for identity and meaning; inability to take responsibility for herself (victim mentality); passivity, entitlement, manipulation; failure to exercise her will.

2. Defiant aloneness (broken left-brain expression): fortifying her heart against feeling pain; detachment; consumed with distancing herself from pain as a defensive move and avoiding emotional vulnerability; consumed with providing for, protecting, and leading herself; dedicated to control, domination, and overpowering threats (real or imagined) to herself.

As much as our stories of wounds and pain vary, sinful responses also vary. Here are several common categories. (This is not an exhaustive list.)[54]

Passive Dependence

- Helplessness; belief that men can and must perform most life functions for her; inability and refusal to exercise gifts or will to act.
- Refusal to take responsibility for herself or her actions; blaming others for bad outcomes; a sense of entitlement to better outcomes.
- Demands to be cared for in ways inappropriate for adult women.

Seduction

- Exploiting physical or emotional gifts to even the playing field of relational power dynamics.
- Becoming an accomplice to evil by exploiting herself for gain or power.
- Gaining men's love or attention simply to reject them and demonstrate a more powerful position.

Neuter / Asexual Reaction

- Erasing biological expression as more plausible and less painful than being a woman or expressing broken left-brain qualities, which caused so much pain.
- No connection to herself as a woman, leading to confusion, desire to erase gender.
- Attempting to become invisible regarding being female or her personhood (detachment).

The "Good" Woman

- Meeting cultural or familial expectations of what a woman "should" do, be, or look like.
- No connection to herself as a woman; existing within culturally appropriate frameworks; playing the role of a woman.
- Not giving free range to the expression of being right/left-brain when it conflicts with cultural expectations.
- "Many of us will place marriage and relationship as of primary importance and concern,

[54]For additional reading on this topic, please refer to the list of resources at the end of this chapter.

even before hearing from and responding to God. Many of us wear a mask of 'woman' rather than being a woman who hears and follows God."[55]

The Restoration and Healing of Women

Facing the right/left-brain qualities that are marred is overwhelming, but God does not leave us in our brokenness. We can bring everything to the foot of the cross: the ways we have sinned; the ways we have been sinned against; and the ways we have perpetuated brokenness in our sinful reactions. God knows every moment of our story and opens wide the door to forgiveness. Internalizing the Gospel through the Spirit's work frees women to flourish in their hearts.

First, *union with God means that any brokenness in our expression as women can be healed.* As we move toward Christlikeness, we can reflect an unbroken expression more fully. We must make peace with being a woman. For women, this chapter might highlight areas in which you may not yet have made peace with yourself as female.

Second, *developing the capacity for being is a spiritual journey.* Mary, the mother of Jesus, shows us her receptiveness to Gabriel's surprising announcement (Luke 1:26–38); in her joy with Elizabeth (Luke 1:39–56); and especially in her heart ponderings after the birth of Jesus (Luke 2:19). To embrace God's design as a woman is a growth in simply receiving from the Father with the posture of Mary: "Behold, I am the servant of the Lord; let it be to me according to your word" (Luke 1:38, ESV).

Third, *God will (when asked and allowed) unveil the healthy partnership between women and men.* Each highlights the strengths of the other, and God has created us to value and cherish these differences in the other. When there is a broken expression through men of the left-brain qualities, women can internalize this assault in devastating ways. In life-giving relationships between men and women, men are called to honor and protect the dignity of women.

Our journey from brokenness to wholeness with God and coming to a place of peace in being female, a woman, is a long process. There is a great need for our healing between now and eternity—but God is at work. He is restoring us at His pace, and we can entrust our full selves to His work.

[55]Comiskey, *Restoring Relational Integrity*, p. 198.

Prayer

Father, I come to You as Your daughter, seeking Your face, seeking Your heart. I come before You bearing my wounds and brokenness. I want to confess the ways I have failed to embrace and walk in my capacity as a woman. Expose the lies I have taken in, which limit my capacity to be the woman You created me to be. Holy Spirit, what are those lies? I choose to lay down before the cross of Jesus any ways I walk in the false self.

Show me if I have been in reaction to being a woman. Reveal to me any ways I have taken on any broken qualities. I now lay them all down before You.

Jesus, I acknowledge that You broke the power of the curse. You have defeated the enemy and his plans, which have kept me focused on my defensive and reactive strivings. Holy Spirit, I seek Your empowerment to renounce that which is false within me. I welcome Your truth to be my foundation. My heart belongs to You. Expose any lies I have believed so I may have Your mind.

Search my heart. I welcome You to meet me in those places where I feel empty, disconnected, or alone. I confess the deep emptiness and aloneness I do feel. I lift to You my broken relationships and where I feel needy. You know where I feel burdened. You know where I am bitter, cynical, or have unbelief. You know where I have become controlling or manipulative due to these emotions. I desire now to have my voice back, to able to speak out these areas of pain and unrest. I seek Your release from all that has limited my becoming the woman You have created me to be. I want to be a woman who chooses truth and life. I want to be a woman who bears Your image to others, bringing the same healing I am now receiving.

Father, align my will with Yours. I stand in the authority of the cross and renounce any brokenness in my family lines that specifically warred against women, which have been made manifest within me. Where women were not blessed, now let that blessing come to me. Enable me to impart that blessing to others. Where there was a lack of affirmation, may it now be present in me.

Lord, I renounce any presence of misogyny or misandry in my family tree. I renounce any broken relational patterns within me. I confess the broken ways I have related to the men and women in my life. Bring release from these broken ways so I may truly enter into community. May I now relate rightly to men and women in relationships that bless and nurture. I want to walk in healthy relationships.

I specifically seek release from any defensive posturing, judgments, fear, self-hatred, or feelings of inadequacy. Help me walk with healthy boundaries with others. May I be authentic and genuine in my relationships, furthering Your Kingdom purposes.

I bring before You any beliefs, lies, or attachments that have restricted the expression of Your design for me to be the woman You intended. By the sword of the Spirit, I cut any ties that have prevented me from having a heart of flesh. I bring before Your cross, Lord Jesus, any stony, unresponsive, parched, and dry areas in my heart. Let Your abundant life and living waters cleanse, renew, and restore my heart. May the fullness of Your being inhabit my soul.

Father, please line up my passions to be one with Your passions. May my will be one with Your will. As I rise up in my true self, as one with You, as Your daughter, may Your love be manifested in and through me.

May I walk in wisdom, discernment, clarity, and understanding as to the woman You created me to be. May I be an instrument of nurturing, life, and healing to others.

And now, Father God, would You come and bless all that is good and true within me? Would You bring blessing where I was not blessed and affirm that which was not affirmed? Holy Spirit, please make real in my heart the reality that I am a beloved and cherished daughter. May my life now bring the fragrance of life to all my relationships and all the areas where You lead me. I choose to have no agreement with the enemy that I am less than, alone, or lacking in any good thing. I am one whom You see and have named. I am Yours, and You are mine.

Soul Work

1. What did I learn about what it means to be a woman from my mother? From my father?

2. Who or what encouraged or discouraged the development Your design in my life?

3. When did I learn that vulnerability was a liability? How did I react?

4. Women: How has your insecurity in being a woman been exhibited in broken ways in your life?

5. Men: How have you not honored or nourished the Godly women in your life?

Journaling Moment

Those dealing with sexual and relational brokenness usually have a distorted view of what is means to be a woman or man—both as it applies to me or to those who are opposite. Ask the Holy Spirit to show you where your understanding has been distorted. Seek how it became, and how it still is, distorted. Wait on the Lord to show you how it needs to be restored.

Resources

- Elliot, Elisabeth. *The path of loneliness: finding your way through the wilderness to God.* Grand Rapids, MI: Revell, 2007.
- Gilliam, Connally. *Revelations of a single woman: loving the life I didn't expect.* Wheaton, IL: Tyndale House Publishers, 2006.
- Kuehne, Dale S. *Sex and the iWorld: rethinking relationship beyond an age of individualism.* Grand Rapids, MI: Baker Academic, 2009.
- Mellody, Pia, Andrea Wells. Miller, and Keith Miller. *Facing codependence: what it is, where it comes from, how it sabotages our lives.* San Francisco, CA: Perennial Library, 1989.
- Meyers, Jan. *The allure of hope: God's pursuit of a woman's heart.* Colorado Springs, CO: NavPress, 2001.
- Proett, Jan Meyers, and Stasi Eldredge. *Beauty & the bitch: grace for the worst in me.* Pikes Peak, CO: Bondfire Books, 2013.
- Rinehart, Paula. *Sex and the soul of a woman: how God restores the beauty of*

relationship from the pain of regret. Grand Rapids, MI: Zondervan, 2010.

- Rinehart, Paula. *Strong women, soft hearts: a woman's guide to cultivating a wise heart and passionate life.* Nashville, TN: Word Pub., 2001.

SEVENTEEN

God's Design for Men

WHEN CHRIST CALLS A MAN, HE BIDS HIM COME AND DIE.

– DIETRICH BONHOEFFER, *THE COST OF DISCIPLESHIP*

Our culture is confused, as we have noted, regarding what it means to be a woman or man. Our culture's attempts to create multiple forms of identity based upon sexuality only further distorts God's holy design, which is contained within each man and woman. The world strives to bury that holy design, supplanting it with ever-changing definitions. The world keeps developing nomenclature because it does not acknowledge the foundational Christian principles established in the book of Genesis.

Are You Man Enough?

What does it mean when we hear someone say, "Man up" or "Be a man"? We hear statements like these in various settings. Aren't those statements subjective rather than objective? Aren't the speakers themselves making judgments according to their standards of what makes an individual "manly"?

Does "manning up" depend on physical appearance, attributes, or performance? What one considers manly in one culture may be the opposite in another. In certain cultures, men walking hand in hand are a sign of friendship and regard. In another, it has sexual overtones. In some cultures, it is an acceptable greeting for men to kiss each other on the cheek; elsewhere, this raises questions. Who or what determines these standards?

Culture, environment, family, and relationships—all affect our perception of what it means to be a man. There is a drive within men to be respected, to fit in, and be accepted. However, what happens when my personality, physicality, or personal preferences do not match with the predetermined norms for the measurement of a man? How do I relate? How do I define myself as a man? How do I see or feel about myself as a man? How do I relate to the men around me? Am I being genuine or building a façade to be one of "the guys"?

What defines a man varies in locations all around the world. What challenges my sense of security in these settings, however, is not the setting itself, but *how secure I feel inside about being a man.* My ease in a particular environment is maintained only when I feel emotionally secure as a man. If I am secure in my identity as a man, that security does not depend on exterior conditions or cultural norms.

Here are the questions I need to ask myself:

- How do I define what it means to be a man and who or what has developed that definition?
- How do I measure up to this definition and standard?
- How are my relationships with men and women influenced by this standard?
- How do I function/exist in my environment based on this definition?

We must always go back to our Creator and His original design. His divine objectivity gives us the capacity to see ourselves aright, replacing the world's parameters. We must let the Spirit of truth bring revelation to any misconceptions or lies we have believed that have limited our becoming.

The Example of Jesus

The Scriptures provide many examples of men who did not illustrate what it means to be a secure man. Due to fear, Abraham lied that his wife, Sarah, was his sister (although she was, in fact, his half-sister), allowing an Egyptian pharaoh to marry her. David's lust sent him down a path of adultery, deception, and murder. Moses and Gideon's passivity deflected God's invitation to embrace their calling.

JESUS' SECURITY AS A MAN WAS ENHANCED BY HIS WILLINGNESS TO OBEY THE FATHER'S WILL.

The Scriptures also give us details of the life of Jesus, the God-Man who provided the example of how we can stand as secure, whole men.

Although we find nothing about Jesus' childhood and early adolescence, we do know that as a young man, he was about His Father's work. At age twelve, Jesus was already teaching in the Temple (Luke 2:46–49). He knew His purpose and calling. Even at this young age, Jesus revealed His commitment to His heavenly Father, making choices that would eventually govern His whole life.

Jesus affirmed and called those around Him to a higher purpose. He renamed Simon Peter, *Cephas*, which means "rock," affirming what that disciple would become (John 1:42). Jesus identified Nathanael as "an Israelite in whom there is no deceit" (John 1:47). Just as an earthly father speaks words of authority, blessing his children, Jesus did that for those around Him, calling forth and blessing what was good in them.

Jesus also upheld the dignity of woman. He spoke directly to the Samaritan woman at the well, shunned by her community, thereby acknowledging her personhood (John 4:4–42). Although the unclean woman subject to bleeding for twelve years touched Him, Jesus did not rebuke her but healed her (Luke 8:43–48). Jesus' encounters with prostitutes in Luke 7 and John 8 resulted in their restoration. The religious leaders of the day avoided and disdained women such as these, but Jesus looked on these women, and He *saw them*. Doing so acknowledged their dignity; they were worthy of grace and mercy. We must also never forget that women were the first individuals to whom Jesus chose to reveal His risen body.

Jesus' security as a man was enhanced by His willingness to obey the Father's will. Jesus yielded His will to the Father's will. That yielding took precedence over every other aspect of His life. Jesus knew there was a higher purpose for His life. This was not blind obedience, cutting off the heart. Indeed, in the Garden of Gethsemane, Jesus asked His Father three times, if He could pass on the cup. No, Jesus' obedience was rooted in His love for the Father and knowing He could trust the Father.

Jesus submitted His authority to that of Father God. On multiple occasions, He could have used His power, but refrained. He would have been justified in doing so. It would not have aligned, however, with His true purpose and calling. Jesus used His power only in ways that glorified the Father.

How have you, as a man, used power which was motivated by ego-centric or narcissistic intentions? How have you justified certain choices which were in contrast to being submitted to the Father's will and purposes? How have you abdicated your responsibility out of fear or passivity?

We all can learn much by meditating on the life of Jesus. How often, when I think of the initials WWJD, (What Would Jesus Do?) do I know quickly in my spirit the answer I seek? Jesus is the way and example of how to be a man of integrity, honor, and purpose.

Dying to What Is False

> The Son is the radiance of God's glory and the exact representation of his being, sustaining all things by his powerful word.
>
> – Hebrews 1:3

When the writer of Hebrews indicates that Jesus is God's "exact representation," he is referencing the action of a signet ring pressed into the melted wax. Just as the wax receives and then exactly reflects the signet ring, so the Son perfectly and exactly reflects the Father. We reflect God's image expressly through the totality of who we are as men. Our image-bearing connects directly with how secure we feel as men. Women also need to have security in their image-bearing as women. If we are insecure, that insecurity manifests itself outwardly (i.e., the broken aspects of the qualities listed in chapter 15).

If we are secure, we relate to others without turning inward questioning our appearance, acceptance, or confidence. When insecurity turns me inward, I begin to have dialogs in my head (i.e., Am I fitting in?). At this point, I've stopped relating and listening to the person with whom I am conversing.

God's image manifests His goodness in us as men. God sets an inspired and secure core into our being. He provides the foundation onto which we build what is true.

Do you find any resistance or hesitation within yourself to this foundation building process? If so, what is limiting this process within you?

Divinely inspired men are redeemed through the work of the cross and being Christ-centered. Any other means of trying to prove ourselves to be men will be at cross-purposes and limit us. As men, we must be heavenly inspired and not earthbound. We must be grounded in the infinite and not the finite. Healthy men are outward-focused and relationally seek to bless, affirm, and advance God's Kingdom purposes. Godly men, therefore, are shaped in community and help to shape it as well.

At the foot of the cross, we choose to die to all broken expressions or actions we've chosen as a means to prove somehow that we are men. We must choose to die to the following broken reactions:

- Passivity and complacency
- Abusive power and control
- Security found through restless activism and achievements
- Hyper-analytical thought that cuts us off from the heart

God wants us to be at peace and secure as men, which directly affects our relational capacity with others. To walk as secure, whole men, we must have healthy, genuine relationships with women. We do not become secure as men in a vacuum.

As we have covered in previous chapters, our parental relationships, environment, and experiences influence our capacity to be engaged in community. The gifted relational qualities we possess, in concert with our biological sex and temperaments, develop further in community. Let us focus for a moment on gaining clarity for how we, as men reflect God's image.

Clarifying God's Design for Men

Men often express the relational qualities to do and to initiate. This capacity can be seen in how men pursue relationships and their drive for accomplishment. Is this due to a cultural or environmental influence? I cannot say. However, the curse on Adam was focused on "doing" as seen in Genesis 3:17, "Cursed is the ground because of you; through *painful toil,* you will eat food from it all the days of your life." (italics mine).

Embracing the capacity to do and initiate is a key component for experiencing security as men. It is stepping out, taking risk, rising up. Men wounded or weakened in this area often exhibit passivity and choose to retreat rather than initiate, as exampled earlier by Moses and Gideon.

The capacity to do often associates with the capacities to give shape, form, and structure. That association is easily observed in those men and women who have predominant left brain physiology. What types of careers do you think men and women typically choose who have a preponderance of these left-brain qualities?

A woman I knew was conflicted regarding her career as an architect. Observing that most architects she knew were men, gave rise to insecure feelings about being a woman. She saw her left-brain giftedness through a biological lens. Freedom from her insecurity occurred upon realizing that having a left-brain approach didn't diminish her capacity of being a woman. Her giftedness was indeed part of the way she, as a woman, imaged God.

Broken expressions of left-brain predominance often have a connection with the misuse of power. For insecure men, this can be particularly difficult. Power, inspired by God, is necessary for men to express God's image in life-giving ways. Inspired power protects, creating a healthy covering for others. It is a power centered in what is true, good, and lovely.

Christ-centered power focuses outwardly on blessing. The right brain qualities—such as receiving, resting, pondering, and intuiting—tend to be inward-focused. Again, this does not make them of less value or significance. It merely indicates that they have different focus and expression.

Right, and left brain thinking often approaches life through different lenses. A predominant right-brain approach often looks for synthesis, unity, and relational harmony. It tends to see the full and unified picture. A predominant left-brain approach looks for definition, differentiation, specifics, details, and gathering of facts. It is visually oriented, looking for what is necessary to make the whole work together.

Have you labeled or categorized others due to their approach to life? How have you done so regarding your self-image?

Men cannot grow in their security as men in a void; it is blessed and affirmed in relationship. Relationally, men sharpen and give further definition to each other. Men can speak into other men and call them out from self-loathing or diseased introspection. Healthy men come alongside one another, as Aaron and Hur did for Moses in the battle with the Amalekites (Exodus 17). They become a band of brothers, standing shoulder to shoulder. ·

My Story

In 1990 I began attending an Anglican church that became my community for the next fourteen years. I had already been leading support groups for two years for those struggling with relational and sexual issues. Feeling insecure as a man, my self- awareness and vulnerability tended toward diseased introspection.

I came out of isolation and joined a home group at church, which was a balanced mix of single and married individuals. I chose to take a risk with these men and women. Even though I was not in full-time ministry, I shared about my past life as a gay-identified man with all of them. The result: I felt welcomed, loved, and accepted. I found a new home.

The men in this homegroup varied in age and background. There were those with whom I would not have connected with in my previous circles. In a short period, however, we became a band of brothers. When I took the risk of becoming transparent with my struggles, pain, and fears, these men reciprocated, and the true intimacy of friendship, I longed for became a reality.

These brothers came alongside me and supported me. I had always felt as if men were on one side of the room, and I was on the other; I felt "other than" them. However, the transparency of these brothers revealed that they, too, were insecure and had fears and difficulties. As a result, I began to realize that the majority of insecurity which I felt had been due to my SSA past were feelings common to all men. I was able to walk from the other side of the room and join my brothers. Here began the decreasing of my unwanted SSA and the growth of security in being a man that has remained to this day.

We need the presence of real and transparent men and women in our lives. Through my experience in the homegroup, I made an interesting discovery. Women drew out my capacity to be a man by blessing it in me, whereas men affirmed me as a man, thereby giving it greater definition and emboldening it. I needed my capacity of being a man to be both blessed and affirmed. A core need for men is also to feel respected. When our vital need to be blessed, affirmed, and respected occurs in community, we further become the men we were meant to be. To grasp the full picture regarding what it means to be a man after God's own heart, we must also understand what creates barriers to becoming the men, the Father created us to be.

The Broken Expression of Man

> By the sweat of your brow you will eat your food until you return to the ground, since from it you were taken; for dust you are and to dust you will return.
>
> – Genesis 3:19

When men experience insecurity, as many do, a shift occurs. Instead of looking up and out of themselves, they focus inward, being aware of their inadequacy as men. Turning inward affects their outward behaviors. This insecurity also has roots going back in time. We are born with a propensity towards brokenness due to the lineage passed down to us from the Garden of Eden.

Genesis 3:19 (see above) clearly states the effect of the curse on man. Man, having lost his center in God, now finds his center in restless activism, tied to the earth, the finite, for his identity and security. This results in a variety of broken expressions:

- The pull to isolate, becoming egocentric and self-reliant
- A diminished capacity to receive
- Turning the capacity to act or do into hyperactivity (e.g., workaholism)
- Finding significance in accomplishments (job, car, physique, power, etc.)
- Creating façades and self-protective barriers to hide weaknesses
- A drive toward immortality, preventing the capacity to rest and to be

In the Garden, Adam chose to remain silent when Eve reached for the fruit of the tree of the knowledge of good and evil. At that moment, he could have spoken up and challenged her. By not speaking, he rooted his guilt in silence. "Since Adam, every man has had a natural inclination to remain silent when he should speak."[56] Here was the diminishing of the good of man's voice, which has had an impact through the centuries.

We see the impact on fathers who fail to affirm, bless, or call forth their children. Silence becomes part of generational sin going back to Adam. Our culture often portrays dads as weak, witless, and worthy of scorn. Without the father's voice to awaken their children, they remain asleep. The voice, which would sharpen them, now dulls them, enhancing their lethargy.

[56]Larry Crabb, *The Silence of Adam: Becoming Men of Courage in a World of Chaos* (Zondervan, 1998), p. 12.

Other expressions of the broken manhood include:

– A disconnect with the heart; the inability to feel or identify feelings
– Being cut off from relationships; the inability to connect on the heart level
– A distorted view of what it means to be a man; symbolized as broken outward behaviors
– Dominating others to compensate for feelings of inadequacy, sought through power and control
– Abdication of power; embracing passivity, complacency, or sloth
– Choosing to remain in an adolescent state rather than face responsibility and maturity; the "Peter Pan" syndrome (i.e., I never want to grow up)

Which aspects in the preceding list are present in your life? Where do you have feelings of being asleep or lethargic regarding being a man? Ask God to awaken the sleeper!

Healing for Men

> [Jesus] compels us toward difficulties, for they compel us toward God, and God compels us toward change.
>
> – Francis Frangipane, *The Stronghold of God*

Redemption of the losses in the Garden of Eden occurred in another garden, the Garden of Gethsemane. Through the humility and obedience exemplified by Jesus, we discern the way He has made for us. To experience security as men, we must renounce the resulting broken expressions of that insecurity through our repentance and humility at the foot of the cross.

We need the Holy Spirit's empowered centering and focus on preventing us from turning to restless activism or retreating into lumpish passivity. Instead of jumping ahead of Him, we must learn to rest. Resting in Him is not passivity:

> To enter God's rest does not imply that we have become inactive, but that God has become active. What we become to Him is far more consequential than all we shall ever do for Him.[57]

To grow in our security as a man begins with a confession of weakness. It is a confession of our inability, our striving for power, or our attempts to prove our worthiness. We may confess

[57]Francis Frangipane, *The Stronghold of God* (Creation House, 1998), p.10, 11.

our passivity, fear of initiation/commitment, or self-hatred/loathing. We confess where we have sought false sources for identity, security, or intimacy.

Will you choose to renounce any attachments you have made to what is false? Where have you made a false peace with your brokenness, allowing it to coexist in your soul? When we confess and renounce, the Holy Spirit begins to give us back our voices.

Experiencing insecurity for an extended length of time allows for the embracing of images and concepts which are false. We must renounce these images and concepts. We need the mind and heart of Jesus to bring His definition once more to our souls. The Holy Spirit is present to us. He will bring the Father's definition and the image of who we are as the men and sons He created us to be. God will redefine our thinking through repentance, enable us to confess any self-hatred or loathing, and allow us to see ourselves as He sees us.

The Sword Between the Sexes

Having now discussed God's design for us as men, and for women in chapter 16, I want to address briefly how the Lord has broken the curse between men and women.

The curse created a sword between the sexes. Through the cross of Jesus, the effects of the curse have been broken and that sword removed. Men and women no longer have to look to their behaviors or others for their security and identity. Jesus made a way to the Father, reclaiming us and restoring our full inheritance as His true children.

We have the capacity and power to rise as men and women of God. We can relate to one another in wholeness without manipulation, control, or bending in to each other for security or identity. We need to continue growing in our process and accept the risk of engaging with each other. Being secure first in who we are in Christ, the fear of community will begin to decrease. Being in process does not limit us from starting to have healthy and whole relationships. We can be less resistant to the power of the other sex to bless us. In healthy relationships,

- Our fears and faulty beliefs are exposed.
- The Holy Spirit brings His revelation, addressing our brokenness.

– Practicing the presence of Jesus centers us to remain present.
– We learn to have holy boundaries.

Secure in who we are in Christ, we can exercise our authority to love aright. We choose to rise, facing, and forsaking our fears. The "giants" that may be in our promised land no longer have the power to rob us of our voices, our ability to stand, or our capacity to become. The only power others have to limit us is what we *abdicate to them*. We can truly enter into that which God has promised us.

As reclaimed men and women, we can promote and protect one another's dignity. Where we see weakness, brokenness, and death, we bring strength, covering, truth, and the fragrance of life. Where there is an injustice, we now have a voice to speak out against it. We can clothe the naked and bring restoration.

Freed from the curse, we become each other's advocate. With the empowering of the Father, we can bless what is true in each other. We call it forth when we see it expressed. Men can be a covering for those who are weak. Women can nurture those who lack connection.

Instead of the sword cutting, stabbing, and destroying others, it now symbolizes victory. It is a sword submitted to God's authority, with the strength to protect and take back what was lost. It is a sword having the capacity to cut any existing ties to that which is false. We do this by being image-bearers of God to one another. We fight to take back the ground the enemy has stolen.

Closing Thoughts

Indoctrinated by what the world believes it is to be a man we may need time to go through the process of detoxification. We must allow time for the Holy Spirit to open our minds and hearts so we can obtain God's understanding and discernment. The Holy Spirit must undo our connection to the finite so that we may embrace the infinite of God.

It is challenging to look at the right/left brain qualities without assigning value or assessing how we express these qualities. We have been taught to value certain traits, and we live in a culture that promotes this activity. Confusion and frustration surround us. The process of becoming the men and women we are called to be takes place in us only through the presence of God. We intentionally need to keep seeking a deeper, more intimate relationship with the Father, Son, and Holy Spirit. We must enter His rest, seeking the capacity to hear His voice, and then wait for Him to speak the healing word.

As you do so, be aware of spiritual warfare. The enemy does not want you to enter the greater understanding of God's inspired design for you. The enemy:

> ... is the one who has dogged your heels with shame and self-doubt and accusation. He is the one who offers the false comforters to you in order to deepen your bondage. He is the one who has done these things in order to prevent your restoration. For that is what he fears. He fears who you are; what you are; what you might become. He fears your beauty and your life-giving heart.[58]

Jesus is your way, your truth, and your life. Seek Him for His objectivity and your healing. His path is ever before you, and He will continue guiding you on your journey of becoming.

Prayer

Father, I come to You with my wounds and brokenness. I confess the ways I have failed to walk uprightly as the man I am called to be. At Your cross, Lord Jesus, I lay down those ways in which I have lived and expressed the false self. I bring to You any ways in which I have abused power in my life. I bring to You any ways in which I have embraced passivity and powerlessness. I ask You to expose all that limits my capacity to walk like a man after Your own heart.

Lord Jesus, would You make real—make alive within me—the reality that through Your cross, You have broken the power of the curse? You have overcome the evil one, smashing the head of the serpent, who wants to keep me bound in pride, arrogance, self-centered egotism, isolation, and addictive compulsions. I seek freedom from my striving, my restless activism, and my weakened capacity to receive. I invite You to come into any places in my heart where I am shut down and cut off. Regenerate within me the capacity to have healthy and true communion with You, with women, and with other men.

Holy Spirit, please come and empower me to release any generational inheritance that limits my capacity to enter into whole relationships. I renounce and release to You any brokenness passed down to me by my father or by other men in my family line. I release to You any ways I have embraced that brokenness and expressed it in my relationships. Specifically, I renounce their silence, detachment,

[58]John and Staci Eldredge, *Captivating: Unveiling the Mystery of a Woman's Soul* (Thomas Nelson, revised and expanded, 2011), p. 91.

outbursts, addictions, false expressions of power, misogyny, misandry, and inability to bless or affirm. I take the sword of the Spirit and break any ties or allegiances with these strongholds.

I offer up to You my heart of stone, which has been unresponsive or unfeeling. I ask You to replace these cut-off, stony places with a heart of flesh. Father, would You do a new work in me as Your son? Holy Spirit, activate the Father's will in me. Lord Jesus, fill me with Your zóé—Your abundant God-life. Root and establish me in the good of Your power and truth.

Father, I take authority over the dishonor I have experienced in relationship with women. I also confess any ways in which I have sinned by being in reaction to the broken women in my life. I take authority over any veil placed on my capacity to be a man by broken women. In Your name, Lord Jesus, through the empowering of Your cross, I remove this veil. I come out from under it, free from any words, expressions, or actions that have limited my becoming the man I was created to be. Lord, free me now to love and honor woman aright.

Lord Jesus, free me to enter into true communion and relationship with women. I cannot become without having godly women in my life. Expose and release me from any false beliefs that prevent me from drawing near to her. My heart needs the reality of how Your image is expressed in and through her. I want to be a man of honor and integrity. I desire to walk in Your holiness. As You heal my brokenness, release me into a true, holy, and authentic desire for her. Father, raise me up as Your true son in Christ. Make me strong in Your truth and love. Reclaim and redirect my heart such that my doing flows out of a centered place of being and rest. In so doing, may I enter into a more profound communion with You, with women, and with other men.

Embracing Your will, may I be resolute and undivided of heart. Release me from fear, doubt, and any feelings of inadequacy which limit me. May I embrace the authority bestowed by You upon me, Father, as Your son. May I walk uncompromised in Your truth. May I be an agent of justice for those who are weak and poor in spirit. Awaken in me Your strong compassion, and realign my desires to be Your desires alone. Advance Your Kingdom through my obedience and devotion to You, Lord.

I forsake the lie that I am self-sufficient. I forsake the lie that I have to hide my inadequacies and insufficiency. I forsake the relational ways that have isolated me.

I need healthy encouragement and blessing from my brothers. Father, teach me to rely rightfully on the men in my community. May I be refined and protected to know and become known to my brothers. Make me like Christ in His capacity to draw near to others, to call out and bless the true self in them. Through me, reclaim the lives for which You died. Help me further Your ways in our relationships and not thwart them. Grant me joy and peace as a man of God. I celebrate this gift from You, standing shoulder to shoulder with other men. Free me to walk in humble honor and dignity. Free me to walk as a man of integrity and truth. Free me to walk in the reality of true sonship!

Father, I receive the blessing You gave to Jesus, Your Son: *You are My son, whom I love. With You, My son, I am well pleased.* Amen!

Soul Work

1. Define in your own words what it means to be a man after God's own heart. What does God require of a true man?

2. How does a cross-centered approach differ from what our culture promotes what it means to be a man?

3. Men: How has your insecurity in being a man been exhibited in broken ways in your life?

4. Women: How have you not honored or nourished the Godly men in your life?

Journaling Moment

Those dealing with sexual brokenness usually have a distorted view of men and women. Ask the Holy Spirit to show you where your view of men has been distorted. Seek how it became, and still is, distorted. Seek the Lord to show you how it needs to be restored. We often lack images in our hearts to be able to see ourselves as God sees us. Ask God to give you the vision to see yourself as the man or woman He has created you to be and write it down.

EIGHTEEN

Healthy Same-Sex Friendships, Singleness, and Celibacy

BY JOYCE SMITH

JUST AS A BODY, THOUGH ONE, HAS MANY PARTS, BUT ALL ITS MANY PARTS FORM ONE BODY, SO IT IS WITH CHRIST. FOR WE WERE ALL BAPTIZED BY ONE SPIRIT SO AS TO FORM ONE BODY—WHETHER JEWS OR GENTILES, SLAVE OR FREE—AND WE WERE ALL GIVEN THE ONE SPIRIT TO DRINK.

– 1 CORINTHIANS 12:12–13

After examining how our desire for intimacy has twisted and bent our identities and our relationships, we can run to Christ for the salvation only He can give. In this chapter, we keep looking to Him as we consider what a positive vision of side-by-side friendships with others might look like. Our identities, as men and women can be solidified in healthy same-sex friendships. And beyond that, we will look at a positive vision of healthy intimacy while unmarried.

Friendship: Wounds and Hope

We all have fears and wounds from same-sex friendships, and some of them have very early roots. Some of the first roots are our connection (or lack of connection) with our same-sex parent. Did that parent affirm and mentor a sense of security in being male or female, or did they disdain and discourage it? We need a secure identity and positive same-sex friendships before we can reach out to the other sex. And although same-sex friendships cannot heal our wounds, God often uses them to mediate His healing in us. In friendship, we see more clearly the image of God in others and are brought to a fuller understanding of His work in our own lives.

Old wounds and patterns may trigger much fear. Perhaps we are afraid to try again after so much rejection from others. Perhaps we are afraid we will slip again into patterns of eroticizing the relationship or becoming emotionally dependent. Perhaps friendship reveals how deep our emotional need truly is, and we would prefer not to face it. Perhaps we have believed safe friendships are possible only with the opposite sex, while we still face the relational loneliness of isolation from our own sex. Perhaps we have believed for so long that deep, safe, same-sex friendships are not something we can enjoy. Regardless of our fears, Jesus himself calls us *friend* and invites us to learn under His gentle care.

Most important, we can trust that God is sovereignly working in our friendships to accomplish His good purposes for our journey. As C. S. Lewis describes it in *The Four Loves*:

> In friendship ... we think we have chosen our peers. In reality a few years' difference in the dates of our births, a few more miles between certain houses, the choice of one university instead of another ... the accident of a topic being raised or not raised at a first meeting—any of these chances might have kept us apart. But, for a Christian, there are, strictly speaking, no chances. A secret master of ceremonies has been at work. Christ, who said to the disciples, "Ye have not chosen me, but I have chosen you," can truly say to every group of Christian friends, "Ye have not chosen one another, but I have chosen you for one another." The friendship is not a reward for our discriminating and good taste in finding one another out. It is the instrument by which God reveals to each of us the beauties of others.[59]

[59]C. S. Lewis, *The Four Loves* (Harcourt Brace, 1991), p. 89. See also http://www.goodreads.com/quotes/183419-in-friendship-we-think-we-have-chosen-our-peers-in-reality.

Why We Need Friendship

We need friends for the same reason that God said of Adam, "It is not good for the man [or woman] to be alone" (Genesis 2:18). No matter how much our culture glorifies the needless, wantless, self-sufficient individual, we are not meant to attempt earthly life on our own. Ecclesiastes 4:10 points out that being completely alone can be a dangerous gamble for frail human beings. We are designed to receive life from Christ and then live in joyful community with one another. God provides for this in His Body, the Church; we are called to learn Christlikeness with and through relating to others.

Jesus Himself had friends during His earthly life—His twelve disciples. And now Jesus calls us friends. Hebrews 2:11 says that "Jesus is not ashamed to call [us] brothers and sisters"—friends. What a magnificent statement about God's relationship with us! We have all known times when someone was ashamed to call us a friend—but Christ's friendship is faithful.

The Bible has many examples of healthy same-sex friendships: Jonathan and David, Ruth and Naomi, Paul and Barnabas, to name just three. These stories are worth further study on their own, and they show true Kingdom friendship that is deep, warm, emotionally expressive, faithful, and God-glorifying. Christian friendship can and should be deeply soul-nourishing. Certain liberals have attributed a sexual component to some of these biblical friendships, but this is a heretical and a self-serving application of the Scriptures.

Also, becoming relationally whole in Christ requires us to look at our need for same-sex friendship. We all have broken areas impacting our sense of security regarding being a man or woman that makes it difficult for us to face our deep desire for same-sex friendships. Friends reveal our emotional need, but we cannot control what they do or what reactions their choices prompt in our hearts: envy, jealousy, contempt, competition, shame, lust, rejection.

When our friends' gifts (in whatever form) appear strikingly better than ours, we are tempted to envy them these good things in unhealthy, destructive ways that build walls of isolation around us. We should take seriously any signs of envy in same-sex friendships, and take them to the cross as we examine our hearts. Other patterns that should prompt spiritual attention include inordinate care-taking, disproportionate anger at the lack of reciprocity, isolation from other relationships, over-dependence on any one friendship for emotional or spiritual support, and patterns of manipulation and control.

Singleness

What is your reaction to a section on singleness? Perhaps you feel that, since it is not your current state, this content does not apply to you.[60] Or perhaps your long-dashed hopes for marriage have made looking directly at singleness a painful prospect. Or perhaps you were once married, and your current state of singleness is one you never wanted to experience.

Before diving in, it helps to note that not all singleness is the same. We all begin life unmarried (never-married singleness). Some stay that way or later embrace a calling of celibacy. Some adults marry but return to singleness at some point, with or without children, due to divorce or death (post-marriage singleness). Each life stage experiences these various types of singleness very differently. Additionally, an individual's desire to be married may wax and wane over time, like this:

Previously married Desires marriage	Never married Desires marriage
Previously married Does not desire marriage	Never married Does not desire marriage

Shifting demographics also impact singleness. As of 2014, more than 50% of American adults were unmarried for the first time since tracking began in 1976 when just 22% of adults were unmarried. Regardless of one's desire for marriage, it has become economically possible and culturally normal to remain unmarried.[61]

No practical advice on how to navigate singleness can address all these variations adequately. Nor does Christian culture have a well-developed theology of singleness. But the Bible does. The goal of this chapter is to discuss the broader framework for singleness and biblical applications to both the joys and challenges of singleness briefly.

[60]If you are the parent of an unmarried child, I ask you to consider this section in light of knowing that God could call him or her to a life of singleness and chastity. How would you parent differently if you knew He might not be calling your child to marriage?

[61]Mythili Rao and T. J. Raphael, "Singles Now Outnumber Married People in America," http://www.pri.org/stories/2014-09-14/singles-now-outnumber-married-people-america-and-thats-good-thing, September 14, 2014.

Singleness in Scripture

Although you have heard many sermons on marriage or family, do you recall hearing many references to singleness? Unlike the sparse references to singleness in the modern church, being unmarried in Scripture is typically significant. And there is a strong thread in Scripture of God's gracious care for and attention to His unmarried children.[62] Ruth and Naomi, for example, were both widowed and childless—the equivalent in their culture of a death sentence. God called Ruth and Naomi, bereft of their immediate community and devoid of economic resources, to follow Him in radical obedience. It turned out that their faithful friendship and God's care wove Ruth into the very lineage of Christ.

While God's faithfulness remains unchanging, there is a definite shift in the language around marriage before and after Jesus. In the Old Testament, singleness and childlessness were an existential threat to the covenant community, which depended on family and children to sustain it. Several times in the first five books of the Bible, God issued the command to "be fruitful and increase."[63] Family was a defining characteristic of God's people; they and their children were set apart under His covenant. Having children and giving them the covenant signs of belonging were absolute necessities. Because of this, being unmarried or barren was a painful, humiliating, and isolating experience often interpreted as God's punishment.[64]

With the coming of Jesus Christ and the advent of the New Covenant, the picture of the covenant community shifted from physical family to spiritual family. Jesus Himself, who was not married, demonstrated this shift, and frequently redefined the family against cultural norms. Because of Jesus, no one is included in or excluded from God's spiritual family based on earthly family status.

This radical reframing of the purpose of family has several key applications for married and unmarried believers.

Calling

Marriage, singleness, and celibacy are parallel vocations for our earthly journey. They are avenues of self-giving love and sanctification. They are avenues of self-giving love and sanctification.

[62]For more on this topic, see Barry Danylak, *Redeeming Singleness: How the Storyline of Scripture Affirms the Single Life* (Crossway, 2010), which is particularly helpful.

[63]See, for example, Genesis 1:28, 9:7; Leviticus 26:9; Deuteronomy 28:11

[64]See, for example, Genesis 30:1 and 1 Samuel 1:5–18..

They are avenues of eternal fruitfulness amidst the thorns of a fallen world. They should not be used to avoid loving God or loving one another. Also, they should not be used to excuse selfishness, including sexual selfishness in whatever form it manifests itself.

Equality

The state of singleness is not inferior to that of marriage (although there often is a subtle or even overt indication of this in church culture). While there are negative cultural connotations to singleness, the Bible does not hold to cultural assumptions. Paul says that, in many cases, singleness is preferable for Kingdom work. In marriage or singleness, the emphasis is always on God! Unmarried individuals can focus on His call on their lives and not on their comfort, pleasure, or social status (regardless of the state we believe would give us more of those things!).

Impermanence

Marriage is a three-dimensional earthly picture of Christ's love for the Church. Jesus makes it very clear that human marriage is a temporary institution that will be replaced by *the* marriage—that between Himself and the Church. Temporal marriage can be of great value, but on the scale of eternity, it is brief.[65]

Fruitfulness

Spiritual fruitfulness is more important than biological fruitfulness. Children have great value, spiritual and physical. (We were all children at one time!) Traditional societies placed great value on marriage and children because these constituted the deepest source of identity, family resources, and societal stability.[66] More recent trends in Western culture have made the individual the center of this framework—with whatever structure of sexual, communal, or economic support each person wishes to create.

The Christian sexual ethic takes issue with both—with the traditional, for worshiping the idol of family; and with the modern, for worshiping the idol of self. Instead of either of these, believers are called to pursue Kingdom fruitfulness, which requires dying to idolatry in any form.[67] God describes the legacy of those without children as better than the legacy of children:

[65]See Matthew 22:30. Francis and Lisa Chan's book *You and Me Forever: Marriage in Light of Eternity* (Claire Love Publishing, 2014), has an extended discussion of this point.

[66]Kuehne, *Sex and the iWorld*, p. 35.

[67]Timothy J. Keller, " *Sexuality and Christian Hope*," April 18, 2004, https://www.youtube.com/watch?v=WaYKyRLjxzI.

> For this is what the LORD says: "To the eunuchs who keep my Sabbaths, who choose what pleases me and hold fast to my covenant—to them I will give within my temple and its walls a memorial and a name better than sons and daughters; I will give them an everlasting name that will endure forever."
>
> – Isaiah 56:4–5

Loyalty

We are called to single-minded devotion to Christ, regardless of marital status. Our loyalty to Jesus is on a higher plane than even our closest family ties. Jesus Himself made this point when asked to prioritize His mother and brothers over His ministry work—and He pointedly identified His disciples as "my mother and my brothers," and "whoever does the will of my Father in heaven [as] my brother and sister and mother" (Matthew 12:49–50).

Desiring Marriage (or Not)

Given these applications, how can we have a balanced view of singleness and marriage without elevating one and undermining the other? How should an unmarried person who desires marriage approach this tension? Here are a few practical thoughts:

Marriage is a good gift. Given the Western experience of painful marriages and frequent divorces, we need to remember that God created marriage before sin entered the world. Marriage is a picture of Christ's love for the Church. All believers are headed to an eternal wedding feast with Christ in heaven. Marriage, although temporary, is a good gift.

Marriage is not earned. No one is "entitled" to marriage (or children). Getting married does not imply that two people are more mature, deserving, or valuable than their single counterparts. Marriage is not a reward bestowed on those whom God finds "ready"; nor is a difficult marriage concrete evidence of having chosen the "wrong" person. And singleness is not a commentary on one's worth.

The purpose of marriage is joy in Christ and sanctification. Marriage is not for enthroning our selfishness but for learning to love in an exclusive way that reflects how Christ loves the Church. It is for refining our hearts in the white-hot furnace of faithfulness, service, and intimacy with the same person day to day.

The purpose of singleness is joy in Christ and sanctification. Singleness is not for our comfort and pleasure, or for hiding from the call to love both men and women in friendship. It is for learning to love in an inclusive way that shows God's generosity and bounty. It is for refining our hearts in obedience and learning to depend fully on Christ.

Suffering comes with both marriage and singleness. The suffering takes different shapes, and it is often difficult for one side to fully empathize with the other. It is easy to assume we understand what it is to be single, celibate, or married in the life of another. But instead of assumptions, we can approach one another with curiosity, compassion, and gentleness. Married or unmarried, we all need honesty, encouragement, fervent prayer, and faithful friendship from other members of the Body of Christ.

False intimacy is always a trap. Especially if we feel cheated in some sense out of marriage, we may experience growing resentment toward God and entitlement toward forms of false intimacy. This can happen for believers either married or unmarried. In singleness, this could be a relentless pornography habit; constant masturbation; exclusive, emotionally dependent same-sex friendships (expecting a friend to play the role of the desired spouse); extreme consumerism in dating; dismissing the opposite sex *en masse*; or intentional isolation from married friends.

The path of true intimacy and learning to love always requires vulnerability, dependence on God, and taking risks.

Singleness, Chastity, and Celibacy

Again, the variations of singleness might approach practical questions of purity from different angles, but they share a central call to chastity. There are no gray areas in this call for those walking in the state of singleness and those walking in the state of marriage. Embracing chastity means living in such a way that we relate to one another in holy, affirming, and honoring ways. Those who have embraced the calling of celibacy have chosen never to marry and have committed to living their lives single. Unmarried adults may find little practical encouragement from others about relying on Jesus to walk out this calling with humility, strength, and joy.

Embodied Love

Celibacy is often framed in negative terms: not having sex, or avoiding sexual intimacy, or denying sexual expression. This is a narrow, self-centered theology that does a serious disservice to married and single believers alike. Unmarried Christians are not at a disadvantage in understanding intimacy. In some cases, much to the contrary! Full-fledged obedience and reliance on Christ for abstinence is often a pathway to the stunningly clear spiritual vision and renewed strength.

We need a much bigger picture of what intimacy and embodied love means. The overarching positive call of the Gospel is to Spirit-powered love. To receive God's love for us in Christ. To love God with all our heart, soul, mind, and strength. To love our neighbors as ourselves. To empty ourselves for the upward call of God in Christ, Jesus. He has very literally *embodied* us and stamped us with His image. When God sent His Son, Jesus was the physical, tangible, embodied Immanuel—God with us.

This call to us as embodied beings to love necessarily includes our physical bodies. The apostle James makes this point by saying that if a person says to someone without clothes or food, "'Go in peace; keep warm and well fed,' but does nothing about their physical needs, what good is it?" (James 2:16). In that case, loving requires tangible, embodied action.

When we think of loving others with our bodies, we usually assume it means sexual intimacy. But I believe God's call to all of us is to love with our bodies, whether or not that includes sexual intimacy with a spouse. God sees getting a cup of cold water for a child as loving that child. God sees caring for the sick, visiting a prisoner, feeding a baby, practicing hospitality, and working with our hands as ways of glorifying God and loving others.

Sexuality in Celibacy

Considering this, what is the role of sexuality in the life of an unmarried believer? If he or she is pursuing Christ and following the call to self-giving love, what is the purpose of the capacity of his or her sexuality?

First, do we think to ask this question about Jesus Christ? Was He less Himself, less alive, less complete, less capable, or less anything because He was celibate during His life on earth? Of course not! He was utterly alive, receiving life from the Father, and grounded in His identity and calling. If we are tempted to dismiss this because He was also fully divine, remember that He, like us, was "tempted in every way, just as we are" (Hebrews 4:15), and longed for home. He had "no place to lay his head" (Luke 9:58) and dealt with betrayal from a faithless friend (John 13:21). He fully and utterly understands the path of celibate, unmarried children of God because

He Himself walked it.

Second, a few practical thoughts:

We are all, married or unmarried, called to live in purity, and we all require spiritual strength and joy to learn to walk that road with Christ. It is far from being a road only unmarried believers walk. All must walk this road. Married believers may face long periods when marital sexual intimacy is impossible—perhaps due to illness, age, or trauma. Learning the discipline of turning our deepest desires for intimacy first to Jesus is non-negotiable.

Unmarried adults are not asexual beings outside of marriage. The healthy sexuality of unmarried adults reflects the image of God as much as the healthy sexuality of married adults. The real issue is how our full and flourishing Christ-given identity integrates being secure as a man or woman and our sexuality as it is healed.

There is real and true suffering in walking the path of obedience to Christ. Our bodies are no exception. In this, it is helpful to remember the words of Christ in the Eucharist: "This is my body given for you" (Luke 22:19). We are following in the footsteps of One who deeply understands, One who sees every tear, every fall, every unheralded quiet decision for purity. And One who has not left us alone!

Last Thoughts: Needing One Another

Living out this vision of same-sex friendship or married or single community requires friendships that supersede life circumstances. It is always simpler to maintain convenient friendships. We need one another, regardless of where we are in life. We need Christ-centered friendships that transcend inconvenience and awkwardness. Married believers need the friendship and perspective of their single friends, and singles need the fellowship and safe familial intimacy that their married friends and family can often provide. Expanding our circle by warmly welcoming others and by being humble enough to accept hospitality from others is a long journey. God has given us His family to share this journey of learning to love, and we miss His bounty when we choose our friendships based on external similarities rather than on shared identity in Christ.

May our joy be full in Christ, and may its overflow nourish friendships in all corners of our lives.

Bob Ragan's Story

In 2004, during a quiet time, Jesus asked me to marry Him. This stark question stopped me in my tracks. At that moment, I discerned that Jesus was not asking me to embrace celibacy, but to embrace a level of relational intimacy married couples pursue. They no longer live independent lives, but choose to share their lives as one. They choose to be present to one another, joining their plans, hopes, and dreams. Jesus was inviting me into a more intimate relationship with Him, becoming less independent and more aligned with His heart.

How did Bob respond?

One day in 2007, as I was about to prepare my dinner, I sensed a tug on my heart. Immediately I knew that Jesus was inviting me into a quiet time. Instead of going into the customary place in my living room, I went straight toward my bedroom. Within seconds, I was on my knees, which turned quickly into what I call "carpet time," being face down on the rug. From the depths of my being rose these words: *Jesus, I have no place in my heart for anyone else but You*. These words kept rising repeatedly.

Nothing unusual had happened that day—no heart-wrenching appointment, no deep revelation. But when those words leaped from my depths, I knew Jesus was calling me to celibacy.

Later I shared with a few friends what had happened, and was immediately confronted with "No, you're to be married!" and "You're going to make a great dad!" Not one individual asked me what God was telling me. I was experiencing the existing prejudice toward celibacy. The reaction was so strong that I stopped telling others about the invitation the Lord had extended to me.

A few months later, a friend I will call Mark gave me a message he believed was from God. Mark had received the word the previous year when I had intended to pursue a deeper relationship with a woman to whom I had been attracted. I had asked Mark to pray for me. The word he received at that time was that God had something more for me. But because Mark could not discern what the word meant, he chose to not share it with me.

Now, when I shared with Mark my perceived call to celibacy, the Lord reminded him of the word he had withheld the year before. Mark then spoke that word—that God had something more for me—and we both knew it was God's perfect timing.

My call to celibacy was not due to a sense of rejection or a passive reaction to loneliness. It was not an acquiescing due to my disappointing relationships with women.

My whole being had responded to Jesus' invitation. It had come unexpectedly, not grounded in a reaction to something from my day or in my life.

Since that day in 2007, I wear a silver ring on my left hand, which has the words I am my beloved's and my beloved is mine. This symbolizes my celibate call unto Jesus.

Is it an easy calling? No. It has proven to be a formative experience. It has challenged me continually to die to self, but without loss of my identity. I am more aware of my daily choices. It has taken my cognitive, doctrinal truths about Jesus and made them far more experiential. I find myself in conversation with Jesus throughout my day.

There is a cost for accepting my calling to celibacy. Since it is a calling, however, an invitation from God, He provides for the cost I have experienced. And the returns from Him far outweigh what I have paid.

Wrapping up

In walking the road of singleness and in navigating same-sex friendships, we must rely on God's Spirit to guide and fill us. He has given us Himself, His Word, and His people to sustain us on our journey. He has not left us alone and will never forsake us.

Prayer

Lord, You state in Your Word that it is not good for man to be alone. You have created me as a relational being. You want me to know You and others in ways that are healthy and life-giving. Entering into community with healthy friendships furthers my process of becoming and overcoming.

I need healthy friendships but am often hesitant about or even fearful of them. My past brokenness has created patterns and attitudes that have limited my becoming known. I have also experienced rejection at the hands of others, which has resulted in my being defensive or reactive. I am too well acquainted with grief, isolation, and loneliness.

Holy Spirit, please search my heart and expose those wounds that limit my capacity to relate to others. Reveal any lack of understanding, faulty beliefs, or misinterpretations that create barriers to engaging with others in healthy friendships. Where am I in reaction? How have I buried Your desire for me to become known in community? Reveal any red flags that arise, signaling past wounds that are interfering with the present. Please help me tear down any defensive walls I have built due to self-protective coping mechanisms.

Lord, You are sovereign and guide my steps. You cause the steps of others to cross my path. Please help me to remain present to those You have placed around me. Help me see them as opportunities—not only for me to receive healing through them, but also for me to be used as an instrument of healing in their lives.

Holy Spirit reveal to me where I have embraced singleness as an identity. Instead of singleness being a state in which I find myself, how do I view it as something wrong with me? How do I view singleness as a "holding tank' until I am married? How have I made an idol of marriage? How do I view my life as worth something less than if I were married?

Help me Holy Spirit to take off the label of single. Help me to see how in my current state of singleness, I am more available for the advancement work of Your kingdom purposes. I confess any ways in which I have despised my current state. Open my eyes to see the wonderful opportunities which exist because of my singleness. Jesus, I bring to Your cross any bitterness, cynicism, anxiety, impatience, and fear. As I do so, please come and fill these places with Your presence, mercy, and love. May I come to know Your joy in the midst of my state of singleness. Lord Jesus, thank You for calling me Your friend. I ask for Your help and guidance to increase my experience of greater intimacy with You. My ability to trust You will rise as I grow in my process of knowing You. As I trust You more, I will be able to extend trust to those You have placed around me.

Jesus, You walked in the state of singleness. You are well acquainted with the challenges I face as one who is single. May I be centered in You as I bear Your image in my singleness. You have established a calling on my life. Holy Spirit, please help me live my life with gladness and singleness of heart, focused on You and not my circumstances. May I live a chaste life that is one of integrity. May my being a gift to others cause them to become all they can be in You, Lord.

Soul Work

1. What fears or hesitations prevent you from being present and engaged in the community around you?

2. How have you viewed your singleness as a deficit or holding pattern until you are married?

3. Put in your own words what it means to be single-minded in your devotion to Jesus. Use examples from your life that illustrate how you display this devotion.

Journaling Moment

We are bombarded through the media with many examples of broken and destructive friendships. "Friends with benefits" (i.e., non-romantic friendships that include sex) and "hooking up" (anonymous sexual encounters) are activities our culture promotes. Romance has become an idol with television channels devoted to it. It is a rare movie or television program that portrays healthy and life-giving friendship. Ask the Holy Spirit to reveal how our society and culture have affected you in your thinking or emotions regarding friendship. Ask Him to reveal how your past has influenced your capacity to be present in close friendships.

NINETEEN

Healthy Marriage

BY BOB AND TERRI PERDUE

THAT IS WHY A MAN LEAVES HIS FATHER AND MOTHER AND IS UNITED TO HIS WIFE, AND THEY BECOME ONE FLESH.

– GENESIS 2:24

As we have journeyed together along this path through the wilderness, it has become clear that one of our deepest desires is intimacy—to know and be known and accepted at the deepest level of who we are. Our struggles with sexual and relational brokenness have almost certainly affected our ability to experience intimacy in meaningful ways. For some, it has meant our putting up walls that keep people and God at arm's length, not risking the potential hurt of an intimate relationship. For others, it has resulted in our throwing ourselves into relationship after relationship, looking and longing for that sense of intimacy.

On a human level, marriage is God's ordained path for us to experience the kind of intimacy for which we were created. But Paul makes it clear that a call to singleness allows one to experience a fulfilling intimacy with God that is less distracted (1 Corinthians 7). For those whose desire for physical and relational intimacy continues to burn within them, marriage is God's ordained path (1 Corinthians 7:9). The decision to pursue singleness or marriage is a personal one that must be made between you and God.

I am sure you have heard that those who are being trained to recognize counterfeit money spend more time studying the real thing rather than the counterfeit because it allows them to recognize the flaws. Let us approach marriage in the same way. There is no question that humankind's fall into sin has affected the way we experience intimacy and marriage. Marriage was instituted by God before the Fall, however, so there is an ideal, a relational flow that was designed to make a marriage work. Let us examine that first.

God's Ideal for Marriage...

We find this ideal for marriage in Genesis 2. It started with God Himself: "In the beginning God..." (Genesis 1:1). He is the source of all things, including relationships. He is the source of life, the source of love, the source of power to choose, the source of our identity. All things flow from Him into us. God, as the source, chose to make humankind in His image. He created Adam as a reflection of who He is. He created Adam in relationship with Himself. (They walked together in the cool of the day.) He gave Adam His identity. (The name *Adam* is the Hebrew word for *man*.) He gave Adam a job to do: He was to work and take care of the Garden. (It makes sense that when man became disconnected from God as his source of identity, he turned to his job as the source. Many men tend to define themselves by what they "do.") He gave Adam the freedom to choose between life and death.

As we read through Genesis 2, it seems that this was the perfect setup. Adam was connected to an all-powerful source in a loving relationship; He was placed in a perfect environment, given a meaningful task to accomplish, and granted volitional freedom. God stated emphatically, however, that it was "not good for the man to be alone" (Genesis 2:18). What was missing? Adam's need for relational intimacy, which was not being met on a human level. In this way, Adam was created "needy."

Some will balk at this word because we have been taught that neediness is a weakness, a flaw. But neediness is a motivator, a driver. Neediness drives us into relationship—with God and with others. Certainly, neediness was complicated by the Fall, but it is clear that man was created with this need before the Fall.

What follows in the narrative of Genesis 2 is a little comical if we interpret it in the light of today's "man." Men historically do not consider themselves needy. God doesn't tell Adam he is needy; He allows him to discover it for himself (as we saw in chapter 9). Right after God says it is not good for the man to be alone, God instructs Adam to name the animals. The animals most likely came in pairs, and the result was that "no suitable helper" was found for Adam (Genesis 2:20). He realized that he needed someone, too. This is when God put Adam to sleep, took out the rib from his side (which speaks of equality), and used it to form Eve.

Eve, like Adam, was created in God's image. She had a relationship with God. She had God as her source. She was taken from Adam (they originated as one), and upon creation, she was brought to Adam (Genesis 2:22). She was *not* given a job; she was given a relationship. (It makes sense that when woman became disconnected from God as her source of identity, she turned to relationships as her source. Many women tend to define themselves by their relationships.)

So now, in this ideal setup, we have three persons. How do they connect and relate? It is clear that God has not replaced Himself as the source for Adam and Eve. They are still fully dependent on Him for all their needs. What He has done is create a channel for meeting those needs. In the ideal marriage, the husband and wife will depend on God to meet their needs while choosing to minister to each other's needs as God's love, power, and grace flow through them. We might illustrate this relationship using a triangle with arrows.

As we depend on God to meet our needs, this dependence draws us into a closer, more intimate relationship with Him. This intimacy with God produces holiness of character in us, which touches the way we act in relationship with others. As we allow God to empower us to minister to the deep needs of our spouse, we are drawn into a closer, more intimate relationship

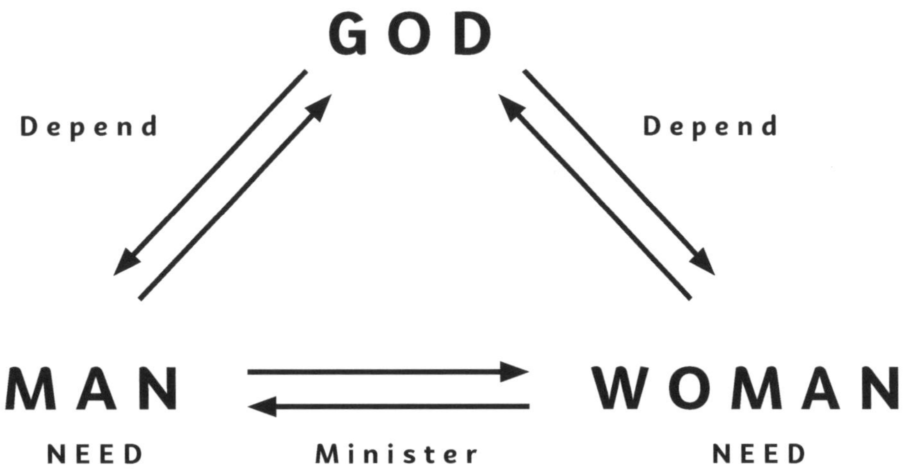

with him or her. This intimacy and holiness is the goal of marriage.

This sacred intimacy between God, husband, and wife is so powerful that Paul compares it to the deep, intimate relationship that Christ has with His Church (Ephesians 5:22–33).

... And My Sexual and Relational Brokenness

We might end the last paragraph with, "And they lived happily ever after." None of us enters marriage, however, with the purity, innocence, and full dependence on God that Adam and Eve did. We enter marriage with our suitcases stuffed with relational, emotional, and spiritual issues. This baggage usually leads to some pretty serious flaws in the marital ideal. Here are just a few.

Depending on Each Other Rather than God

Entering into marriage without a vital, dependent relationship with God sets us up for relational idolatry. We look to the other person to meet our needs. The list of needs we bring into the marriage varies, based on our history, but there are two common themes:

- Significance—the sense that I matter, that I have value and make a difference in the world.
- Love—a convinced awareness that I am cherished, accepted for who I am unconditionally.

Although both men and women need significance and love, Paul's commands in Ephesians seem to indicate that men primarily look for significance over love and women primarily look for love over significance:

> However, each one of you also must love his wife as he loves himself, and the wife must respect her husband.
>
> – Ephesians 5:33

You can see how this is a setup for us, in our fallen state, to fail. We are not capable of fully meeting another person's need for love or significance. We can minister to that need in tangible ways, but we cannot meet it. Only God can do that. When we depend on our spouse to meet our needs, we will always end up disappointed and disillusioned.

Reacting to Hurt

Since depending on a person to meet our needs is a setup for failure, husbands and wives will experience hurt. When someone hurts us, we tend to back away. Intimacy is moving toward another, but hurt causes us to move away into isolation. In isolation, we tend to wallow in our hurt and allow negative self-talk to dominate our minds. We rehearse all the past failures of our spouse that connect with this current failure and begin to build up a wall of resentment, creating emotional distance.

This emotional distance makes communication difficult and often results in hurling "missiles" at each other over the emotional walls—missiles that start with the word *you*. These accusatory statements cause the other to retreat further and perhaps launch a counterattack of *you* statements meant to self-justify and equal the score. Sometimes a spouse chooses to hurl not verbal missiles but torpedoes of silence under the emotional walls—passive-aggressive behaviors meant to hurt the other person.

Resignation

At some point, without meaningful conversation and reconciliation, couples make an internal decision to accept the emotional distance as the norm and make the best of the situation. Living like roommates, they can function, be cordial, go on vacation, and appear happy. However, they are not experiencing the intimacy for which they long.

Looking Elsewhere to Get Our Needs Met

The desire for intimacy and the need for significance and love do not go away. Some people can shut down their desire while others go looking for other avenues of fulfillment.

Men can try to find significance in their jobs, burying themselves in work to be successful or to get praise. Other men become obsessed with sports, identifying with a winning team, and finding some sense of significance in that connection. Some men believe the lie that, while their wives are not able to meet their needs, there may be another woman out there who can, so they open themselves to an extramarital affair or a fantasy life filled with pornography.

A woman's need for love may find some fulfillment in motherhood. Pouring love into her children and receiving from them in return can be very fulfilling. Other women seek security in material things when security in love is not happening. The perfect house, the perfect body, or the perfect social status may become a driver. And some women believe the lie that another man can meet their need, opening themselves to an extramarital affair or an online fantasy life.

Jesus and Your Marriage

After reading the subtitle just above, you may be asking, "What does Jesus have to do with my marriage?" My answer is, "Everything!" Since Jesus came to reconnect us to the Father as our source (John 14:6), He makes it possible for me to make all the choices needed to repair a broken marriage.

Here are a few choices that will get you moving in the right direction.

Choose to Depend on God

You can fully depend on God as your source because Jesus has completely reconciled you to Him. This begins with "firing" your spouse from this job. You have to relinquish the right to have him, or her meet your needs. You must give up and surrender every expectation to God. This does not mean you have no hope that your spouse will ever minister to your needs in a meaningful way. Ministry is essential for intimacy to be experienced between two people.

However, the truth is, your spouse may have shut down trying to minister because your expectation to have your needs met is so high. So fire him or her! Confess to God that He alone is the One who can meet your needs. Instead of spending your time trying to fix your spouse, spend your time cultivating a vibrant, dependent relationship with God. Focus on intimacy with Him because He promises, "You will seek me and find me when you seek me with all your heart" (Jeremiah 29:13).

Choose to Forgive

The emotional walls and distance that have been built up by marital hurt can be torn down only through forgiveness. We dealt with forgiveness in chapter 13, and I won't review all that is involved in that process.[68] Remember that you can forgive because Christ lives in you and He is a forgiving person.

Also, remember that forgiveness and reconciliation are not the same things. You are releasing your spouse from the expectation that he or she can repay the "debt" you feel you are owed, but you are not yet rebuilding the relationship.

Choose Reconciliation through Ministry

Loving ministry to your spouse is possible through the love of Christ that is in you. Since hurt has caused you both to move away from each other into isolation, with the walls torn down through forgiveness, you can now begin to move toward one another into intimacy through ministry.

[68]I have written a chapter on forgiveness, with an exercise to help guide you through it, in my book *Ten Life Choices* (CrossHouse, 2010).

Clearly communicate with each other the needs you are bringing into the relationship. Talk about tangible ways those needs can be ministered to while releasing your spouse from the expectation that he or she can fully meet those needs. Wake up every day and ask God to show you some way to practically minister to the needs of your spouse that day.

A fuller explanation of the role of needs and how to minister can be found in *The Marriage Builder* by Larry Crabb (Zondervan, enlarged edition 2013). Tangible ways to love your spouse can be found in the book *The 5 Love Languages* by Gary Chapman (Northfield, 2015).

A Word About Love

In his book, Sacred Marriage, Gary Thomas states, "Any mature, spiritually sensitive view of marriage must be built on the foundation of mature love rather than romanticism."[69] Those of us who struggle with sexual and relational brokenness must be aware that we may have eroticized and romanticized our concept of love to such a degree that the realization of our ideal is impossible. The culture we live in idolizes romantic love, while God promotes a mature, selfless, intimate love. Romanticism is not love itself; it is an expression of love.

In seeking to move into an intimate, loving relationship with another person, it is not mandatory that it begins with romanticism. This part of love can be very difficult for a sexually broken person to access until a mature, loving relationship is established. In pursuing a relationship, be honest about this struggle and open to how God may want to bring healing into it.

A Word About Infidelity

God's desire that a man and wife "become" one flesh is not just about the physical act of sex. It is a process of moving toward intimacy in body, soul, and spirit. When someone goes outside the marriage and forms a one-flesh union with another person sexually, it violates the marriage bond and profoundly hinders the move toward intimacy. Do not take this lightly. Jesus felt so strongly against infidelity that He called it grounds for divorce—even though God's ideal for marriage is that it is for life.

[69]Gary Thomas, *Sacred Marriage* (Zondervan, reprint edition 2015), p. 16.

I don't believe Jesus was saying that all infidelity leads to divorce. The truth is, when one spouse is unfaithful, divorce becomes an option for the wronged spouse. That spouse should seek God in full dependence for direction and guidance as to whether to forgive and seek to reconcile or to forgive and seek to divorce. If the decision is to reconcile, the wronged spouse should seek wise counsel to set boundaries and accountability. The guilty spouse must fully own the sin without excuse or rationalization and submit to a reasonable plan of rebuilding trust.

Remember that reconciliation cannot happen without forgiveness. Seeking to reconcile before fully forgiving the guilty spouse will result in ambivalence, resentment, and a desire for revenge.

A Word About Same-Sex Attraction

When it comes to the question of whether someone who struggles with same-sex attraction should seek a heterosexual marital relationship, there are no easy answers. Again, this is a highly personal decision, made while fully leaning on God for direction and wisdom. Perhaps a few reminders of truth may help steer you in the right direction.

1. You are not defined by your sexual attraction. There is much more to you than which sex you are attracted to.
2. Marriage is based on mature love, not romantic love. Romantic love is an expression of love that grows in intimacy.
3. Entering into heterosexual marriage will never "cure" same-sex attraction.
4. Intimacy with God is to be sought before intimacy with a potential spouse. As we grow in dependence on Him, the path ahead becomes clear.
5. Singleness is a calling from God and not "settling."
6. Honesty is the only basis for a lasting, committed relationship. Cultivating a relationship with someone without sharing the struggle with same-sex attraction is a violation of the relationship.
7. No matter what your sexual attraction, marriage is monogamous. We are never justified in seeking sexual satisfaction outside of our marriage.

A Personal Testimony from Terri Perdue

After over 40 years of marriage to a man who struggles with same-sex attraction and sexual addiction, the Lord has taught me many things. I have learned that my worth as a woman and a wife does not come from my husband but from my Heavenly Father who loves me unconditionally and can be trusted 100%. This involved two choices on my part. I had to choose to relinquish my husband and choose to fully surrender to God and His truth.

At the beginning of our marriage, my relationship with my husband was very codependent. I was trying to get life out of him and leaned into him for my identity and worth. Through a series of events including my husband's severe health issues, the loss of five babies to miscarriage and a complete emotional breakdown that led to a stay in a psychiatric hospital, I began a real personal RELATIONSHIP with God and making Him my source for life and identity.

Years later, when I became aware of my husband's infidelity, it became clear to me that I could not fix him or heal the brokenness, I needed to relinquish my husband to God completely. My own journey over these years had prepared me for this choice. Notice I did not say abandon. I never stopped praying for him or ministering to his needs, but I stopped trying to fix him or fix our marriage. This freed me to focus on my own healing and allowed God to work on my husband in His own way. I always say that when I finally got out of the way, God was free to work.

Of course, just like with every other part of healing, relinquishment is both a choice and a process.

When I made the choice to relinquish my husband God impressed upon me to symbolize my choice by taking a picture of my husband and nailing it to a small wooden cross which I kept in my drawer and about which my husband knew nothing. In the weeks and months that followed, anytime I would start trying to fix him or make the situation better, I would look at that cross and remember the decision I made and say to myself, "God's got this and I can trust Him!"

Trusting God is key to this whole process. To let go of my husband, I needed to learn to fully trust God and surrender to Him. But before I could trust Him, I needed to know who He really is. God had me on a journey of learning and experiencing who He is since my breakdown. I had begun to learn that God is good, and He will meet my needs because I am His daughter, and He loves me unconditionally. Now it was time to fully surrender to those truths. God used the process of journaling through some truths from His Word to prepare me for this surrender.

God is faithful – Psalm 145:13b
God is with me – Isaiah 43:2-3a
God is my provider – Philippians 4:19
God is my refuge – Psalm 62:8
God is my rest and hope – Psalm 62:5
God is my Father – Psalm 89:26, Galatians 4:6-7
God is my peace and strength – Isaiah 26:3-4

God used an illustration from The Marriage Builder by Larry Crabb to help me with this surrender. In this illustration, I am standing on a cliff of safety with an abyss of fear in front of me. In my past, my husband had been that cliff of safety, but now it was clear that I could not fully depend on him. I needed to see myself connected securely to God so that when my husband could not love me or meet my needs, I did not fear falling into the abyss of rejection (fear, loneliness, the feeling that I don't matter) but would be held securely by a loving and powerful Father. This also freed me to minister to my husband through the pain because my needs were being met totally by God during this time.

Stepping off of that cliff of safety (relinquishing my husband) was difficult because initially, it felt like I was free-falling into the abyss until I experienced the Father's embrace. At that point,

I did know that God loved me and that I mattered to Him. However, I wrongly believed that this meant He would protect me by letting me know if my husband acted out again. Even though I wasn't aware of it, I was not simply trusting God, I was trusting Him to protect me in the way I wanted to be protected, by letting me know if my husband acted out.

After years of sobriety, while I was trusting God, my husband acted out sexually again, and I felt like God let me down. While my relationship with God kept me from falling into the abyss of rejection, I experienced many of the negative feelings associated with that abyss and even began to doubt that I could count on Him. Struggling through my emotions with God, He began working on me to release my fears further and surrender fully to His love. This was no longer about Bob, this was about me and my relationship with my loving Father.

Several years later, God would deepen this experience when my husband and I went zip-lining in Hawaii. When my husband asked me to go zip-lining God clearly impressed on me that this was His way of helping me fully release not just my husband but all of my fears about the future of my life and marriage. On each platform I envisioned my Father's arms and Him saying, "Jump, I have you, you can always trust me, don't let your fears in life have any control over you, I've got you… JUMP and experience me in EVERY area of life!"

I cannot completely trust that my husband will not act out again or that God will let me know if he does, but I can trust that God loves me, He is with me, I matter to Him, and I will be okay.

Learning all of this has given me the security and strength to forgive my husband for his infidelity and to be open to the risk of building trust again. I have learned to go to the Lord for my needs to be met and to communicate honestly with my husband about ways we can minister to each other.

I never imagined I would experience this kind of pain when I said my marriage vows, but I am so thankful that God has and still is bringing deeper intimacy and healing in our marriage. I love and respect my husband today in a deeper way than I ever have and look forward to that increasing in the years ahead. God has shown me and can show you that He makes beauty from ashes. God is good!

A Personal Testimony from Bob Perdue

As I write this chapter, I am moving toward my fortieth wedding anniversary. I have struggled with same-sex attraction since puberty and married at nineteen in hopes that it would fix the problem. I have spent many years in recovery ministry and developed a deep, intimate relationship with God, but my sexual attraction has not changed. I do not find myself looking at women sexually the way I do men.

During our forty years of marriage, I have gone through two periods of infidelity. Both times, my wife sought the Lord diligently and sensed Him telling her that she was to remain married to me. This was certainly from the Lord and not due to anything I deserved. Both times we followed the steps that I have outlined in this chapter. We sought counsel, worked on our individual relationships with God, set up boundaries and accountability to rebuild trust, and committed to minister to each other's needs.

I can honestly say that I love my wife; and because that love has grown and matured through pain and joy, I can express my love to her in romantic and sexual ways that are satisfying to both of us. It has not always been easy, and we have not always been "happy," but we have experienced a level of intimacy that I fear most couples lack since my wife and I have chosen to share life together in our brokenness and our healing.

Prayers

For Those Not Married

Father, I surrender my future afresh and anew to You. I ask You to lead my mind and my heart as related to the subject of marriage. I am willing to remain single if this is Your plan for my life, and I am willing to seek marriage if You call me to it. I will strive neither to be single nor to be married but will stay fully surrendered to Your plan for my life. I refuse to allow any of my current brokenness to define me fully or to disqualify me from marriage. I choose to believe that You can bring the healing and wholeness I need.

For Those Who Are Married

Father, I surrender my marriage afresh and anew to You. I choose to align my will with Yours as it relates to my marriage, and I ask that You empower my will to choose:

- To relinquish any dependence on my spouse to meet my needs.
- To stop looking to other people, accomplishments, or pleasures to meet my needs.
- To totally depend on You, my Source, for all my needs.
- To receive forgiveness for my sins against my marriage.
- To extend forgiveness to my spouse for his or her sins against our marriage.
- To pursue my spouse by ministering faithfully to his or her needs.
- To ask You to fill my heart with a mature love for my spouse.

Soul Work

1. Write an honest paragraph about how you feel about being married. Allow yourself to express the thoughts that normally flow through your mind as you think about the prospect of marriage, the state of your current marriage, or whether to remain married. It is important not to write about what you "should" be feeling but how you feel. Satan uses negative self-talk disguised as truth to help us form opinions that keep us stuck in our present state. After you have written your paragraph, ask God to reveal how much of what you "feel" is His truth and how much is the voice of Satan speaking through your past, your brokenness, or your lack of faith.

2. As you read through the ideal for marriage in this chapter, which part seems the most difficult? Dependence on God? Realization of your own neediness? Commitment to minister to another? Dealing with hurt in the relationship? Are you opening your heart to intimacy?

3. How might the definition of mature love in this chapter help you as you pursue intimacy?

4. For those who struggle with same-sex attraction, how do the truths shared in that section of this chapter help you as you move forward?

Journaling Moment

The chart in this chapter reveals how we are to depend on God for meeting our needs as we minister to one another as husband and wife. Ask the Holy Spirit to reveal where you may be depending on your spouse rather than ministering to him or her. Where am I transferring my needs onto my spouse rather than going to God first for those needs? Seek the Lord's direction on how to shift your dependency onto Him.

SECTION 4

LOVING OUR PROCESS ARIGHT

Addressing what is required for us to live lives of holiness and integrity.

Loving Our Process Aright

Many who read *Path*, struggle with addictions in one form or another. Common sense would place chapters 21 and 22 earlier in the book. However, without the understanding gleaned from preceding sections, the focus would be on *doing* instead of *being*. We would be looking for a method rather than the Personhood of Jesus. Section 4 will reveal how approaching our process through forms of behavior modification and performance eventually will fail.

Chapters 1-19 revealed how the true nature and character of God impacts our souls. They revealed what issues and challenges limit us in our capacity to become and overcome. Section 3 especially explained how the world has greatly drifted from what God intended for us to be as women and men. Without knowing the way we were designed to be in relationship, we remain in illusion and non-reality.

Chapter 20 illuminates why the presence of suffering is a reality in every Christian's walk and part of our becoming process. We will see in chapter 21 how temptation, instead of shaming us, can bring revelation of what God has accomplished in our lives. Addressing addictions in Chapter 22, we will learn how grace, rather than sobriety, frees us from the legalistic prison of performance.

We are strangers in a strange land. We are sojourners on pilgrimage, journeying to the home God has prepared for us. You have been on a journey with me coming through *Path*. It is a journey in which I pray you have gained a greater capacity to know and see God aright. My prayer is that you will know how God has been leading and guiding you since you drew your first breath and will continue to do so until you draw your last. Then you will see His face unveiled, saying to you, "Welcome, My child. You are home with me now and forevermore."

TWENTY

Holiness and Suffering

YOU SHALL BE HOLY TO ME, FOR I THE LORD AM HOLY AND HAVE SEPARATED YOU FROM THE PEOPLES, THAT YOU SHOULD BE MINE.

- LEVITICUS 20:26, ESV

Sexuality and sensuality saturate the world around us. We can hardly get through a day without a visual encounter with a sexual or sensual image. Sex is the hook that draws our attention and entices us to linger or give a second look to an advertisement. Companies promote their products this way because it guarantees attention. They know their markets and target audiences.

But we are called to be separate from the world. God's Word provides instructions for the proper expression of our relationships and sexuality. We must search the Scriptures for ourselves to ascertain God's parameters for our sexuality. In my own story, I could not simply rely on others who stated that homosexual behavior was unacceptable in God's eyes. I had to read the Scriptures for myself and discern what God had defined as holy, pure, and righteous. This discerning applies to everyone.

No matter what form of relational or sexual brokenness you may struggle with, searching the Scriptures for His truth is non-optional. We must, as Joshua 24:15 states, "choose for yourselves this day whom you will serve."

God's intent for our relationships and sexuality does not conform to current societal norms. Once our culture threw out the centrality of the Scriptures, it opened the door for an ever-growing variety of sexual expression. Christians must determine what we know to be true and right in God's eyes, and then, through the power of the Holy Spirit, choose to act on those beliefs. We must be set apart from secular cultural and societal influences.

The question remains, Is Jesus truly Lord of our lives, or only a Savior.

Walking in Holiness

We find many references in the Scriptures to holiness. Leviticus 20:26, quoted at the beginning of this chapter, indicates that we are to be holy because God is holy. When we are in a true relationship with Him, holiness manifests itself within us. Holiness is found, then, in being—a state of "aliveness" within our personhood. God says not to try to achieve holiness, but to be holy. Holiness is not simply the result of a choice of behaviors but is a state of being and identity.

The Hebrew and Greek words commonly used for *holy* or *holiness* in the Scriptures imply separation, consecration to God. Holiness is being in the right and sacred relationship with God. Our sanctification process, through the presence of God's love and grace, changes us into the likeness of God. This is an ongoing progression as God establishes His character in us. God, Himself sets us apart. Once Jesus is our Lord, our right doing is the fruit of His first setting us apart.

Holiness involves being intimately devoted to God. As believers, we follow His commands and conduct our lives by His guidelines, including those regarding our relationships and sexuality. We walk with holiness as a forethought, living our lives in a holy manner. As the Lord indicates in 1 Peter 1:14–15:

> As obedient children, do not conform to the evil desires you had when you lived in ignorance. But just as he who called you is holy, so be holy in all you do.

Holiness is more than living a sacred life. It requires a deeper knowing. Essentially, holiness is being characteristically Godlike. It is the ongoing process of becoming more Christ-like, bearing the fullness of His image. Holiness is rooted in who *we are* in Christ and who Christ is *in us*.

When I speak in men's groups on purity, I frequently ask three questions. First, I ask, "Is there anything you can do to make yourself more righteous?" The quick and resounding answer is no. We find our righteousness in Christ alone. He is our true center, our true self, where we find our righteousness.

Then I ask, "Is there anything you can do to make yourself more holy?" There is some hesitation in answering yes or no to this question. We do not find our holiness in what we do but rather in who we are in Christ. If I try to be holy, then I am striving with restless activism, caught up in doing instead of being. I lose sight of the fact that I cannot make myself more holy than I already am through simply abiding in Jesus.

Let me clarify a point before going further. For us to stand and remain in holiness requires action on our part. Obedience to God's Word makes holiness manifest within us, as we align our will with His. But we must never think it is our actions that make us holy. The cross of Jesus restored our right and holy relationship with the Father. The Holy Spirit (as we saw in chapter 7) empowers us to rise in our true selves. We rest upon the righteousness and holiness of Jesus as we stand in our true selves. Nevertheless, obedience is required for us continuing to stand and live out of our true selves.

My final question to the men's groups, which often yields puzzled looks, is this: "Is there anything you can do to make yourself purer?" Although there is some hesitation, the typical response I hear is yes, of course, we can make ourselves purer.

But this question reveals whether we are finding our identity in Jesus or finding it in our behaviors. As soon as I think I can make myself purer, the emphasis is on my doing rather than in my being.

The question I need to ask myself when tempted with impurity is not what I must do maintain my purity. The question to ask is, "*What is motivating me toward unrighteousness*"—being unholy and impure? Yes, practical steps are helpful here, as I will discuss in chapters 21 and 22. However, I need to focus on why this temptation is drawing me out of my true center in Jesus.

Part of our process in embracing holiness is embracing our bodies as holy. We do not cover up our genitals because they are unclean, but because they are sacred and holy unto God. Holiness involves recognizing that our bodies are holy because God created them to reflect His image and that He loves them. Holiness enables us to see, live, and experience God's plan of love and communion in our bodies.

To embrace holiness, we must embrace the fullness of God. It is opening body, soul, spirit, to all that pertains to God Himself. Our God-given desire to know and be known connects our yearning with that which is good, holy, and true. If we are to embrace holiness in our sexuality and relationships, we must grasp the larger reality of the holiness that encompasses every aspect of our lives.

Purity of Heart

Create in me a pure heart, O God, and renew a steadfast spirit within me.

– Psalm 51:10

Our calling as Christian men and women is intentionally to follow God's truth and goodness. Before inviting Jesus to be both Lord and Savior, our hearts focused narcissistically on the pursuit of egocentric happiness and pleasure. We were self-focused. Once we are born again, however, we open ourselves to God and, through His redeeming work within, become new creations. Redemption has allowed us to return to the purity of heart that existed in the Garden before the Fall.

To embrace purity is to live a life free from immorality. Living a pure life goes beyond it being a concept or theory. It is not Pharisaical, focused solely on outward appearance. Living a holy and pure life, one that is chaste, is not living according to a list of rules and regulations. A pure and holy life is living not with the absence of something but with the presence of *Someone*. To be pure in heart is to live out of our true center, our true self, in Jesus.

In Matthew 5:8, Jesus says that the pure of heart "will see God." Notice Jesus associates being pure in heart with vision. Being pure in heart is embracing the capacity to see with God's eyes and knowing His heart. Purity is a state of being and a state of mind. Being pure in heart is living each moment with

A PURE AND HOLY LIFE IS LIVING NOT WITH THE ABSENCE OF SOMETHING BUT WITH THE PRESENCE OF SOMEONE.

forethought, walking intentionally in a state of purity regarding all that we see, think, and do.

Purity is not exclusively exterior. Being pure in heart focuses us on our inner being first, which will result in exterior change. Our hearts are circumcised unto the Lord; we are in covenant relationship with Him. David cried out in Psalm 51 for a pure heart, after his sexual fall with Bathsheba. God does create new hearts in us, but He does not prevent us from choosing to be impure; choosing to stand in the false self.

Pursuing moral living, based on the idea that this is what a Godly man or woman must do, will ultimately fail. Timothy says we go after what is holy out of a pure heart: "Flee the evil desires of youth and pursue righteousness, faith, love, and peace, along with those who call on the Lord out of a pure heart" (2 Timothy 2:22).

There is something sacramental, holy, and pure about how we, as men and women, walk relationally together in unity. The creation of Adam and Eve was the pinnacle of God's creation. Moral goodness and purity of heart abounded in this original body creation.

Wholeness and purity of heart affect our thinking, relationships, attractions, desire, and behavioral choices. Walking in a state of purity is living, moving, and having our being in Jesus (Acts 17:28). Purity of heart is a redemptive result of walking in our true selves, being one with Christ. We can be pure in heart because Jesus made a way for us to do so. It is a state of being rather than a state of doing.

Drawing a Line in the Sand

> But among you, there must not be even a hint of sexual immorality, or of any kind of impurity, or of greed because these are improper for God's holy people.
>
> – Ephesians 5:3, NIV

> Let it not be once named once among you. (KJV)

> Must not even be mentioned among you. (NRSV)

Paul is emphasizing a serious point regarding sexual immorality. Not even a hint of it, he said, should be spoken of among us. In our sexually saturated world, it requires true dedication and commitment to ensure that there is no hint of it in our lives. It is very clear that we as believers not be associated with sexual immorality of any kind.

A key Greek word in Ephesians 5:3 is *porneia*, which is translated "sexual immorality." This is the root of the word for pornography. Those in Paul's time understood this word to refer to *any* immoral form of sexual behavior between any individuals outside of marriage.

The same word is used in Matthew 15:19, where Jesus warned that "out of the heart [comes] … sexual immorality (*porneia*)." Likewise, those to whom Jesus was speaking understood its meaning.

Those today who insist that Jesus said nothing about homosexual behavior do not comprehend these verses from Matthew and Ephesians. It was not necessary for Jesus or Paul to provide a list of unacceptable sexual behaviors; the word *porneia* covered them all.

Any form of sexual behavior outside of heterosexual marriage is considered fornication and unacceptable in God's eyes. Are you willing to walk with this knowledge and truth? What allowances do you make that, if measured out, is more than "even a hint"? Too often, I see that those who make small allowances eventually descend into paralyzing addictive behaviors. Where have you drawn a line in the sand regarding your sexual activity, saying, "I will not cross this line," only to cross it and then create a new line of demarcation?

Our culture makes the experience of sexual intimacy into an idol and necessity. Sexual intimacy is the world's primary way to become known because God no longer figures into the equation. Here are some of the lies the world promotes:

- Sex is necessary in order to be happy or content.
- You have to be sexually active. (Animalistic drive is considered normal.)
- If you are chaste or celibate, something is wrong with you.
- Masturbation is a physical need that must be met.
- All men think about is sex.
- A woman must give of herself sexually to please or keep a man.

This worldly philosophy bombards us constantly through media and entertainment. Because we tend to go into a passive mode when we watch multiple forms of media, our minds absorb these lies through repetitive exposure. Unless we have studied the Scriptures and determined what God's truth is, we are in danger of believing the lies we have absorbed. We need wisdom and discernment regarding what we place in our field of vision.

The world accepts lust as part of human relationships. This normalization was not so at the beginning. Christopher West writes, "If God's love constitutes man's origin, vocation, and destiny, then lust constitutes the antithesis of man's very existence."[70] Lust is a separation from God's love, focusing on the satisfaction of self apart from Him. Lust is an issue for both men and women. This is why lust is such a serious matter and not "normal" for us as believers. It is normal to fallen humankind but not to redeemed humankind.

Herein lies the danger of walking in worldly understanding. If we buy the world's lies about sex, the door for lust remains open. We must address our misbeliefs about sex and sexuality with singleness of heart. We must address what place of authority the Scriptures truly have in our lives. We must remain centered in the righteousness, holiness, and purity of Jesus.

Suffering

To embrace a life of relational and sexual integrity is to embrace a life of self-denial. "He must become greater; I must become less" (John 3:30). A life of denial requires self-sacrifice. Suffering is part of self-sacrifice. "Son though he was, he learned obedience from what he suffered" (Hebrews 5:8).

If one thing is required of us, it is to obey. Living a holy and pure life requires obedience. Embracing obedience causes change on multiple levels:

- Through the work of the Holy Spirit, my will and passions become aligned with the Father's.
- I deny myself and bear my cross daily.
- I live a chaste life with integrity regarding my relationships and the expression of my sexuality.
- Growing in intimacy with Jesus shifts the motivation for my obedience from the law and trying to be perfect to that of love.

I mentioned earlier how we draw shifting lines in the sand regarding our behaviors. Jesus has drawn and established the line for our lives. He set the standard, which in our own strength

[70]Christopher West, *Theology of the Body Explained* (Pauline Books, rev. ed., 2008), p. 228.

is impossible for us to achieve. Knowing this, however, He met the requirements of that standard, enabling us to live according to that standard through, in, and by Him.

As we see in the Hebrews text above, Jesus learned obedience through suffering. The two—obedience and suffering— are connected. If I am to live the life of Jesus, I, too, will experience suffering. I draw comfort and strength, knowing that Jesus already bore my infirmities, sorrows, and shame. Nothing catches God by surprise, and He lays out the path before us. The question is, will you follow that path? Henri Nouwen wrote:

> Suffering invites us to place our hurts in larger hands. In Christ, we see God suffering – for us. And calling us to share in God's suffering love for a hurting world. The small and even overpowering pains of our lives are intimately connected with the greater pains of Christ. Our daily sorrows are anchored in a greater sorrow and therefore a larger hope.[71]

Suffering as Part of the Christian Walk

> Enter through the narrow gate. For wide is the gate and broad is the road that leads to destruction, and many enter through it. But small is the gate and narrow the road that leads to life, and only a few find it.
>
> – Matthew 7:13–14

To enter the small gate requires that we make choices that call us to die to ourselves. Instead of going the way of the world, which can seem more appealing, we take the road that looks less appealing. Dying is not an easy experience, and suffering is part of that process. We experience suffering when

– we break away from sources of false intimacy;
– we break away from false sources of life;
– we choose to face our brokenness coming out of any area of denial or illusion.

Not only is the gate small, but the road is narrow. I have found that the road becomes

[71]Henri Nouwen, *Turn My Mourning into Dancing* (Thomas Nelson, 2004), p. 11.

narrower as I proceed on my journey home. In the process of sanctification, by excluding the ways of the flesh, world, and the devil, I make choices that narrow my path. These choices are not made through fleshly legalism, but being Spirit-led and motivated by love.

My choices often carry a degree of suffering as I continue to die to self. The great mystery of this journey is that, with each denial I make, I experience new life. What feels like restriction results in newborn freedom. The death embraced with the crucifixion became resurrection life. I keep my eyes on Jesus, who is the path ahead of me.

The reality of following Jesus is that we will—not might, but will—experience suffering in some part of our lives. Suffering arises from different sources and for different reasons. We suppress or run from our pain so often that we may also do so when we experience suffering. Therefore, it is helpful to recognize the sources of our suffering so we may know how to process it aright.

Suffering Due to Past Wounds

In section 2, we identified wounded areas from our past. It helped us identify how we reacted to those wounds and to those who inflicted them on us. The quality of relationships from our past affects our identity, our emotional well-being, and the choices we make. Experiencing broken relationships results in suffering. The suffering originates in the past but is experienced now, in the present.

When a bone is broken and not treated correctly, it does not heal properly. Doctors may have to reset it by breaking it again, to achieve true healing and proper function. Reliving the trauma of our past can be like breaking a bone again to set it aright to achieve healing.

By contrast, we are accustomed to avoiding suffering. Usually, we do not want to suffer through the facing of our pain because

- if I start to cry, I will never stop;
- if I let the pain come up, it will be too much for me;
- if I get in touch with my anger, I will lose it;
- if I relive that memory again, will it result in healing for me?

Two questions we must face are these: If I allow the pain and suffering to come to the surface, will God or others meet me in that place. Will my pain and suffering be so intense that I will never fully recover? When our bodies experience trauma, we suffer pain as our body heals.

Those who undergo knee replacements must start walking within 24 hours post-op. It is painful, but the immediate walking prevents scar tissue from forming, which will be of detriment to the healing process. Suffering is required to be able to walk later without pain.

Suffering Due to Self-Denial

Relational dysfunction in our current culture is widespread. The pursuit of sex devoid of relationship exacerbates the intimacy void within. The egotistical pursuit of pleasure and happiness narcissistically centers on me.

Our culture panders to individual rights and demands. How often have I seen individuals explode with service staff because their needs are not being met quickly enough? When individuals routinely talk on their cell phones while making purchases, they are treating sales staff as non-entities, unworthy of direct conversation: "My cell phone conversation is more important than engaging with you as a person." If the service person asks a question, I've seen individuals react as if to say, "How dare you to interrupt me with your question."

Why am I stating the above? Because to deny oneself, to any degree, is to experience suffering. Our individualistic culture, which caters to the self, urges me to balk when it comes to denying what I want, whenever I want it. I do not want to wait. I am entitled to be happy. If something makes me feel good, why should I give it up? When it comes down to holiness and purity, Satan's question recorded in Genesis pops up: *Did God really say?* It is easy to avoid suffering or rationalize it away.

But, as we stated earlier, to die to self is to embrace suffering. I may have to end a relationship, which requires me to walk away from someone I love. I may have to close down a social media account because I am living vicariously through other people. I may have to change my eating or television habits. Suffering will be part of these choices. Caught in this individualistic culture, we can find self-denial a major challenge. We need to be open to the spiritual practice of self-examination: "Holy Spirit, search my heart and expose where I am resistant to self-denial."

What are you unwilling to give up? Even when God says, *I have something so much better for you.*

Self-denial can result in the experience of grief. There are five recognized stages of grief: denial, anger, bargaining, depression, and acceptance. Self-denial that requires the severing of a relationship may cause grief. Loss of relationship may also result in suffering through a season of loneliness. Because grief and suffering can occur together, it is helpful to recognize the stages of grief.

Denial of self is the denial of ego. It requires placing God first, as our priority in our everyday living. It also requires the relinquishing of my control. I submit myself to a higher authority. I relinquish my rights at the foot of the cross, yielding myself to Jesus. Jesus had every right to defend Himself before Caiaphas and Pontius Pilate. He had every right to pass by the cup of suffering.

But Jesus was submitted and committed to doing the will of the Father. "He was oppressed and afflicted, yet he did not open his mouth; he was led like a lamb to the slaughter, and as a sheep before its shearers is silent, so he did not open his mouth" (Isaiah 53:7). "For the joy set before him, he endured the cross, scorning its shame…" (Hebrews 12:2). Jesus denied Himself for the will and purpose of the Father. He is our example.

Why Do I Have This Struggle?

Tim Keller writes,

> Some suffering is given in order to chastise and correct a person for wrongful patterns of life (as in the case of Jonah imperiled by the storm), some suffering is given "not to correct past wrongs but to prevent future ones" (as in the case of Joseph sold into slavery), and some suffering has no purpose other than to lead a person to love God more ardently for himself alone and so discover the ultimate peace and freedom.[72]

It is not infrequent that those who struggle with unwanted SSA ask the question, "God, why do I have this struggle?" Why won't these attractions go away? Why do I have this life-dominating issue? My reply is limited because only God knows the direct answer to these questions. God sees the entire picture of our lives, and we do not. As Tim Keller indicates above, one purpose of our suffering may be that we may love God with a deeper passion.

But what is the question behind the question? The question seems to indicate an underlying belief that I should not be suffering this way. Where did that belief originate?

[72]Timothy Keller, *Walking with God through Pain and Suffering* (Penguin, reprinted 2013), p. 47.

- God says that with Him, all things are possible. So why does my continuing struggle seem to be exempt from this promise?
- Why do I have to make choices that, for other Christians, are not required?
- Why, when I see Christians who seem to be experiencing freedom in life, do I have to maintain certain restrictions that appear to limit my freedom?

What is your question? How has suffering taken predominance in your daily life? Do you have tunnel vision regarding suffering such that it has obscured your capacity to see other aspects of your life? We can go through seasons of suffering that feel as if they will never end. It feels like there is no hope to rise above it.

A while back, the wife of a good friend received a very difficult, terminal cancer diagnosis. The cancer had spread and was aggressive. Her husband is a gifted ministry leader. I heard him share their story at a conference. He stated that when both he and his wife heard the diagnosis, they made a choice not to ask God why this was happening. They chose instead to accept their situation and stay present with God, together, facing the road ahead. They shared some very meaningful years before she recently passed away.

We need a change of perspective.

Some conditions—like blindness, paralysis, or amputation—will not change without divine intervention. These individuals are faced with living in the "what is" with the tension of the "not yet." Is that tension dominated by hope or despair? In all these situations, the real question is this: How will I, as a unique individual, walk through my circumstances? Can I be an overcomer amid my suffering?

Here are some questions that may be helpful to consider:

- Has suffering blocked my capacity to engage with others and God?
- Have I embraced self-hatred, self-pity, or cynicism?
- Have I become demanding of God?
- Am I unwilling to follow God farther unless He heals me?
- Am I blind to those things in my life for which I can be grateful?

Jesus took on flesh for us, knowing He would have to endure suffering the likes of which we will never experience. This is not to diminish the depths of your suffering but to encourage you to gain some perspective. Prolonged suffering can cause us to become overly self-aware and self-focused. As Jesus promised, however, He is our way. There is light at the end of the tunnel if we will but hold onto to His grace and mercy.

I firmly believe had I not battled with unwanted SSA; I would not be as in love with my Beloved as I am today. The suffering and denial I have experienced have drawn me into depths of knowing Jesus. Even so, I feel I have only scratched the surface of knowing Him.

I encourage you, then, if you are asking why you have a particular struggle, to press in with God and be real. If you question Him, avoid becoming demanding. Ask, but be open to the reality that Jesus is your way. Release what you think your life needs to be, and allow God to shape it into what He knows it can be. Allowing Jesus into your suffering, He will prove Himself faithful to walk you through it.

Processing Our Suffering with Jesus

…weeping may stay for the night, but rejoicing comes in the morning.

– Psalm 30:5

Jesus was abandoned, rejected, abused, shamed, and cursed. The pain and suffering He endured were more than we can ever fathom. Jesus, as the Son of Man, did this on our behalf. Since He identified with our suffering and humanity, we have One we can turn to who personally knows what it is like to live on this earth.

The challenge of dying to self, to walk in holiness, is difficult. It does require us to experience suffering. It does call us to deny what the world offers and what the world tells us is good. It means having to let go of the person or relationship that has become an idol in our life. It requires us to seek the Lord to meet us at the core of our suffering.

Suffering is a deeply personal experience. It often feels as if we are alone. However, we are truly never alone because Jesus dwells within, inhabiting our being. We are one with Him. To process your suffering with Jesus, you

– must allow your pain and suffering to rise to the surface
– seek the Holy Spirit to identify what you are feeling, being brutally honest

- ask the Holy Spirit to identify a specific wound or hurt so you can bring it to Jesus
- invite Jesus into the wound and suffering
- choose to remain present to the pain and suffering
- let the pain, suffering, and emotions be absorbed by His broken body on the cross
- ask Him to re-symbolize your wounds, no longer to see them as a source of victimization or defeat but as a place where Jesus' healing presence now remains
- allow Jesus to help process, reclaim, and restore that which was lost
- ask Him to strengthen you to extend forgiveness where it is needed
- ask Him to give you new vision to see this hurt or suffering
- establish the cross of Jesus in the memory of any wound

The Lord meets us in our place of suffering. Focusing on our suffering, we can become lost in it, sinking into diseased introspection. We can become bitter, angry, and cynical. We can retreat from God and community. This is why we must spend time at the foot of the cross, sitting in our pain and suffering. We allow Jesus to process it with us. We look up and out of ourselves, so our suffering does not become internalized toxicity.

Allowing Jesus to inhabit our suffering is a redemptive act. God does not allow us to suffer for the sake of suffering. By embracing the suffering in our lives, we are embracing the sufferings of Jesus. Following the above steps, Jesus redeems our suffering, causing it to become something of benefit to us. If we see life with Jesus only as suffering more, then we have stopped short of pursuing the blessing of surrender to His will and goodness.

- We benefit from His comfort: "For just as we share abundantly in the sufferings of Christ, so also our comfort abounds through Christ" (2 Corinthians 1:5).

IF WE SEE LIFE WITH JESUS ONLY AS SUFFERING MORE, THEN WE HAVE STOPPED SHORT OF **PURSUING THE BLESSING OF SURRENDER** TO **HIS WILL** AND GOODNESS.

- We benefit in His glory: "Now if we are children, then we are heirs—heirs of God and co-heirs with Christ, if indeed we share in his sufferings so that we may also share in his glory" (Romans 8:17).
- We benefit in knowing the power of His resurrection: "I want to know Christ—yes, to know the power of his resurrection and participation in his sufferings, becoming like him in his death" (Philippians 3:10).
- We benefit by becoming overjoyed: "But rejoice inasmuch as you participate in the sufferings of Christ, so that you may be overjoyed when his glory is revealed." (1 Peter 4:13).

Wrapping Up

As our world distances itself from God, calling evil good and good evil, walking in holiness grows ever more challenging. Every day the road continues to become narrow. Hatred of God and what is good, is intensifying. Christians are increasingly being labeled as fools, ignorant, and judgmental. Just as Jesus was despised, so are we in greater measure.

Too many of us have sought victory over our sin through doing and behavior modification. Doing so, we become caught up in restless activism. We are so prone to pursue a method rather than a Person. It hardly seems possible that achieving a holy life happens by first resting in the holiness of Jesus.

That is the good news! Remaining centered in the righteousness, holiness, and purity of Jesus frees us from perfectionism. It is not a complacent, passive faith. Remaining centered involves obedience.

I pursue intimacy with Jesus first, changing me at the core of my being. That inward change results in outward change, being obedient to the will of the Father. The Pharisees had it backward. They thought they achieved holiness by cleaning the outside of the cup. Jesus countered, "Blind Pharisee! First, clean the inside of the cup and dish, and then the outside also will be clean" (Matthew 23:26).

We must battle the world's definitions of relationships and sexuality. We must know deep in our spirit that the only sexual union God ordained and blessed is that between a man and woman married to each other. All other forms of immoral sexual activity are *unacceptable* in His eyes. God has drawn a line in the sand before you. Are you willing to stay behind that line?

Will you remain committed to the expression of God's design in your relationships and sexuality? Even if your attractions do not change? Even if you remain in the state of singleness? Are you following God only if He provides your exact requests? Are you willing to wait on Him, submitting to His Lordship and sovereignty? Will you follow His timetable for your process?

We need God's divine objectivity to see suffering is a reality and worthwhile. Suffering can be an emotional awareness of our inner wounds. Rather than walk in outward denial of our wounds, and suffer in silence within, we must see suffering as a signal of our need for Jesus. We turn upward instead of inward.

When we suffer as the result of self-denial, dying to the false self, we are sharing in the sufferings of Jesus. Suffering because we choose to follow Jesus is part of our sanctification and maturing process.

Living, moving, and having our being in Jesus will result in some degree of suffering. Knowing this, however, and knowing that Jesus will meet us there and help us process it, enables us to practice endurance and perseverance. The result: our transformation into the men and women, God created us to be.

Prayer

Lord, where would I be without Your presence? How can I possibly live a life of holiness, righteousness, and purity? With You, all things are possible. Jesus, You tell me You are my way, truth, and life. In You, I live, move, and have my being. Therefore, I can live a life of integrity. You are at work, completing this work You have begun in me so that I will become and overcome.

Show me, Jesus, where I am striving to achieve holiness rather than resting in being centered in You. How has being perfect become a burden that I must achieve through my performance? Help me choose to trust Your perfecting of me. May it not become a passive abdication, but rather a balanced pursuit of resting and doing. Holy Spirit, empower me to do what Jesus asks of me, relying on His strength, and not my flesh. Reveal the will of the Father for me; then will what You command in me.

I admit I would prefer a life without suffering. If I am to live Your life in me, then suffering will be part of my journey home. Please guide me through my wounds and pain. Please help me not to become tunnel-visioned, such that I can perceive my life only through a lens of suffering. Renew my vision with Your divine objectivity to see my pain through Your eyes. Help me accept the reality that the suffering I endure is redemptive and part of my sanctification process.

Holy Spirit, guide me through the process of being able to abide in my pain with Jesus. Meet me in my fears that if I allow my pain to surface, it will annihilate me. May I begin to see my self-denial as an opportunity for experiencing greater life and freedom. Please help me not to turn inward with diseased introspection and narcissism, but to look up and out of myself toward You. Father, would You speak Your healing word to my suffering? Restore unto me the joy of Thy salvation, and renew a right spirit within me.

Soul Work

1. How have you strived to achieve holiness and purity in your life? How has it become a burden?

2. Provide some examples where you have drawn a line in the sand regarding some behavior, only later to wipe away that line and draw a new line to make allowances for sin to remain. What steps can you take to keep from making any more such allowances in your life, moving the line you have established?

3. How has suffering shifted your focus from God onto your pain?

4. What are the specific steps you can take to see suffering in a new light in your life?

Journaling Moment

In the section "Processing our Suffering with Jesus," there are four benefits listed for embracing our suffering with Him. Ask the Holy Spirit to reveal how embracing your suffering will benefit you with (1) His comfort, (2) His glory, (3) knowing the power of His resurrection, and (4) becoming overjoyed. This journaling may require more than a moment! I suggest seeking a contemplative time devoted to addressing only one benefit at a time.

TWENTY ONE

Temptation

JESUS CHRIST WAS TEMPTED, AND SO SHALL WE BE TEMPTED WHEN WE ARE RIGHTLY RELATED TO GOD.[73]

– OSWALD CHAMBERS

There is an interesting trick said to trap monkeys. Attached to a pole is a hollowed-out coconut. The coconut has a small hole carved into it, through which a monkey's paw can fit. The coconut contains rice, which is a temptation for the monkey. But when the monkey reaches into the hole and grabs the rice, its clenched fist cannot fit back through the hole. The monkey is caught in the trap because it is reluctant to let go of the rice.

Temptation is very similar to this trap. Like the rice, something tempts us. Once we attain the focus of our temptation, we resist letting go of our "precious" (just like Gollum in the Lord of the Rings). The temptation, in and of itself, is not sin. However, following through with the temptation—obtaining what enticed us—results in sin.

Does the Oswald Chambers quote above feel like bad news? We may not want to hear it, but temptation is an ever-present reality in the life of every Christian. What challenges most of us is our perspective regarding it. I hope that, after reading this chapter, you will agree that we can benefit from temptation.

First, let's begin to unravel the nuances of temptation.

[73]Oswald Chambers, *Biblical Psychology* (Marshall, Morgan and Scott, 1962), p. 191.

What Is Temptation?

Temptation is a trial that takes place when we are enticed or drawn to someone, or something that does not fit within the parameters God has determined are best for us. It may also be an enticement to take a shortcut or become complacent in our sanctification process. If an object or person does not align with our particular predilection, it will not tempt us. This is why one individual in a particular situation may sense temptation, whereas another individual may not. Temptation specifically aligns with your personal areas of brokenness.

Stop for a moment. What are your specific areas of temptation? Sexual temptation is a generic term. Beneath it are specific areas of weakness or triggers that make sex tempting. Some of these might be feeling inadequate, jealous, or envious. Seek the Holy Spirit's counsel to reveal the hidden depths and nuances of the temptations designed to fit in accordance with your brokenness.

Facing temptation requires our fortitude and courage in denying ourselves.

> "I have the right to do anything," you say—but not everything is beneficial. "I have the right to do anything"—but I will not be mastered by anything.
>
> – 1 Corinthians 6:12

Sometimes we may be tempted toward something that has the appearance of being good, but that, in the end, is not beneficial. There are situations we clearly define as temptations. However, other at other times, it may require greater sensitivity and discernment to classify the situation as a temptation.

Entertainment that is not beneficial can lead us into enslavement later. For example, we may watch a movie that has scenes bordering on sensuality. Although they may not cause us to sin at the moment, they may weaken us for later sexual temptation. Buying that bag of candy, that pair of shoes, that extravagant purchase on a whim—any of these may open the door a crack to

TEMPTATION SPECIFICALLY ALIGNS WITH YOUR PERSONAL AREAS OF BROKENNESS.

later, more significant temptation. We must discern what increases our vulnerability and makes us more susceptible to temptation.

Adam and Eve were tempted by what looked good and appealed to their senses. They saw the fruit of the tree of knowledge of good and evil as being *good for food* (Genesis 3:6, my italics). I need food to live, so why does God deny me something I need? Temptation will tweak my God issues. *Are You going to help me overcome this temptation? Why am I under constant temptation? You are so unfair. You know I am vulnerable right now. Why are You allowing this temptation to occur?*

Those questions are valid because they rise within us—not because they reflect right theology, but because we are feeling them. It is crucial to bring such questions to the Lord and seek His counsel regarding our feelings, preconceived wrong attitudes, and any transference issues. If these questions remain unchecked, the result can be the beginnings of anger, bitterness, or cynicism.

Temptation diverts us to make sinful choices that provide momentary escape or euphoria. The paradox is that it feels like freedom but later leads us into bondage and slavery. Yielding to temptation attacks our humanity at its weak points and limits our becoming.

The purpose of all temptation is to make me "god." Stop and read that sentence again. Ponder the spiritual reality that is being communicated. I *am* choosing to meet my needs or to escape from an emotionally challenging situation according to my plans and timetable. I *choose* to turn my back on God's guidance. I *get* to decide what is best for me. I *am* not submitting to God's knowledge of what is best for me; I *am* choosing to be in control. Do you see the shift of focus?

Going Deeper

> …but each person is tempted when they are dragged away by their own evil desire and enticed. Then, after desire has conceived, it gives birth to sin; and sin, when it is full-grown, gives birth to death.
>
> – James 1:14–15

The first area James identifies is recognizing that I allow myself to be "dragged away" or "enticed." Notice that he indicates "each person," indicating it is an individualized temptation. As was previously stated, only those things to which I am personally susceptible tempt me.

James also points out that temptation connects with my evil desires. These desires do not align with the healthy desire to know and to be known. They do not align with our true self and God's will. These are desires aligned with the false self, arising from me choosing to step out of my true center in Jesus.

God has caused goodness to be present in my heart and has made a way for me to renew my mind. Nevertheless, I still can make choices that are contrary for my good. As I become vulnerable—either mentally, emotionally, physically, or spiritually—I increase the susceptibility for my heart to make wrong choices. I allow the false self to redirect my desire to settle for false intimacy rather than true intimacy.

Temptation is the "sperm" seeking to enter the womb of my heart to "conceive" death (using James' metaphor, above). "Conception" occurs when my desire, through an act of my will, joins with what is false. The more I open my heart to darkness, the greater will be the deadly consequences. By making allowances for things that are not beneficial, the more susceptible I make myself to temptation.

I must take ownership of my divided heart. I start with the assumption that I have allowed mixture to enter my heart. I have allowed the misalignment of my passions. I and I alone are responsible. I humble myself before the Lord, therefore, and seek His forgiveness. At the root of temptation is choosing to be in control and satisfying myself with that which is temporal and finite.

Two other sources of temptation are the devil and the world around us. The world will tempt me only if I become vulnerable to it. This is why I must take care of myself mentally, emotionally, physically, and spiritually. I must keep present and alert to discern when each of these particular areas exhibits weakness.

I must also discern when I deflect responsibility within myself. I can blame-shift the temptation onto the devil or the world when it is actually coming from my heart. I need the Holy Spirit to search my heart and reveal my culpability.

Satan is a liar and knows humankind well. He has had millennia to perfect his attack. The devil observes us to learn our vulnerabilities, weaknesses, wants, and desires. He slyly tries to distort our thinking with lies as he did in the Garden ("Did God really say?"). Satan hates God's creation and seeks its destruction.

Satan and Jesus are not equal opponents. Jesus defeated Satan on the cross. Never forget Jesus crushed Satan beneath His feet. He no longer has spiritual authority over you. Distortion through the devil's lies is his only power.

Jesus prayed that Simon Peter's faith would sustain him while being sifted by Satan. Jesus is always present to you when you are experiencing trials or temptations. Ask for the empowering of your faith. Endurance gives birth to perseverance within you. Each victory over temptation adds to the foundation on which you stand. Each failure is an opportunity for learning, which God will work towards your good. It is all part of your process of becoming.

Battling Temptation

There are several ways to combat temptation. This section will discuss various ways to address temptation, especially when in the heat of battle. Here are some questions to ask when you are being tempted or for further reflection:

- Why am I being tempted?
- What triggered this temptation?
- What am I feeling?
- What is drawing me to this particular person, place, or thing?
- Deep down, how does this temptation represent a false source of intimacy or escape?
- For what am I truly searching?

The Lord will teach you through the experience of temptation. Seek the Holy Spirit for His revelation so that you may glean wisdom from your particular experiences.

The enemy tempts us, utilizing our five senses. The perfume or cologne someone wears may remind you of a previous emotional or sexual encounter. The appealing taste of food may entice you toward gluttony. A physical touch may cause an abreaction, a body memory to surface (i.e., when a touch in the present causes the body to react due to a past physical experience). We may hear a piece of music reminding us of a previous difficult situation.

Visual Temptation

One of the more common avenues of temptation is sight.

> If your right eye causes you to stumble, gouge it out and throw it away. It is better for you to lose one part of your body than for your whole body to be thrown into hell.
>
> – Matthew 5:29

If we apply this Scripture literally, there would be many Christians lacking a right eye! Matthew is making a strong point about what we do with our eyes. Job addressed the visual temptation he experienced by making a pledge with God: "I made a covenant with my eyes not to look lustfully at a young woman" (Job 31:1). Moreover, Jesus taught, "Your eye is the lamp of your body. When your eyes are healthy, your whole body also is full of light. But when they are unhealthy, your body also is full of darkness" (Luke 11:34). We must be cautious as to what we allow visually to enter our bodies.

An ancient Greek proverb states, "Beauty is in the eye of the beholder." Individually, we respond or react to what we see. Depending on our state of vulnerability, a work of art may present a temptation one day and not the next. Someone overly sexualized due to sensuality or pornography may be triggered by the most innocent pieces of art or sculpture.

We must be aware of our current state of being. What are your cues which indicate a present vulnerability to visual temptation? What boundaries do you embrace when you feel this way? As we saw in chapter 20, maintaining our state of purity is a forethought and not an afterthought. What precautions do you take when you sense you are in a state of vulnerability?

We cannot always control what crosses our field of vision. We are responsible, however, for how we respond or react. A wise and observant friend once told me, "The first look is free, but the second look is a sin." When visually tempted, do we take a second look or perhaps let our vision linger too long? How do we know when we have crossed the line when temptation becomes sin? The line is crossed when we are no longer remaining and abiding in Jesus. Allowing our minds to linger often makes us vulnerable to sinful behaviors. We will discuss further in chapter 22.

To discern whether something I am viewing is appropriate, I imagine Jesus, my pastor, or my accountability partner sitting next to me. How would each respond? Trust your "spiritual gut" when you first sense something may be inappropriate. Let the Holy Spirit guide you as to what is safe or unsafe for where you are in your process.

Advance Choices

> And if your right hand causes you to stumble, cut it off and throw it away. It is better for you to lose one part of your body than for your whole body to go into hell.
>
> – Matthew 5:30

Maturing in our Christian walk, we are more aware of what makes us susceptible to temptation and sin. In certain seasons of our overcoming process, we may have to cut off specific activities or even relationships. If something is causing us to stumble, then we must establish healthy boundaries for our safety and well-being. For example, discontinuing going to a beach in the summer may be necessary due to visual sensitivity.

Tempting Activities and Relationships - My Story

I am very fond of classical music and especially opera. I have met many world-renowned opera singers. Backstage at one performance, the great tenor Luciano Pavarotti introduced me to all four of his daughters. Also, I participated in two Metropolitan Opera performances as a supernumerary. (I was an Egyptian slave in *Aida* and a sacristan in *Tosca*.) Opera has been a significant part of my life.

However, listening to opera became a way for me to escape my unresolved emotions. I had a collection of nearly one hundred opera recordings. When I wanted to escape, I would use alcohol or inhalants to heighten my listening experience. Opera was a "drug" to which I turned. Rededicating my life to the Lord in 1987, I knew I had to dispose of the pornography I owned. I did not do this with my opera recordings. But I learned how to identify my coping mechanisms and no longer sought opera as an escape. Having the recordings at home did not create a temptation for me. I chose to err on the side of caution and stop listening to opera. Another of the boundaries I created was not to attend any live opera performances.

Years passed, and I began to wonder if opera would be safe for me. I left this in the hands of the Lord. Shortly after doing so, friends contacted me who knew I enjoyed opera. They offered me free tickets to attend a few performances. God opened the door for me once more to enjoy opera. It no longer tempted me as an escape mechanism.

Why do I share this story? To provide an example of a temptation that is not sexual or appears wrong to the casual observer. My love for opera looked perfectly acceptable and even commendable. However, I knew what it had represented to me.

What areas of temptation are present in your life that, to those around you look perfectly acceptable?

Questions frequently arise concerning the continuance of engaging in a particular relationship. When asked, my response is always the same: Does this relationship draw you closer to God or pull you farther away? If it is drawing you away from God, then you need to set boundaries.

Resistance to do so may indicate that the relationship is a source of temptation or an idol.

Places of Temptation

> And if your foot causes you to stumble, cut it off. It is better for you to enter life crippled than to have two feet and be thrown into hell.
>
> – Mark 9:45

> A person's steps are directed by the LORD.
>
> – Proverbs 20:24

God does order the steps of the righteous. (Remember that your righteousness is in Jesus and not in what you do.) We also have the free will to disregard His ordering. To not place ourselves in harm's way, we must discern where we are going. The wise individual knows where they are not to walk or linger.

Those who struggle with alcohol addiction are wise not to walk into a bar, go out with certain friends, or traverse the wine aisle in a grocery store. Those struggling with sexual addiction (as stated earlier) are wise to avoid the beach in the summer. This is not to put us back under the law but to exercise wisdom and discernment.

In the work environment, we may have to orchestrate our steps in such a way as to avoid encountering someone who is a temptation to us. We may have to avoid a certain street because a business, home, or location may tempt us. Once we learn of our vulnerabilities and weaknesses, the Holy Spirit will guide us through the minefield of temptation.

Physical Symbols

In a secular job, having a cross on your desk or a Scripture verse on your wall is likely not allowed. Nevertheless, we can find ways to associate an object symbolically with our Christian walk. A stone on your desk, which you collected on a contemplative walk with the Lord, can remind you of His presence. Seeing the stone reminds you of God's fellowship and His strength to overcome temptation. Perhaps you can place a small cross in a desk drawer, which, when opened, reminds you of Jesus' presence.

When I worked in a secular job, I wore a cross under my shirt. If I experienced a temptation during a meeting, I could rest my fingers on my chest in an innocuous way. I would feel the cross with my fingers and practice the presence of Jesus. No one had a clue what I was doing. The cross had weight to it. There were times I became aware of it on my chest, and I was reminded of Jesus. I still wear that cross to this day.

There are multiple ways we can bring symbols into our everyday lives, which connect us at the moment with God. Place them in your car or by your bedside. They have no special power; they remind us of God's presence when we become tempted or troubled. I have a small icon of Jesus under my computer screen. I see it in the periphery of my vision. It is a constant reminder that Jesus is with me.

The Armor of God

> Finally, be strong in the Lord and in his mighty power. Put on the full armor of God, so that you can take your stand against the devil's schemes. For our struggle is not against flesh and blood, but against the rulers, against the authorities, against the powers of this dark world and against the spiritual forces of evil in the heavenly realms. Therefore, put on the full armor of God, so that when the day of evil comes, you may be able to stand your ground, and after you have done everything, to stand. Stand firm then, with the belt of truth buckled around your waist, with the breastplate of righteousness in place, and with your feet fitted with the readiness that comes from the gospel of peace. In addition to all this, take up the shield of faith, with which you can extinguish all the flaming arrows of the evil one. Take the helmet of salvation and the sword of the Spirit, which is the word of God.
>
> – Ephesians 6:10–17

How can I discuss temptation without addressing the armor of God mentioned in Ephesians 6? Many wonderful commentaries go into detail about the various pieces of the armor. I want to address only a few key points from this Scripture passage.

First, it is vital to recognize that we are in an actual battle. There are spiritual rulers, authorities, and powers shooting flaming arrows at us in the form of temptation. Because we are in a battle, I encourage you to seek commentaries that discuss the spiritual significance of each piece of armor. Each of these pieces is valuable when we battle temptation. Be a wise warrior.

It is important to recognize that the armor does not attach to us on its own. Paul says we must "put on the full armor of God." In other words, we must make an intentional, active choice to put on the armor of God. A soldier would never go into battle and leave his weapons or protective gear behind. How often do we do so?

Next, a soldier rarely operates individually. He is part of a unit or troop. Likewise, when we are battling temptation, it is good for us to rely on our brothers and sisters to help us. We can contact a friend when we sense temptation is coming our way. The words of encouragement and affirmation are a valuable resource for battling temptation. The simple act of texting a friend when you are being tempted shifts your focus, and connects you with community.

In Ephesians 6, Paul does not say, "Now go out and do battle." No, he says, "Having done all, stand your ground." Paul is indicating that we stand in a place of authority. The battle is already won. Because a soldier falls into a specific ranking, he trusts those above him to develop a battle plan. We do not go out to do battle without God's plan. As Paul indicates, we stand, waiting on our Commander-in-Chief, the Lord Jesus Christ, for His orders and His plans.

God's Promise

> No temptation has overtaken you except what is common to mankind. And God is faithful; he will not let you be tempted beyond what you can bear. But when you are tempted, he will also provide a way out so that you can endure it.
>
> – 1 Corinthians 10:13

This is a significant statement from Paul. It reminds us of hope. It helps keep us from turning to fear or despair. Paul experienced much abuse from the hands of others and waged many battles with temptation.

"Common to Humankind"

The first part of this verse speaks against any feelings of chronic uniqueness—that is, "*Only I am going through this experience.*" "*No one else has it as bad as I do.*" Paul reminds us that we are not isolated due to our temptations but are part of a larger community. We are all together in the same boat.

I want to speak specifically to those who struggle with unwanted same-sex temptations. How are these temptations common to humankind? Same-sex temptations are often composed of lust, envy, jealousy, and control, which indeed are common to all. The temptation is not that man or woman, but how he or she triggers you emotionally. Also, I may see that individual as a way to take control, using him or her as a means to escape my pain or stress. More deeply, it is trying to meet our ache for true intimacy through illegitimate ways.

The writer of Hebrews states, "For we do not have a high priest who is unable to empathize with our weaknesses, but we have one who has been tempted in every way, just as we are—yet he did not sin" (Hebrews 4:15). Was Jesus homosexually tempted? Applying what I stated in the previous paragraph, I believe Jesus was tempted to lust, to feel envious or jealous, and to escape His pain. The issue is why I am vulnerable to that particular object or person. Your temptations do not define or label you.

Stop and ponder this for a moment. How often have you let the enemy or your self-hatred define you by the type of temptation you experience? Does temptation for alcohol define you as an alcoholic? No! It means you are a child of God who struggles with alcohol. Never forget that your identity and true self are centered in Jesus alone.

As recorded in Luke 4, Satan began two of the three temptations of Jesus in the desert in the same way, by saying, "If you are the Son of God…." What was Satan attempting to do? Jesus knew who He was. He did not have to prove or affirm His identity. The real temptation was not to change the stone into bread or hurl Himself off the Temple mount. The focus of the temptation was not the activity Satan was asking Jesus to do. It was trying to make Jesus prove His identity and authority.

Likewise, your temptations are an attempt by the devil to make you forget who you are in Christ. He wants you to believe *the lie* that I can become "god." He has been repeating the same temptation ever since that day in the Garden with Adam and Eve. The temptation is to confirm that God is impotent and untrustworthy. *You* must take control. *You* must determine your path apart from Him.

There is nothing new under the sun, nothing.

"More Than You Can Bear"

I find comfort in Paul's words. No temptation has the power and authority to push you over the edge! Does this mean you will not struggle or, especially early on in your process, white-knuckle it? Memorize this Scripture and recite it when you are in the midst of temptation. Tell yourself the truth that this temptation cannot destroy you. Learning to walk through temptation teaches you how to endure, persevere, and overcome.

"Because he himself suffered when he was tempted, he is able to help those who are being tempted" (Hebrews 2:18). When you feel as if you are going under, call on the powerful name of Jesus. Jesus identified with our humanity, and He exactly knows how you are feeling. He knows your fears and anxiety. Shift your focus from the temptation itself and onto Jesus. You may need to run as Joseph did from Potiphar's wife. However, wait for the Commander-in-Chief to instruct you what to do.

"A Way Out"

Once again, Paul's words are comforting and hopeful. God will provide a way out. He knows your state of being and the condition of your heart. You do not have to tell Him how you are feeling; He already knows. Look up and out of yourself and seek His face. He is faithful to provide a way for you.

Note, however, that Paul promises that God will "provide a way out" so you can endure temptation. You may not be able to flee or change your circumstances. However, in those very situations, God will provide in such a way that you will be able to endure it. This particular temptation may even be part of your training to stand and take authority in your position as the Father's daughter or son.

Let me set a scenario for you. Let's say you are on a dock and, out in the water, you see a man drowning. Would you say that the man was *struggling* to survive or that he was *persevering* to survive? The correct verb is that he was struggling to survive. Why was he struggling instead of persevering? If I am struggling, it is because I am uncertain of the outcome. If I am persevering, I know there is light at the end of the tunnel.

Early in our process, we struggle with temptation, feeling it is excruciating and long. Through each temptation, I am learning and growing. Listen again to Paul's promise in Romans 8:28: "And we know that in all things God works for the good of those who love him, who have been called according to his purpose." God will work the experience of temptation for your good. He will prove Himself faithful as you endure temptation. If you fall, even then He will turn it for your good. Eventually, you will go from white-knuckling and struggle to a place of endurance and perseverance.

Extending Grace

> For I have the desire to do what is good, but I cannot carry it out. For I do not do the good I want to do, but the evil I do not want to do—this I keep on doing. Now if I do what I do not want to do, it is no longer I who do it, but it is sin living in me that does it.
>
> – Romans 7:18–20

Don't you love Paul's honesty and transparency? He is real with us. We are in the process of sanctification and will be so until the day we go to be with our Beloved. Temptation is not a sin. Sin is the fruit when we embrace temptation and follow through in thought, word, or deed. We abdicate our true self, embracing the false self and choose to sin. We choose false intimacy. Oswald Chambers' quote at the opening of this chapter indicates that being rightly related to God means we will be tempted. As the Apostle John writes to us intimately in 1 John 2:1: "My dear children, I write this to you so that you will not sin. But if anybody does sin, we have an advocate with the Father—Jesus Christ, the Righteous One." John reminds us that when, through our humanity, we fail, Jesus is our advocate and righteousness. As we mature into overcomers, however, we will still be tempted, but we will sin less.

Giving in to temptation often leads to shame and diseased introspection. I want to remind us all of what we learned in chapter 13 on forgiveness. Embrace the practice of extending grace to yourself. The same grace Jesus extends to you, apply to your falls after temptation, which will lead you to repentance. Resist letting temptation limit or define you.

The Bottom Line

Having provided you with all the previous understanding let me discuss in closing one final aspect of 1 Corinthians 10:13. If I will not be tempted more than I can bear, this means that, when tempted, I *already have* the capacity to overcome the temptation. Let me provide you with an example.

Walking down the street, I come across an open garbage can. I see there is pornography in it. If this occurs when I am not walking with the Lord, I may retrieve the pornography for my addictive use.

However, let's say this happens after I commit my life to the Lord. I can now respond differently. Knowing that the temptation cannot overwhelm me, I know I have the capacity to defeat it. The temptation is showing me that God has accomplished such a healing work in my life that I can keep walking past the pornography. The temptation is an *opportunity* for me to rejoice in God's faithfulness to complete the good work He has begun in me.

Let that sink in, my brothers and sisters.

Instead of seeing temptation as something to dread, you can now see it through God's perspective. It truly is an opportunity to see what He *has done* in your life.

But let me say that this applies to when we have not orchestrated our temptation. For example, I am not about to walk into an adult bookstore to "test" the degree of how much I am healed. God forbid! When temptation occurs not due to your own devices, the Lord will reveal the depths to which He has been at work within you. Here is a thought from Oswald Chambers worth contemplating, "Temptation in the life of faith are not accidents; each temptation is part of a plan, a step in the progress of faith."[74]

I highly recommend studying 2 Peter 1:5–8:

> For this very reason, make every effort to add to your faith goodness; and to goodness, knowledge; and to knowledge, self-control; and to self-control, perseverance; and to perseverance, godliness; and to godliness, mutual affection; and to mutual affection, love. For if you possess these qualities in increasing measure, they will keep you from being ineffective and unproductive in your knowledge of our Lord Jesus Christ.

There is an important order in the way Peter encourages the qualities we need to add to our faith. Note how self-control comes before perseverance. Through our failures and successes with

[74]Oswald Chambers, *Not Knowing Whither* (Marshall, Morgan and Scott, 1934), p. 117.

temptation, we learn self-control, which matures into perseverance. Peter's list of the qualities we need to pursue helps us in our becoming process.

Temptation is an opportunity through which we can experience further transformation as an overcomer. It reveals our amazing God, who is completely committed to us.

Prayers

Lord, I thank You that You know me completely in my humanity. You are fully aware of my weaknesses, inadequacies, and fears. You are at work in the depths of my being, perfecting, and leading me in my process.

I admit my struggles with temptation. There are times when it feels overwhelming. I acknowledge that I cannot overcome temptation unless I am centered in You, Lord Jesus. In my vulnerability, I can focus so easily on the temptation and turn inwardly with condemnation and diseased introspection. Please reveal where I have let temptation to limit and define me.

Holy Spirit, I need Your presence to reveal the ways I become vulnerable to temptation. Would You reveal how I have become weakened emotionally, mentally, physically, or spiritually? Where am I complacent or passive? Where have I entered into sin? Expose any lies or transference issues that make me more susceptible to temptation. Bring Your truth and empower me to walk ever more aligned with the will of the Father.

Lord, what aspects of temptation appeal specifically to my weakness and brokenness? What are my emotional or behavioral patterns that give rise to temptation? Reveal where there are underlying issues with envy, jealousy, self-hatred, and self-loathing. What lies beneath my feelings of lust? I need Your insight, wisdom, and discernment.

Lord, help me not dread temptation but begin to accept it as an opportunity for growth and becoming. I invite You to change my thinking so that I no longer see temptation as an indication of failure or defeat. Help me extend grace to myself. Help me look up and out of myself into Your loving face.

Thank You that no temptation has the power to overwhelm me. Lord Jesus, thank You for taking on my humanity, for being tempted in every way and yet not falling into sin. Thank You that You will always provide a way for me in the midst of temptation. Thank You for always being present to my needs.

Soul Work

1. How do you know when your temptation has drifted into sin?

2. How have you allowed temptation to define you and your process?

3. Reflect on what your most difficult experiences have been with temptation. How did the object or person toward which you were tempted reveal underlying emotions, personal vulnerabilities, and faulty beliefs in you?

4. Give an example of how an experience with temptation revealed how far the Lord had brought you into your process.

Journaling Moment

Journal about what each piece of the armor of God described in Ephesians 6:10–18 represents to you. (For example, how does the helmet truly represent salvation to you?) Reflect on your position in Christ regarding each piece of the armor. How does each affirm your true self?

TWENTY TWO

Addiction

... ADDICTION ATTACHES DESIRE, BONDS AND ENSLAVES THE ENERGY OF DESIRE, TO CERTAIN SPECIFIC BEHAVIORS, THINGS, AND PEOPLE. THESE OBJECTS OF ATTACHMENT THEN BECOME PREOCCUPATIONS AND OBSESSIONS; THEY COME TO RULE OUR LIVES.[75]

- GERALD MAY

We hunger at our very core (as we saw in chapters 9 and 10) for true intimacy. This hunger affects every aspect of how we interact with our environment, including our relationships. It takes us in many directions, often wrong ones, especially in the form of addiction.

Addictions are rooted in unresolved relational issues. Our journey in *Path through the Wilderness* has revealed thus far where we have reacted to the relational deficits and wounds of our past. Our desire for true intimacy is met by addressing any defensive reactions in the past, which then allows us to engage in healthy relationships in the present. To experience freedom from addictions, in which we no longer battle dominating, addictive urges, we must pursue healthy relationships. This is not an option but a necessity. To overcome addiction, *we must* be in healthy community, a community existing outside of programs or support groups.

There are many books written on addiction. However, this chapter will specifically

[75]May, *Addiction and Grace*, p. 3.

explore and address addictions on a practical, physical, and spiritual level. Gaining wisdom and understanding is of great benefit for our recovery. The more we understand how and why we are "triggered," and how addictions affect our bodies and spiritual reality, the better we can enter healthy community.

A void within us, the ache for true intimacy, longs for fulfillment. We must learn how to navigate our deepest desire to know and be known in a world full of sensuality, of compelling sources of false intimacy, and of avenues to escape our pain. The battle is whether to give in to immediate gratification with the finite or to persevere, holding out for the infinite. Do we want illusion or reality?

We are born into this fallen world with a predilection to seek sources for our life apart from God. We all, at some time, face the pull towards addiction. For some, it is less of a battle. For others, it can be a daily source of great anxiety. Addictions can take on the appearance of socially acceptable behaviors. Some people fail to see that they are entangled in addictive behaviors. Each of us must let the Holy Spirit search our souls to reveal where we have opened the door to addiction.

Are you willing to let Him search you on this level?

God wants to be our source of knowledge, satisfying and fulfilling our innermost being. Immanuel, "God who is with us," inhabits our souls. Jesus longs for us to stay present to Him when our needs, hurts, and desires rise, beckoning—dare I say screaming?—for attention. Through the centering and empowering of the Holy Spirit, we can find the place of peace and rest.

When are you most vulnerable to addictive behaviors? What sends me down the path of addictive cycles? Why do my addictions drive me so? Why do the objects of my addictions have such a hold on me? What will happen if I let go of my false sources of intimacy?

The Holy Spirit provides us with His gifts of discernment and understanding. Facing your addictive behaviors requires willingness, honesty, and relinquishment. As we explore many aspects of addiction, seek the Lord's help to remain present and open to His revelation.

The Establishment of Addiction

You were created because of the incredible love of God. Love is the core of your existence. Created in the love of the Beloved—that is, Jesus—you were created for love. Remember those innate questions with which we are born: *Do I have worth? Do I have value? Am I lovable?* You were born with these questions as part of your being. They are part of your process of becoming. God wants you to know ecstatic love and joy in your heart. He wants to be your source for identification, being, and affirmation. Addictions replace God as that source. They divert you from knowing and becoming known. All addictions are rooted in this alternate source of being. They are a replacement for life-giving, healthy relationships with God, others, and yourself.

May writes, "Addiction is a state of compulsion, obsession, or preoccupation that enslaves a person's will and desire."[76] The word *state* equates addiction with a condition of the mind and heart. It is a state in which I live. I view the people and the world around me through a filter created by that state. Addiction is a condition to which I have abandoned my reason and will. Addiction consumes my will and desire, resulting in my eventual enslavement to it.

Attachment is the foundational reality of addiction. Addiction attaches our desires and passions, by our own volition, to something other than God. All too often, we deflect our culpability, our responsibility, for making this choice. To walk in freedom, I must take ownership of the reality that *I have* allowed attachment to occur.

As we see in the opening quote of this chapter, there is *energy* in desire. The source of that energy is our longing for true intimacy—what drives me within. Through my choice (are you beginning to dislike that word?), I align that energy either toward God (true intimacy) or toward something other than God (false intimacy).

Are you more God-centric or more egocentric?

Emotions trigger addictions. The reason we turn to a particular behavior or person or thing is a feeling of insecurity, inadequacy, or unacceptability. However, we must not blame-shift for choosing sources of false intimacy—for example, "She gave me the apple" or "The serpent beguiled me." My idolatry, envy, lust, or desire for control are to blame. It is my sin.

Emotions trigger us to seek control when we find ourselves in a vulnerable situation. Our minds begin to think up ways to address the problem, to feel okay or safe once more. Not centering ourselves relationally in Jesus, we attach ourselves to false sources of life and intimacy. Adam and Eve experienced this attachment the moment they bit into the fruit of the tree of knowledge of good and evil. Attachment to knowledge and control replaced healthy attachment to God.

[76]Ibid., p. 14.

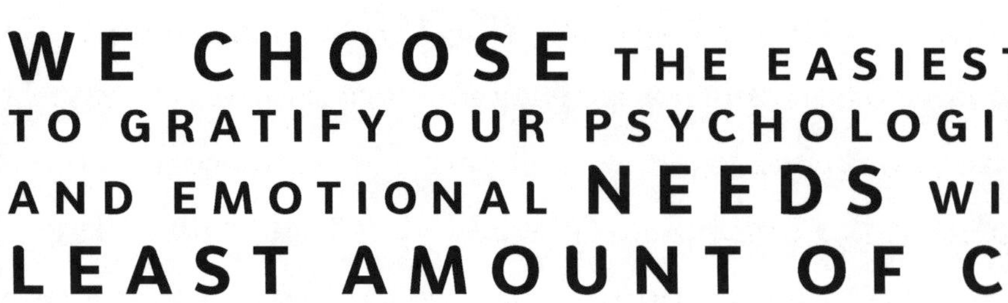

Addiction attaches our desires to lesser sources of fulfillment which are finite and temporal. We choose the easiest ways to gratify our psychological and emotional needs with the least amount of cost. However, as is so often the case, that "least cost" ends up being extremely costly to the well-being of our souls and bodies.

The attachments we make become an established part of our lives. If I turn to food to escape pain, I have made an attachment to it. Whenever I feel pain, I immediately feel the urge to eat. If I have turned to pornography to escape pain or loneliness, the urge for it will increase when these emotions arise. You can substitute drugs, alcohol, religion, workaholism, shopping, romance novels, and many other sources for whatever you turn to in place of God to meet your needs. *Emotions and attachment are at the core of addiction.*

Here is an equation showing the flow of addiction:

Vulnerability > Attachment > Pleasure > Repetition > Obsession

Triggered by something in our environment, we experience a growing sense of vulnerability. Our brains compel us to search for an attachment to assuage this vulnerability. Because we experience pleasure or release due to our attachments, we repeat these behaviors. Repetition creates habits and neural pathways in our brains. Eventually, addictions become obsessive, enslaving us.

Descending into Addictions

As Paul makes clear in Romans 1, when we turn away from God, we will turn to His creation to satisfy ourselves. Trapped into seeking or making false gods, we find it more difficult to turn back to God as our true source of intimacy. Our brains search to find a mental state of equilibrium, longing to feel happy, good, or connected. Attachment is an attempt to deaden our pain by seeking non-reality, which makes our brain feel okay. The problem is that addiction only provides a false, temporal sense of being okay.

To what have you attached to feel okay?

Addictions take us down to the lowest denominator, directing desire toward the easiest and quickest way of escape. Our addictions paralyze us, trapping us in non-becoming. My identity is earthbound, turning inward, away from God.

The transformation of Sméagol into the piteous creature Gollum, as portrayed in *The Lord of the Rings* films (based on J. R. R. Tolkien's trilogy), clearly illustrates the fruit of addiction. After Sméagol comes under the control of the power of the one Ring, he retreats from community, hiding from the light in a cave. He forgets the taste of bread (illustrating no longer being able to connect with the Bread of heaven). Finally, Sméagol admits that he has forgotten his name (his original identity), and becomes Gollum (a broken identity).

Descending into addiction, I start to lose the sense of who I am. My godly inspired passions are now earthbound, limited, and separate from my Creator. Consumed by desire, becoming the sensualist as described in chapter 10, I experience addiction as a psychological malignancy that drains me of energy. It decreases my availability and capacity to be available for healthy relationships and pursuits.

Addiction consumes and enslaves me in these ways:

- Mentally I become obsessed with repetitive thoughts.
- Emotionally my heart seeks false intimacy and broken relationships.
- Physically my body is altered through behaviors and the consequences of my actions.
- Spiritually my will becomes atrophied so that eventually I end up despairing of hope.

Aspects of the Addictive Cycle

Ultimately, we turn to addiction to assuage unmet, legitimate needs. Let that sink in for a moment. Beneath all the various forms of addiction is a legitimate need for love, acceptance, and community. The deepest need at our core, as you have read multiple times in *Path*, is our need for true intimacy. When we do not trust God to meet those needs in His way and His timing, we take control to meet them in ways we think will work, only to find that they fail. (Remember our discussion back in chapter 1?) We internalize shame, build self-protective walls, and isolate.

When addictions become our center, we experience a pervasive sense of neediness. As we saw earlier, our brains seek a steady state of equilibrium, a state of feeling okay. Repeated behaviors used to achieve this state create neural pathways. We have automatic neural pathways for walking or talking. Repeated activities linked with addictive behaviors become automatic as well. Before we even realize it, we enter into our addictive cycles. They can eventually become so ingrained that they feel like a necessity for life.

The previous paragraph illustrates what Paul states in 1 Corinthians 6:18 "Flee from sexual immorality. All other sins a person commits are outside the body, but whoever sins sexually, sins against their own body." Addiction creates physical consequences, an altering of brain physiology, in our bodies.

Addiction is a thief:

- It robs us of love: It taints *philia*, *agape*, and *storge*, and twists *eros*.
- It robs us of integrity and self-esteem: We continue to pay the price for our addictions, which is ever rising, increasing the cost of the consequences of our sin.
- It robs us of being able to see: We become blind to consequences, retreating into self-pity, narcissism, and cynicism.
- It robs us of hope, encouraging us to embrace despair.
- It diminishes our sense of greater purpose for God's kingdom.
- It robs us of well-being: We lose our true center, Jesus.
- It robs us of freedom: Addiction becomes, in Gollum's words, "our master, our precious."

Twelve-step programs use an acronym called HALT. When you are *H*ungry, *A*ngry, *L*onely, or *T*ired, you are to halt. These triggers open the door to our cycles. I typically add another letter to the word, making it HALTS, with the *S* standing for *S*tress. We must learn what makes us tick. Getting in touch with our emotions and realizing when we are vulnerable will help us minimize the impact of being triggered. Emotions challenge us, which lead to thoughts and actions. The emotional identification form in appendix 1 is a helpful resource in this area.

When challenges arise, halt and ask four simple questions:

1. What am I feeling?
2. What has led me to feel this way?
3. What is my broken reaction to these feelings and where are they taking me?
4. God, will You meet me where these feelings are coming from and center me in You?

The purpose of these questions is to shift our focus. We can shift out of descending into the triggered emotions and being consumed by them. We can ask for God's revelation regarding our feelings. Seeking His truth will help us make wise decisions on how to proceed.

We have three choices (that word again!) to turn to at the moment when we halt:

1. To God: for direction, understanding, comfort, discernment, wisdom, and more.
2. To relationships: for support, counsel, comfort, accountability, and more.
3. To addictions: for escape, frustration, condemnation, and despair.

When we turn to addictions rather than to God, we seek to *S*uppress, *A*void, or *P*acify our present emotions—an acronym called SAP. It is not that we are saps but that addictions sap us of life. We enter into established rituals. Our mind and body go on autopilot. We enter into the excitement of the hunt for that which will allow us to escape. The hunt causes the release of adrenaline, and our bodies respond with physical sensations. We lose touch with reality, seeking only our emotional and physical high. Eventually, we feel shame, make resolutions (which fail), and become vulnerable once more. Eventually our will atrophies, our hearts shut down, we become cynical, and we go into isolation.

Resisting Performance and Pride

> As soon as one tries to control any truly addictive behavior by making autonomous intentional resolutions, one begins to defeat oneself.[77]

The obvious first focus chosen to overcome addiction is behavior modification. However,

[77]Ibid., p. 28.

as Gerald May suggests in the preceding quote, choices in the flesh, not centered in Christ, are self-defeating.

Where did you focus when you first entered the process of stopping your addictions?

> Since you died with Christ to the elemental forces of this world, why, as though you still belonged to the world, do you submit to its rules: "Do not handle! Do not taste! Do not touch!"? These rules, which have to do with things that are all destined to perish with use, are based on merely human commands and teachings. Such regulations indeed have an appearance of wisdom, with their self-imposed worship, their false humility and their harsh treatment of the body, but they lack any value in restraining sensual indulgence.
>
> – Colossians 2:20–23

Paul's admonition to the Colossians is startling. He reminds us of who we are in Christ, having died to the ways of the world. We are not to put ourselves back under the law. The law says for us to do in order to be accepted, but grace says, "Done. You are accepted." The rules Paul highlights put the focus on behavior and a record of sobriety. They appeal to the flesh and pride. They emphasize doing and achieving.

Let me take a moment to address keeping a sobriety record. My breaking free from my addiction to pornography and masturbation took time. Early on in my process, when I had not masturbated for more than a year, and I felt good about it, I began sharing my record. You guessed it. I fell. The problem was, I had identified my "righteousness" with my record and stepped out of who I was in Christ.

The only way I can walk in a state of purity is to recognize that my purity, holiness, and righteousness are in Jesus alone (as discussed in chapter 20). Granted, it is not a passive choice or abdication because I must rise and obey what Jesus instructs. Nevertheless, it is only through the strength I find in Him that I can become and overcome. I realize my freedom only when I stop keeping a record and trust instead in Jesus.

Initially breaking free from our addictions, we can find encouragement in sobriety records. We can rejoice with brothers or sisters when they experience sobriety. The danger is when that record—or "chip," as some call it—becomes an emblem of pride rather than humility. For me, a one-day record or chip is just as powerful as one that is twenty or thirty years in the making.

Why? Because it always boils down to our daily choices.

Truly breaking free from an attachment means I must make some difficult and painful choices. First, I must begin pursuing a deeper relationship with God. I need the reality of His being constant and present to me every moment of the day. Second, I make the difficult choice to turn away from my false sources of intimacy and life. I deny my immediate gratification and choose to persevere for what will fulfill my deepest longings. Third, I commit to God to walk increasingly in His ways in my life. It is not a passive, lumpish choice that tells God, "You do it." It is an act of the will, an active choice. It is the belief that "By Your strength, O Lord, I will overcome."

Growing in Intimacy with God

> His divine power has given us everything we need for a godly life through our knowledge of him who called by his own glory and goodness.
>
> – 2 Peter 1:3

Experiencing greater freedom from addiction, as we have just said, requires intimacy with God. Peter indicates in this passage that knowing God will enable us to live godly lives. The knowledge Peter refers to is a complete knowledge—knowledge both of the head and the heart. It is not only having a doctrinal knowing of God's character and nature but also *knowing* Him relationally.

Those struggling with addiction have difficulty pursuing intimacy with God. This pursuit requires a foundational knowledge of God based on unconditional love and not performance. We must not only know His love that is freely given but also have the capacity to receive it freely. God is fully present to us, and we, in turn, grow in becoming fully present to God.

Growing in this intimacy is challenging for addictive strugglers because

- they fight to be present to their interior pain and wounds and so are cut off from their hearts and resistant to intimacy with God
- they often pursue restless activism—doing anything to avoid the ache or emptiness within—so they cannot rest or be quiet to discern the voice of God
- due to shame and self-hatred, they resist being transparent and vulnerable with God

- after years of defeat and failure to overcome addictions, they have to battle the misbelief that God is incapable of bringing the freedom they are seeking
- they often embrace despair which creates an inability to receive God's grace, mercy, and forgiveness

The bottom line: Those struggling with addiction are alienated from themselves and God. It takes courage, perseverance, and community to surround and help the addictive struggler enter a deepening level of intimacy with God. Breaking free of addictive attachments necessitates a focused pursuit of a growing consciousness of God and His commitment to our overcoming. "You will seek me and find me when you seek me with all your heart" (Jeremiah 29:13).

We must seek to re-establish what was lost, letting God enter in to renew and transform our desire. As we saw in chapter 10, we must find the balance of walking as a sojourner, a stranger in a strange land. We continually invite God to enter any void or ache within our souls. We allow Him to transform that void into a space for Him to inhabit.

God desires to do this redemptive work in you. Are you willing to let Him do so?

The empowering of the Holy Spirit redirects the energy I sacrificed to pursue my idols and false intimacy toward the things of God. I shift from pain-awareness to God-awareness amid my struggles. I cry out to the Father to align my passions with His passions, my will with His will.

Becoming an Overcomer

You may have noticed that in the previous section, I do not refer to someone as an addict but as an addictive struggler. Overcoming a problem begins with the essential realization that I do have a problem. However, that problem is not a label or identity which defines my personhood. In the beginning stages of my process, I did not refer to myself as a sex addict. The spiritual reality was that I am a son of the living God and that I struggled with sexual addiction. Saying, "I am a sex addict" shifts my identity from who I am in Christ Jesus. Repetition of that "I am" statement elevates my behaviors as having *the authority* to define me. Only God has that authority.

How you think about or define yourself influences your behavioral choices. As we discussed in chapter 4 regarding shame, if I believe that I am shameful, I will choose behaviors that confirm that belief. Likewise, if I continue to define myself as an addict, I am allowing myself to be defined my addiction and creating a hindrance to my overcoming process. We do need to realize we are powerless in and of ourselves to overcome addictions. We are not hopeless, however, because Jesus lives in us. In Jesus, "we live, move, and have our being" (Acts 17:28).

Overcoming involves major risk-taking by becoming known to God and becoming known in community. It is beginning to believe we have worth, value, and are lovable. Can we place trust in God to complete the good work He has begun in us? Emotions have been misleading for us. Are we willing to believe in God's love and presence even when we cannot feel them? Overcoming requires being real with God. It requires saying aloud that we do not trust Him. It requires confessing that we have trouble believing He loves us unconditionally.

Often in my process, I have cried out, asking God to meet me in my places of unbelief, lack of trust, and sense of despair.

God already knows what you are feeling. Invite Jesus into these feelings that He may resolve them.

The Lord is always initiating toward me. His grace, mercy, and love are constant. Rising up as an overcomer is a process; sometimes, I cooperate, and other times I resist. However, I do not give up on the battle. God will prove He is trustworthy, which eventually translates into my growing trust in Him. Over time, my diseased self-awareness will transform into a greater God-awareness and healthy awareness of those around me.

Truly breaking free from addictions means we enter into life-giving relationships. The roots of our brokenness and suffering, the roots of our addictions, originated in disappointing relationships. To become overcomers, we must become known in community. We must learn how to love others aright and be able to receive love in return. I have learned that it is far easier to love others than to be able to receive their love.

Do you have difficulty receiving love from others? If you do, ask the Lord to help you specifically in this area.

We have often used our imagination to create sinful, illusionary fantasies. Because of this, we may have forgotten how to use the good of our imagination. We fear or resist it believing it will take us back into sin. God does redeem our imagination. How can you read the book of Revelation without incorporating the good of your imagination?

Some of my own healing experiences with the Lord have been through images He has given birth to in my mind's eye (the good of my imagination). I have seen images of Him walking with me, of His arm around my shoulder, or of Him holding me as I break down in His arms. These images spoke to my heart in ways that reading words on a page could not achieve.

To build intimacy in our relationships, we must make quality time for them. Imagine if every time you met with a friend, all you did was talk about your problems, pain, and struggles. Then, after doing so, you said goodbye and left. How long do you think that friendship would last? How often do we similarly treat God? How often do we do a file dump on Him (as we discussed in chapter 8) and then walk away, just when He wants to speak a healing word to us? Is our time with God concentrated solely on our issues or pursuing intimacy with Him?

Yes, early in our process, our issues feel so overwhelming that we often focus on them. However, as we mature, we begin to see that it is more important to connect with God's heart first and then let Him bring a healing word for our souls. To grow in intimacy with God is to spend quality time with Him, engaged in a dialogue and not a monologue.

The same is true with our friends. Yes, there are times we may be in crisis and need extra time to process with our friends. But do we give our friends time to be likewise with us? Do we seek to know their hopes and dreams? To be free from addiction is to live in close community. It is to experience the freedom to be yourself and giving others the freedom to be themselves, foibles and all. It requires risk-taking.

Here are some pointers in becoming an overcomer:

- Be willing to live by God's parameters for your well-being and relationships.
- Accept God's guidance, even when it feels uncomfortable or painful.
- Acknowledge that things may get worse before they get better.
- Give up on the quick fix and be willing to commit for the long haul.
- Be content with small victories, and don't get caught up in performance.
- Yield your idea of a time frame and trust how God is establishing His presence and healing in your life.
- Walk this process day by day, not projecting yourself into what you want your life to look like in a week, month, or year. Anticipate the "not yet" but embrace what God is doing in the "what is."
- Accept where you are each day, trusting that *He* is completing His good work in you.
- Walk with patience, endurance, and holy anticipation of what God is doing in your life.

Wrapping It Up

Those who cling to worthless idols turn away from God's love for them.

– Jonah 2:8

As stated earlier in this chapter, there are many books and programs dealing with addiction. Each may have a particular method or approach. It is indeed helpful to gain wisdom and understanding of the nuances of addiction. I trust that the Lord guided your steps to read this book. I believe He guides our steps to the specific resources which will benefit us where we are in our becoming process.

Many have walked before you in this journey of overcoming addictions. When you talk to them, you learn that it is not an easy process. I learned that turning inward after failing, and not extending grace to myself, kept my vision earthbound and immersed in self-pity and self-hatred. Gerald May writes, "To be alive is to be addicted, and to be alive and addicted is to stand in the need of grace."[78]

So I have had to learn how to apply grace to my process. Although God is completing His good work in me, I will not achieve perfection this side of heaven. If I am steeped in self-hatred, I will sense being incomplete and unacceptable in God's eyes. I must come to a place of peace with my incompleteness, then, resisting complacency, sloth, and despair. The wondrous truth is that my incompleteness is like a magnet for God. My incompleteness is the very place He wants to meet me. He is at work, committed to its restoration and longing to inhabit it. Therefore, as I walk with divine objectivity, I will view my incompleteness as an opportunity to experience more of God's love, grace, and mercy. Moreover, when I can accept this reality about me, I will be more willing to accept it in others.

Resisting diseased introspection or restless activism makes me more of a willing vessel for God to fill. Not only will He fill me, but will do it abundantly. From that abundance, I can be a gift to others. That which I have received, in the proper season, I can extend to others in need.

So would you rather remain in a state of illusion and fantasy, despising your weaknesses and deficits? Or will you see your life as opportunity after opportunity for God to prove His love

[78]Ibid., p. 11.

for you? Will you let Him lavish His love on you, welcoming you at this very moment, without deflecting it or projecting it away? Here is where the ache becomes less. Here is where your life becomes motivated more from a place of love than of performance.

Let the Holy Spirit make Philippians 1:6 truly alive in you: "Being confident of this, that he who began a good work in you will carry it on to completion until the day of Christ Jesus."

Prayers

Lord, unite us with Your love. Lord, help us see that our hearts' greatest desire is not for sex, romance, or anything apart from You. Holy Spirit, You cry out within us for love to have its perfect way. Help us be more fully released to love You. Lord, may every part of who we are begin to embrace this deepest desire to love You above all. Help us also be able to love ourselves and others aright. Lord, bring out from our depths—those deep, buried places—the reality of Your profound desire for us. Help us yield more fully to You, Holy Spirit. May Your desire become more firmly grounded, more real in our hearts.

Father, we yield to You the long-standing patterns of relational addiction that have marked our lives. We confess to You as sin the ways we have sought to deal with our stress and pain in false, empty ways. Lord God, we lift the desires that have become ensnared by false objects of release. We have exchanged Your glory for that of lifeless, worthless idols—created things that cannot impart true life to us. Lord Jesus, we bring these false patterns to the foot of Your cross, confessing them as sin. We ask that, by the power of Your blood, the hold of these patterns is broken.

Holy Spirit, bring Your truth and revelation to our addictions. Free us to become known in our addictions, calling us out of isolation. Help us see how we have tied our identities to them; escaped our pain through them; and been blinded by them. Use our addictions as a means by which we learn to rely more wholly on Your grace. Help us detach ourselves from our objects of addiction so we can learn how to face pain maturely and redemptively. Draw us closer to Yourself. As we begin to face the burdens and longings of our hearts, reclaim the true desire deep within us.

Lord, call up and out of us that truest desire to know You and You alone. Shelter us, Lord, as our desires are being reclaimed, reborn, and renewed within us. Help us stand in Your presence as we are transformed more and more by the freedom of Your grace. Feed us spiritually with good things. Lord, we long to be the good gift You created us to be from the very beginning of time. As we become freer in You, may we truly be the fragrance of life to those around us.

Soul Work

1. To what do you attach or turn to when experiencing emotional challenges in your life? How does it affect your relationship with God, others, and yourself?

2. Explain how any addictive or broken behavior(s), or feeling pulled toward them, may be rooted in pain or distress from your past.

3. Read the following Scripture passage:

> How can you say, 'I am not defiled; I have not run after the Baals'? See how you behaved in the valley; consider what you have done. You are a swift she-camel running here and there, a wild donkey accustomed to the desert, sniffing the wind in her craving—in her heat who can restrain her? Any males that pursue her need not tire themselves; at mating time they will find her. Do not run until your feet are bare and your throat is dry. But you said, 'It's no use! I love foreign gods, and I must go after them.'
>
> – Jeremiah 2:23–25

Identify and explain how this passage captures the steps of ritualization and consequences for sexual addiction.

4. Prepare a thank-you list for what your addiction has represented to you. List the ways your addiction has seemingly "helped you." Take the time to let the Holy Spirit reveal how your addiction functioned or still is functioning for you. State what your addictive behavior or addictive relationships felt like or provided for you, without any judgment regarding the validity of each. For example:
   - You were always someone I could turn to.
   - You were always there.

- You were someone who always made me feel good.
- You always made me feel more like a man/woman.
- You were the mother/father I never had.

5. Now make a list of why you are leaving your addiction behind by identifying the consequences of the addiction or person in your life. To do this, take your thank-you list and add the word but after each, indicating what else was true. For example:
   - You were always someone I could turn to, but you weren't real.
   - You were always there, but you only took life from me.
   - You were someone who always made me feel good, but the emotions I thought you made me feel were temporary and non-fulfilling.

Journaling Moment

The roots of addiction are formed through attachment—attaching our desires and unmet needs to an object or person or behavior. Ask the Holy Spirit to reveal where you have made attachments in your life, where their roots are, and how He is leading you to break those attachments.

Recommended Book Resources

Addiction and Grace, Gerald May. San Francisco: HarperOne, 2007.

Falling Forward, Craig Lockwood. Grandview, MO: Desert Stream, 2000.

The Game Plan, Joe Dallas. Nashville: Thomas Nelson, 2005.

False Intimacy, Understanding the Struggle of Sexual Addiction, Dr. Harry W. Schaumberg. Colorado Springs, CO: NavPress, rev. ed. 1997.

The Bondage Breaker, Neil Anderson. Eugene, OR: Harvest House, 2006.

TWENTY THREE

The Unexpected Journey

"THE ROAD GOES EVER ON AND ON

DOWN FROM THE DOOR WHERE IT BEGAN.

NOW FAR AHEAD THE ROAD HAS GONE,

AND I MUST FOLLOW, IF I CAN,

PURSUING IT WITH EAGER FEET,

UNTIL IT JOINS SOME LARGER WAY

WHERE MANY PATHS AND ERRANDS MEET."

– J. R. R. TOLKIEN, *THE FELLOWSHIP OF THE RING*

Bilbo Baggins and, later, his nephew Frodo Baggins, two of the main characters in J. R. R. Tolkien's trilogy about Middle Earth, began their epic journeys without a clue regarding the path ahead of them. Both started their journeys with excitement about the unknown and with limited knowing what lay ahead. Something more significant was necessary, however, to motivate them to complete their heroic journeys.

Bilbo and Frodo discovered that a deeper calling and higher purpose governed their journeys. The initial purpose for each transformed into something far more profound, which eventually affected not only the lives of those they knew but also the lives of all who lived in Middle Earth. They faced not only life-threatening dangers but also, even more challenging, their inner fears and inadequacies. They experienced great loss. However, in the end, both became much more than they could ever have imagined.

Something about your journey led you to connect with *Path*. At the start, you had only a glimpse of what lay ahead. I feel sure you looked at the table of contents, seeking the chapters that would apply directly to your need. Each chapter opened the door to another topic upon which to reflect and ponder. You had no idea of the revelation the Lord would bring. Some chapters contained information that may have been familiar. The Lord used other chapters to bring new and needed insight.

When we first invite Jesus to be Lord of our lives, we often experience an initial euphoria, as if a burdensome weight is no longer present. We have no clue, however, what remains buried deep in our hearts. An enemy, previously unseen, or recognized only marginally, now becomes a real adversary. Our eyes begin to see the bigger picture, and we grasp the reality that we are part of something much bigger than we could ever have imagined.

Living in our Egypt

Before connecting with *Path*, you discerned that something was wrong in your life and not working for you. You had a vague sense that there had to be something better. You were living in the world but somehow lacking freedom. So you sought resources and places of support.

Our early relationships and environment often do not meet all our love needs. Shame frequently inhabits the places where these deficits exist. Burdened with shame, we experience broken attachments to behaviors, people, and false identities. At the same time, we are unable to name or recognize the false self. We are in the midst of a drought and famine. In our brokenness, we look for a place to rescue us. Like the Israelites under the new Pharaoh, however, our personal Egypt eventually enslaved us.

At first, our "designer" Egypt feels comfortable. We seek resources for life, community, and security. And initially, we feel welcomed and experience a sense of freedom because we are in control. We are the master, the one making the decisions and choices. Egypt is the master, however, and soon we enter into bondage, enslaved, and controlled by it. The path of our making becomes cloaked with shame and filled with doubt and hopelessness.

Like the Israelites, we cry out and pray for release from our imprisonment. Being impatient with God, we try multiple resources looking for help, but get caught in the branches of good of the Tree of Knowledge, which ultimately fails. Thinking we have discerned rightly what our problem is—for example, specific behaviors or attractions—we embark on paths that lead only to further confusion and disappointment. Then we grow weary of our brokenness. Some of us begin to question whether God exists, thinking He must be impotent or that He does not care. Like the Israelites, we remain captive in our personally designed form of Egypt.

God's Plan of Rescue

God chose Moses, a broken eighty-year-old man, to deliver the Israelites. Here was once a mighty prince of Egypt who "was educated in all the wisdom of the Egyptians and was powerful in speech and action" (Acts 7:22). Yet at the strange sight of the burning bush, Moses told God repeatedly that He had the wrong man, that the Israelites might not believe him, that he was "slow of speech" and not eloquent (Exodus 4:10). Moses' fall from power and authority in Egypt had resulted in a man now filled with feelings of insecurity, inadequacy, and fear.

Let's pause here for a moment. Midian, where Moses was living, had become a prison, just as Egypt was for the Israelites. However, the actual prison Moses experienced was in his *thinking*. Moses defined himself by the consequences of his past choices and his present surroundings. Shame and self-hatred had crippled Moses to such a degree that he argued directly with his Creator on how God defined him!

Reflect on what you have learned in *Path*, Sections 1 and 2. Have you allowed anything regarding your past, your particular struggle, or your present actions to shroud you once again with garments of shame?

In Exodus 6:6–8, God instructed Moses what to tell the Israelites regarding His promises:

> Therefore, say to the Israelites: 'I am the LORD, and I will bring you out from under the yoke of the Egyptians. I will free you from being slaves to them, and I will redeem you

with an outstretched arm and with mighty acts of judgment. I will take you as my own people, and I will be your God. Then you will know that I am the LORD your God, who brought you out from under the yoke of the Egyptians. And I will bring you to the land I swore with uplifted hand to give to Abraham, to Isaac and to Jacob. I will give it to you as a possession. I am the LORD.'

It is crucial to see that the Israelites were freed through God's power and actions. In the Scripture above, note that seven times God says, "I will," and three times, He says, "I am the LORD." God wants His people to know who He is, how He wants to relate to them, and what He has done and will do for them. He wants them to know He has not forgotten about them and that He has compassion for them. He wants them to be His people.

The Israelites had lived in Egypt for 430 years (Exodus 12:40). How do you think they felt about God as their initial freedom under Joseph's leadership turned into captivity and bondage? How had their circumstances and struggles tainted their view of God?

Section 1 in *Path* described the true character and nature of God as Father, Son, and Holy Spirit. I detailed how we can transfer onto God our disappointments and pain, thereby distorting our view of Him. How do you relate to God today regarding your current struggles and circumstances? How do God's promises to the Israelites apply to you and your current emotional state and well-being?

God's Request to Pharaoh

Then you will know that the LORD makes a distinction between Egypt and Israel.

– Exodus 11:7

Several earlier chapters in *Path* addressed the issue of idol worship and attachments we have made to false life sources. In Exodus 20:5, God indicates that He is a "jealous God." Since God knows what is best for His creation, He is jealous for His children when they stray into false intimacy and make non-life-giving attachments. Out of love, God has set His people apart for Himself. He demonstrated this love in the Garden of Eden and on the cross where Jesus died.

What were the reasons Moses gave Pharaoh for releasing the Israelites from bondage?

TRUE FREEDOM FROM BONDAGE OCCURS WHEN WE ENTER INTO TRUE WORSHIP OF GOD.

Twice Moses told Pharaoh to release the Israelites, so they might hold a festival to the Lord and offer sacrifices in the desert. Seven times, however, Moses told him to let the Israelites go so they could worship God in the desert. Significantly, God did not tell Pharaoh to free His people so they could leave their bondage. No, the freedom God wanted for His people was for them to worship Him aright. God could have told Pharaoh to release His people so they could build Him a temple at Mount Sinai or in the Promised Land. Instead, God told him to let His people go so they could worship Him in the desert.

In the desert, there are minimal distractions. There are no competing idols but the stark simplicity of God's creation around them.

True freedom from bondage occurs when we enter into true worship of God; our eyes are transfixed on Him and nothing else. God desires true intimacy with His children, which is the core desire He imparted to us and is in our hearts (see chapter 10).

> Yet a time is coming and has now come when the true worshipers will worship the Father in the Spirit and in truth, for they are the kind of worshipers the Father seeks.
>
> – John 4:23

When we enter into worship centered in the Spirit and truth, we are standing in our true selves. God wanted to shift the Israelites' sight from their bondage onto Him. He was making a distinct line of demarcation between Egypt and Israel. He wanted their vision no longer earthbound.

In reality, it was their return to an earthbound vision—they saw with earthly eyes, fearing the giants who lived in Canaan—that later cost them forty years in the desert until they were allowed to enter the Promised Land.

God also shifted Moses' focus and vision from Exodus 2 and 4, where we see a broken and insecure man, to the shore of the Red Sea, where we see Moses become secure in the fullness of who he was and in his calling. Moses addressed the fear of the Israelites in Exodus 14:13–14 by saying,

> Do not be afraid. Stand firm and you will see the deliverance the LORD will bring you today. The Egyptians you see today you will never see again. The LORD will fight for you; you need only to be still.

God had changed Moses through his experiences in Egypt and Midian. The Lord brought the Israelites and Moses together at the right time. He changed their focus from their brokenness and circumstances, redirecting it to a higher perspective.

The Lord has brought you through this journey of *Path* in a similar fashion to redirect your vision. Throughout *Path*, how has the Lord addressed any fears you had at the beginning? How has God shifted your perspective regarding your brokenness and struggles? What place does worship have in your current process of becoming?

Leaving Our Egypt

Crossing the Red Sea, the Israelites entered the Desert of Sin between Elim and Mount Sinai. The Israelites had left their familiar surroundings and were facing the hardship of the desert. They had become accustomed to their bondage because it had provided some comforts and escape from their struggles. Those comforts were now gone, and all that was left was the harsh reality of the desert and their journey ahead.

Likewise, we in our brokenness have found comfort in false intimacy and fleshly escape patterns. We, like the Israelites, to leave our comforting, false life sources, must experience sacrifice, suffering, and even grief. This separation means we will enter a desert where God is asking if we will worship Him alone.

Are your current choices resulting in your flight from Egypt or your return to it?

The Israelites witnessed amazing ways in which God stood in the gap for them in Egypt. They saw destruction, pestilence, even the death of Egypt's firstborn. How soon after they crossed the Red Sea—with waters heaped up miraculously on either side as they crossed over on dry ground—did they begin to grumble, forgetting the signs and wonders God had performed? They complained about the food and lack of water. "…The Israelites quarreled and … tested the LORD saying, 'Is the LORD among us or not?'" (Exodus 17:7). They failed to see God's true character of love. They focused on what they had given up rather than look ahead with the holy expectation to what God promised He would provide.

How many individuals, first hearing the Gospel message, focus on what they have to give up rather than on what they are gaining? Abandoning our false sources of life, security, and comfort, we will be tempted to grumble and disobey God. Breaking free from our brokenness requires challenging our carnality, immaturity, narcissism, and established patterns of acting out.

Having left our bondage, traveling through the Desert of Sin, we experience the pull to return to Egypt. We make allowances for other "gods" to escape our pain. We seek the familiar, instant gratification of false intimacy. Egypt, connected with the false self, beckons us back. Our brains will prompt us to seek our old patterns and drug(s) of choice to achieve equilibrium. However, what we are trying to escape is the ache within, the drive for true intimacy. We want to numb the ache by diverting it towards sources of false intimacy. The reality is that we want the temporary absence of the drive so we can feel okay.

Turning our backs on Egypt means we have to stop listening to familiar voices. After Moses disappeared up Mount Sinai for forty days and nights, and before Aaron cast the image of the golden calf, Aaron said to the Israelites, "Take off the gold earrings that your wives, your sons, and your daughters are wearing, and bring them to me" (Exodus 32:2). The idol he cast, then, consisted of gold earrings, which I suggest symbolize a desire to "hear" from false gods. Listening to false gods, we forget what God has done. We lose the capacity to hear His gentle, loving voice. But we are called to become bondservants to the Lord, offering ourselves freely to Him.

In ancient times, individuals allowed their earlobes to be pierced on a doorpost (a shedding of blood) to indicate that they were now in servanthood to that house. Breaking free from bondage requires dedication, discipline, and the empowering of the Holy Spirit. We make an allegiance, a bond of servanthood to One who is greater than us; One who shed His blood on our behalf to secure our freedom.

God sets apart those who will worship only Him. You will become that on which your heart is set. To leave your Egypt behind, you must look up and out of yourself. You join the royal priesthood of Christ. You now bend the knee only to Him.

On the Edge of the Promised Land

Soon after the children of Israel left Egypt, the Promised Land came into range. Moses sent twelve scouts to survey the land. Only two, Joshua and Caleb, saw the land with spiritual vision, with divine objectivity, while the other ten saw through the eyes of their flesh. Even though they saw the land as fruitful, the dangers and giants who inhabited the land overwhelmed them. As those ten scouts described the threat, their fear stirred up the people.

Caleb came before Moses and the people, challenging the message of fear. He said, "We should go up and take possession of the land, for we can certainly do it" (Numbers 13:30). Caleb saw and discerned what God was laying out before them.

Like Caleb, with Egypt behind us, we must face our fears. We seek God for the gift of faith to believe in His promises. We seek the empowering of the Holy Spirit to rise and take hold of what is rightfully ours. Instead of practicing the presence of fear, we must see the "not yet" ahead of us with divine expectation. It is attainable. It will happen with God's help.

To whose report will you listen and give credence? Will you trust God to lead you to the Promised Land according to His design?

The Israelites, believing the bad report, turned inward and reacted. They wept aloud, giving themselves over to despair, bitterness, and cynicism. They cried out melodramatically, "If only we had died in Egypt! Or in this wilderness!" (Numbers 14:2). They could see only the desert because they were no longer focused on the path, the journey home. Having received the fear of the ten spies, they had lost hope, focusing on themselves and turning inward to self-pity.

They also exclaimed, "Why is the LORD bringing us to this land only to let us fall by the sword? Our wives and children will be taken as plunder. Wouldn't it be better for us to go back to Egypt?" (Numbers 14:3). Now they were accusing God. Their perception of what would happen in the Promised Land was wrong. They were focusing solely on their own strength and inadequacy to complete the task ahead. Yes, indeed, in themselves, they were inadequate, but God was on their side. How quickly they had forgotten the plagues, the column of fire, and the parting of the Red Sea!

Finally, they turned on Moses and indicated they needed a new leader to take them back to Egypt. "And they said to each other, 'We should choose a leader and go back to Egypt'" (Numbers 14:4).

God had made a way out of Egypt for the Israelites, but the path He had provided was no longer available since the Red Sea had closed back up. To return to Egypt, the Israelites would have to find their own way back.

If we plan to return to bondage, to our vomit, we have to create a path of our own. God does not make a way for us to enter back into sin. Here we must be wary of false teachers who teach a hyper-grace message that returning to our vomit is okay in the eyes of God. The enemy tries to distract us from God Himself. The Israelites tried to create a solution of their own because they felt God had failed them.

In our path through the wilderness, we can acknowledge feelings of despair, bitterness, cynicism, and self-pity. As we have learned, we need to identify our feelings, so they do not become toxic or redirect our focus. We are to walk by faith, not by feelings, by earthbound vision, or by false reports.

Moses, Aaron, Joshua, and Caleb attempted to speak the truth and change the minds of the Israelites. "The land is exceedingly good," they said. "The Lord will lead us." They asked the people not to rebel or be afraid, reminding them that the Lord was with them. But the Israelites, with their ears blocked and vision corrupted, wanted to stone them.

How have you transferred anger or hurt onto others when you felt disappointed in your journey? How have your emotions impaired your capacity to hear the truth? We need good community and the wise counsel of others. Yet do we, like the Israelites, want to stone those who speak the truth to us?

Entering Our Promised Land

> Israel's release from Egypt is often called their deliverance. God saw their misery and was moved to action. But remember, it was not just a deliverance from but a deliverance to. God freed them from hard servitude, and that alone was deliverance. But it was also a means to an end, the end being the Promised Land. There, they'd make new conquests, establish their homes, develop their community, and enjoy a better life.[79]

Our past lies in Egypt, but we find our long-term future in Canaan. There will be battles. We have to face our fears, doubts, and unbelief. We have to make difficult choices and keep our focus on the Lord. We must resist despair, sloth, and complacency.

[79]Joe Dallas, *The Game Plan: The Men's 30-Day Strategy for Attaining Sexual Integrity* (Thomas Nelson, 2005), p. 196.

GRACE WITHOUT REPENTANCE IS A **DECEPTION.**

The cross of Jesus has indeed wrought our freedom, but we must enter into the process of walking out that freedom daily. We are in the process of becoming and overcoming. A holy tension lies between the "what is" and the "not yet." We are walking through the process of sanctification.

In chapter 20, I spoke of the holiness we have in Christ. It is *positional* holiness with Him, like our righteousness and purity. We also have *relational* holiness, however, worked out in our daily lives. God extends grace to us as the result of the shed blood of Jesus on the cross for our sin. Grace is always associated with blood. Grace has a direct connection with sin. Grace without repentance is a deception. Our journey, our lifelong process, means that we receive grace as we practice repentance.

Grace does not mean we have a license to sin. God clearly defines the parameters for our behaviors. "Whoever says, 'I know him,' but does not do what he commands is a liar, and the truth is not in that person" (1 John 2:4). We renounce the hyper-grace message, then, that makes allowances for behaviors that God says restrict us from entering the Kingdom of God (1 Corinthians 6:9–10).

We battle with being satisfied with the immediate rather than holding out for what will truly fulfill us. We tend to settle for less because it is challenging to hold out for something more. Have you noticed that, until you get used to them, artificial sweeteners have an odd or bitter aftertaste? We settle for artificial sweeteners when our taste buds long for what is truly sweet. Our hearts yearn for the real, but we settle for that which is imitation and non-real.

In our forward journey, we must embrace authentic humility. We must learn to embrace the "what is" as a temporary condition. We must accept the reality of setting our hearts on pilgrimage (Psalm 84:5). We will always be in the state of becoming until we are finally with Him. On your journey home, you will experience ups and downs this side of heaven. There will always be some aspect of your soul that needs God's revelation, restoration, and reclamation. There is no shame in this.

This is what the LORD says: "Stand at the crossroads and look; ask where the good way is, and walk in it, and you will find rest for your souls. But you said, 'We will not walk in it.'"

– Jeremiah 6:16

Will you trust God with your journey or seek your own path? Will you continue to come up with solutions that fail because you cannot discern the real problems? In the quote from Jeremiah just above, note the action words: *stand*, *look*, *ask* (twice), *walk*, and *find rest*. Our journey requires an active faith connected with those words. We press into God by our active pursuit of and with Him in our journey. Our faith is one of taking action, but not through fleshly striving, which cannot rest.

Transparency and honesty are vital aspects of our journey. By admitting we are still in process, we open ourselves to continued opportunities for God to manifest His mercy, grace, and love. I will always need my Savior and my God—as did Moses, Joshua, Gideon, and many others. Shame no longer needs to be my identity, a defining factor for my soul. I will not allow myself to turn inward and shut down. I must resist the urge to shift my focus from God onto myself. I make an active choice to resist self-hatred and refuse to allow the enemy to define or label me. I will make mistakes on my pilgrimage home, but this does not mean I am a mistake, hopelessly flawed, or less than any of my brothers or sisters.

My particular struggles do not define who I am. Instead, they reveal my—our!—shared humanity. We have been freed from our chronic uniqueness and autonomy, our overt self-focus and diseased self-awareness. We turn up and out of ourselves to the One who created and knows us. We embrace the healthy self-love that says, "I am my beloved's and my beloved is mine" (Song of Songs 6:3).

The challenge we all face is entering the crucible of obedience. Through obedience, the remnants of the false self are continually ground down. Here lies the one choice we all have to make: Will I embrace the nothingness of sin or the radiant real of God? Temptation, suffering, and pain are a reality. So are hope, joy, and comfort.

The Israelites had to face many challenges before they became established in the Promised Land. I live with the reality of my smallness compared to the majestic holiness and righteousness of God. But I also live with the reality that this amazing God not only sees and knows me but likes me! I walk in holy fear, in reverence for God; but I also know that Jesus has made a way for me to approach His amazing throne.

Our greatest and deepest growth occurs not on the mountaintop but in the valleys. With patient perseverance, we learn our constant need for and dependence on God through every challenge and battle. All the great women and men in the Bible faced adversity and were imperfect in their process. Either we learn our lessons, or we will face them again. We must release our perfectionism. Through the process of learning self-control, we move on in the process of embracing perseverance.

Within our souls, we hold onto the expectancy for the "not yet." The incarnational reality of God (i.e., "God is alive and living within me!") enables us to embrace hope as the belief that it will turn out well for us. Knowing we can do all things through Christ who strengthens us (Philippians 4:13) helps us not only to overcome but also to rise again when we fall.

So we set our eyes on the real prize, which is knowing true intimacy with our Beloved, Jesus; with our loving Father; and with our precious Holy Spirit. The prize is not our healing, victory, or change. The prize is God Himself. We rest not in a presumed air of familiarity, a sentimental, "sloppy *agape*" knowing of God, or making Him into our own image, but in knowing His promise to complete the good work, He has begun in us., Healing, victory, and change are the fruit we can experience as a *byproduct* due to our knowing of God.

In Closing

> Whether you turn to the right or to the left, your ears will hear a voice behind you, saying, "This is the way; walk in it."
>
> – Isaiah 30:21

In J. R. R. Tolkien's book *The Hobbit: Or There and Back Again*, Gandalf shows up at Bilbo Baggins' home and invites him on an unexpected journey. Bilbo is initially reluctant to leave his cozy hobbit hole, fireplace, and books. But Gandalf breaks through Bilbo's comforts and stirs up his desire for adventure buried deep inside. Much the same way, Jesus meets us and invites us on an unexpected journey, stirring the deep desires He has planted within us from the very beginning of time. We take the first step of faith, choosing a road that "goes ever on and on."

To be on the journey home is to turn to God, inviting Him into my fears, insecurity, and doubts. I embrace my life, able to rejoice in the reality that I am a work in progress. No longer do I let my weakness and inadequacy be the standard on which I base my worth, value, or lovableness. I refuse to embrace "religion," which is based on laws and performance-based acceptance. Rather, I embrace the reality of grace with repentance, truth with love, and mercy with hope.

I am a stranger and sojourner in a strange land. I fix my heart on the spiritual reality that is not yet visible with my earthly vision. Because Jesus is alive in me, walking with me each step on this path through the wilderness, I know I can become and overcome. I become less as He becomes more. I begin to experience the life He has intended for me since the very beginning. I am becoming more and more like Jesus, bearing His image in my unique way.

> "Little by little, breath by breath, love dissolves the illusions and fears born of our estrangement from the infinite love that is our very life."[80]

> Therefore, my dear brothers and sisters, stand firm. Let nothing move you.
>
> – 1 Corinthians 15:58

Prayer

Lord, You have carried me through every chapter in this book. I started in one place, but You have brought me to a new place. Even if I cannot sense a profound difference within me, I choose to trust that You have been working deep within me. You guided me to read this book, and now I turn it back to You and say, have Your way. Write the truth You have revealed to me on my heart, that I may not forget it.

Lord, I want to believe that You are completing the work You have begun in me. I seek the gift of faith to establish this as a living reality within me. I have lived so long letting my feelings, the input of others, and the extent of my circumstances define me. It is a challenge not to let those things have power over me. I pray to remain open to Your healing word for me; for Your truth to speak to any lie or faulty belief within me.

[80]James Finley, Richard Rohr's Daily Meditation, August 5, 2017, WeeklySummary@cac.org.

You spoke the universe into being by Your words. Help me to hear and receive Your voice speaking life and transformation into my soul and being.

I pray that You grant me gladness and singleness of heart to follow after You alone. I pray that my primary goal is not the pursuit of change but intimacy with You. I want to focus not on the healing of my soul but the Healer of my soul. I humbly accept where I am today and trust You with my future.

Lord Jesus, I want to be able to answer yes to Your two questions: Will you trust Me? Will you follow Me no matter what the cost? I long to base my devotion and commitment to You solely on love, with no strings attached. Even if I do not change according to my timetable or expectations, help me base my yes and amen solely on the choice I have made to be obedient to Your will alone.

I seek Your empowering, Holy Spirit, to embrace my journey home with commitment, fortitude, and devotion. May my eyes be set ever heavenward, fixed on the prize of knowing You. Thank You for the blood covenant. Thank You for never leaving or forsaking me. Thank You that You will always provide the way set before me.

I look forward to the day when I see You face to face with no veil of separation. Thank You for Your great faithfulness and lovingkindness. I choose to remain centered in the reality of hope that it will turn out well for me.

Soul Work

1. Describe your personal Egypt. In what ways has God provided for your deliverance from it?

2. What does the Promised Land look like for you?

3. Draw another picture of you with God. Compare it to the drawing you made at the beginning in Section 1. How has it changed, and why?

Journaling Moment

Ask the Holy Spirit to reveal how God has been proving Himself present and faithful as you have been journeying home. How has He been carrying you as you have progressed through *Path*? Now that you have completed the 23 chapters of Path, what is His specific healing word for you?

Glossary

antinomianism: the heretical belief based upon the principle of salvation by faith and divine grace which indicates we are no longer under the law thereby giving permission for lawlessness, being able to partake in sinful behaviors which are forbidden in the Scriptures without consequence; the concept of hyper-grace

becoming: the process of growing and being transformed into the man or woman that God has created us to be; it is the process of becoming an overcomer

being: my oneness with God in body, soul, and spirit; my personhood

bentness: our broken capacity to lean into others for our identity, security, or peace

celibacy: a calling, not a temporary season, which involves one's choosing to remain unmarried and single

chastity: living our lives so as to relate to one another in holy, affirming, and honoring ways

condemnation: word or feelings which indicate I am bad, deficient, or inadequate; the source for condemnation is three-fold being the devil, the world, and our own self-hatred or loathing (flesh); an emotional reaction which prompts to run and hide from God

conviction: a work of the Holy Spirit speaking truth into our broken choices for false intimacy and unhealthy attachments; conviction confronts our doubt or denial that we have taken control and chose to stand in the false self; it addresses every aspect of how we live in thought, word, and deed

deflection: an emotional reaction of shifting our attention, shutting down our emotions or thoughts, when what is present reminds us of a past hurt or wound

despair: the belief that it will not turn out well for me; the antithesis of hope

diseased introspection: an inward self-consuming focus on my faulty beliefs, broken attitudes, and unresolved emotions; allowing our brokenness to dominate our vision; the inability to look up and out of ourselves into the loving face of God; it is the abandonment of hope and the embracing of despair

divine objectivity: our capacity to see our brokenness and lives through the eyes of God; learning to see my life experiences as opportunities for me to "become" rather than a form of punishment

false intimacy: seeking to know and be known through broken behaviors and relationships; relationally expressing *agape*, *eros*, *philia*, or *storge*, through broken behaviors, being motivated by control and self-gratification; making attachment to that which cannot give life

false self: living our lives based upon self-protective mechanisms, performance-based-acceptance, or identities associated with our brokenness and sin; that part of me which does not identify or affirm who I am in Christ

fulfillment: the ultimate meeting of the deepest desire of my heart to know and be known by God and others; goes beyond gratification or satisfaction which are momentary and fleeting; the meeting of all my needs in God

grace: receiving that which we do not deserve

hope: the belief it will turn out well for me because of the reality that the Creator of the universe, God Himself, lives in me

incarnational reality: the relational awareness that God dwells and lives within me as Father, Son, and Holy Spirit as described in John 14:20 and Acts 17:28; God being incarnate, embodied within me

knowing: a relational connecting which engages both the mind (mental capacity) and the heart (emotional capacity); seeking to be connected in whole and true relationships

living in the flesh: being centered in my control, faulty thinking, diseased attitudes, and behaviors rather than being centered in Jesus; not being Spirit-led; living a self-focused life centered in the soul

lust: allowing my choices to put my own happiness, security, and need above that of others; objectifying others to satisfy my brokenness

magnanimity: the virtue of realizing that I can become much more than I could ever imagine because God, the Creator of the universe lives and dwells within me

matrix: : an illusionary grid and world of our own making due to being in reaction to our experiences; it originates in our minds as a means of self-protection and escape from reality; a non-reality

mercy: not receiving that which we do deserve for our sins

misandry: the hatred of men

misogyny: the hatred of woman

non-being: choosing to live apart from Christ; when we embrace thinking or doing which hinders our "becoming" process

"not yet": the future which lies ahead for us as Christians; the holy anticipation of the day when we are with the Lord without barriers or obstacles, seeing Him clearly

old man/self: all that we allow to define us before accepting Jesus as our Lord and Savior

performance-based-acceptance: finding my acceptance in relationships and the world by how

I perform rather than who I am in Christ: finding my identity through my outward behaviors/ striving rather than resting in who God has called and named me to be

practicing the presence: making the choice to acknowledge in the moment and relationally embracing the incarnational presence of Jesus being alive within and present to me; it is shifting our focus from whatever is preoccupying our attention to the reality of God who is with us

process: is our daily choices and series of actions directed toward our becoming the man or woman God has created us to be; this is the choice to trust Jesus and to remain committed to follow Him no matter what the cost

redemptive suffering: the allowance of our pain and wounds to rise to the cross of Jesus knowing He will meet us in our place of suffering, ministering to our abuse, hurt, or disappointments; it is not a reliving of our pain for pain's sake but inviting the presence of Jesus to inhabit where it dwells and establish His healing touch and peace

religion: creating my own standards and rules, to feel acceptable to God

restless activism: the inability to remain still and enter into rest; an act of avoidance to keep busy not to face our pain, disappointments, and wounds; not allowing our unresolved emotions to surface so that we have to acknowledge their existence; living in denial

sanctification: the process whereby the brokenness in our lives, the unresolved emotions in our hearts, and the faulty belief systems in our mind come under the control of God; the realigning and perfecting of our will to be one with the Father's; being set apart for God

self-awareness: is the capacity to know and be familiar with oneself; in negative terms, a diseased self-awareness often keeping us turned inward, creating levels of self-hatred/loathing, and the decreased ability to stay present to others; negative self-awareness is rooted in insecurity, comparisons, or control

self-hatred: an emotional reaction derived from our faulty belief systems that indicate we are tainted, defective, inadequate, etc.; a state of being whereby we become consumed with negative thoughts about ourselves thereby blocking the grace, mercy, and love of God and others

self-love: is a virtue through which we realize that we are loved, accepted, cherished, and welcomed by God; it is the healthy knowing that I am part of God's greater purposes and vision; unhealthy self-love is egocentric and self-serving

sense of being: the inner realization that I am one of God's creation and having the capacity to connect with God, others, and myself; knowing that I am welcomed and part of something bigger

separation anxiety: the result of becoming detached from a source of life, identity, or security

sloth: is the choice to stop becoming, to acquiesce to passivity, complacency, and non-being

transference: the unconscious redirection of unresolved feelings from a person or event in our past to a person or circumstance in the present

Trinitarian: of or that which corresponds to the tri-expression of God as Father, Jesus, and Holy Spirit

true intimacy: the capacity to know and be known without masks, facades, or defenses; standing in the true self and relationally connecting where *agape*, *eros*, *philia*, and *storge*, are in true expression without the presence of control, narcissism, or self-gratification

true self: my identity in who I am in Christ (incarnational reality); living in the reality that I am the Father's daughter or son because of Christ living in me; no longer being defined by my past or present sin, nor circumstances

vain imaginations: being lost in our diseased thinking and attitudes; practicing the presence of my pain through the creation of fantasies as a reaction to our wounds, disappointments, or circumstances

vulnerability: : there are two forms of vulnerability: being in a situation whereby we find ourselves at risk for abuse or attack; being open and willing for the healing or restorative presence of God or others

"what is": that which reflects our current circumstances and existence

wholeness: being made complete in Christ and living out of His true center; walking in right and healthy relationships; having an unhindered relationship with God

Appendix 1: Emotion Identification Sheet

This sheet is helpful for identifying emotions. Check each emotion which you believe applies to you. The numbers correspond with a category which reveal possible lies associated with them. Select the three most prominent emotions for item #2 of the forgiveness form located in chapter 13. (This form is used with kind permission from Grace Ministries Inc.)

Emotion		
1-Abandoned	____	____
3-Agitated	____	____
5-Annihilated	____	____
3-Anxious	____	____
2-Ashamed	____	____
2-Awful	____	____
2-Bad	____	____
2-Blamed	____	____
6-Belittled	____	____
2-Betraying	____	____
6-Betrayed	____	____
8-Bewildered	____	____
6-Broken	____	____
4-Browbeat	____	____
2-Cheap	____	____
4-Childish	____	____
2-Condemned	____	____
1-Confused	____	____
4-Choking	____	____
6-Cold	____	____
4-Confined	____	____
8-Confused	____	____
4-Constricted	____	____
4-Cornered	____	____
2-Corrupt	____	____
3-Cowardly	____	____
5-Crazy	____	____
2-Criminal	____	____
5-Cureless	____	____
5-Cursed	____	____
5-Damaged	____	____
5-Damned	____	____
6-Deceived	____	____
2-Deceitful	____	____
7-Defeated	____	____
4-Defenseless	____	____
5-Defiled	____	____
6-Denied	____	____
6-Depleted	____	____
2-Depraved	____	____
4-Depressed	____	____
4-Deprived	____	____
1-Deserted	____	____
3-Desperate	____	____
6-Despised	____	____
6-Devalued	____	____
6-Disapproved	____	____
6-Devastated	____	____
4-Distressed	____	____
2-Disloyal	____	____
6-Disgraced	____	____
4-Disarranged	____	____
6-Disposed	____	____
8-Dizzy	____	____
6-Despised	____	____
1-Displaced	____	____
1-Discarded	____	____
4-Disordered	____	____
4-Disjointed	____	____
3-Doomed	____	____
6-I don't matter	____	____
6-Drained	____	____
3-Dreadful	____	____
8-Dumbfounded	____	____
3-Dying	____	____
2-Embarrassed	____	____
4-Entangled	____	____
2-Evil	____	____
3-Excited	____	____
2-Exposed	____	____
2-Failure	____	____
2-Fake	____	____
7-Fatigued	____	____
2-Fault	____	____
3-Fearful	____	____
5-Flawed	____	____
2-Filthy	____	____
2-Foolish	____	____
1-Forgotten	____	____
1-Forsaken	____	____
2-Foul	____	____
1-Friendless	____	____
4-Frail	____	____
4-Frustrated	____	____
2-Gross	____	____
2-Guilt	____	____
2-Gullible	____	____
4-Helpless	____	____
1-Homeless	____	____
7-Hopeless	____	____
2-Homosexual	____	____
2-Humiliated	____	____
3-Hysterical	____	____

2-Ignorant ______ ______
4-Impaired ______ ______
3-Impending Doom ______ ______
4-Impotent ______ ______
2-Improper ______ ______
2-Incompetent ______ ______
8-Indecisive ______ ______
2-Indecent ______ ______
7-Indifferent ______ ______
2-Inept ______ ______
6-Inferior ______ ______
6-Insignificant ______ ______
6-Insufficient ______ ______
6-In the way ______ ______
4-Intimidated ______ ______
4-Jittery ______ ______
3-Jealous ______ ______
2-Lazy ______ ______
1-Left Out ______ ______
2-Lewd ______ ______
4-Little ______ ______
2-Loathsome ______ ______
1-Lost ______ ______
6-Loser ______ ______
3,8-Manic ______ ______
6-(a) Mistake ______ ______
6-Mistreated ______ ______
6-Misunderstood ______ ______
2-Nasty ______ ______
6-Not Wanted ______ ______
3-Nervous ______ ______
6-Numb ______ ______
2-Obnoxious ______ ______
4-Oppressed ______ ______
4-Overpowered ______ ______
4-Overwhelmed ______ ______
6-Outcast ______ ______
1-Outsider ______ ______
4-Out of Control ______ ______
3-Paranoid ______ ______
2-Pathetic ______ ______
3-Panic ______ ______
2-Perverted ______ ______
6-Petty ______ ______
2-Phoney ______ ______

4-Pressured ______ ______
2-Regretful ______ ______
6-Rejected ______ ______
2-Repugnant ______ ______
2-Repulsive ______ ______
6-Revengeful ______ ______
2-Rubbish ______ ______
5-Ruined ______ ______
2-Sabotaged ______ ______
3-Scared ______ ______
5-Screwed Up ______ ______
6-Second Class ______ ______
2-Shameful ______ ______
2-Sickening ______ ______
2-Sinful ______ ______
2-Sleazy ______ ______
2-Slut/Whorish ______ ______
2-Smutty ______ ______
4-Squashed ______ ______
4-Stretched ______ ______
2-Stupid ______ ______
7-Suicidal ______ ______
3-Suspicious ______ ______
5-Tarnished ______ ______
3-Tentative ______ ______
3-Tense ______ ______
3-Terror ______ ______
3-Tormented ______ ______
4-Torn ______ ______
4-Trapped ______ ______
2-Trashy ______ ______
2-Ugly ______ ______
6-Unacceptable ______ ______
6-Unappreciated ______ ______
2-Unclean ______ ______
3-Undecided ______ ______
2-Unfit ______ ______
6-Unloved ______ ______
2-Unrighteous ______ ______
6-Unsuitable ______ ______
3-Untrusting ______ ______
2-Unworthy ______ ______
2-Valueless ______ ______
2-Vulgar ______ ______
5-Wasted ______ ______

4-Weak ______ ______
4-Weepy ______ ______
3-Worried ______ ______
6-Worthless ______ ______
2-Wrong ______ ______
2-Yucky ______ ______
OTHER: ______ ______

Revengeful Emotions ______ ______
Angry ______ ______
Bitterness ______ ______
Confronting ______ ______
Critical ______ ______
Defiant ______ ______
Depressed ______ ______
Hate ______ ______
Judgmental ______ ______
Murderous ______ ______
Offensive ______ ______
Sullen ______ ______
Violent ______ ______

Lie/Emotion Identification Sheet

Category	Possible lies producing emotions.
1. Abandonment	"I am all alone. I have been overlooked. I will always be alone. They do not need me. I don't matter. No one even cares. They are not coming back. There is no one to protect me. God has forsaken me too. No one will believe me. I cannot trust anyone. I am afraid they won't come back."
2. Shame	"I am so stupid, ignorant, an idiot. I should have done something to have stopped it from happening. I allowed it. I was a participant. I should have known better. It was my fault. I should have told someone. I knew what was going to happen, yet I stayed anyway. I felt pleasure, so I must have wanted it. I was a participant. It happened because of my looks, my ender, my body, etc. I should have stopped them. I did not try to run away. I deserved it. I am cheap like a slut. I was paid for service rendered. I kept going back. I did it to him/her first. I am bad, dirty, shameful, sick, nasty."
3. Fear	"I am going to die, he/she is going to hurt me. I do not know what to do. If I tell they will come back and hurt me. If I trust I will die. He/she/they are coming back. It is just a matter of time before it happens again. If I let him/her/them into my life they will hurt me too. Something bad will happen if I tell, stop it, confront it. They are going to get me. Doom is just around the corner."
4. Powerlessness/ Trapped	"I cannot stop this. He/she/they are too strong to resist. There is no way out. I am too weak to resist. The pain is too great to bear. I cannot get away. I am going to die and I cannot do anything about it. I cannot get loose. I am overwhelmed. I don't know what to do. Everything is out of control. I am pulled from every direction. Not even God can help me. I am too small to do anything."
5. Tainted	"I am dirty, shameful, evil, perverted, etc., because of what happened to me. My life is ruined. I will never feel clean again. Everyone can see my shame, filth, dirtiness, etc. I will always be hurt/damaged/broken because of what has happened. I will never be happy. I will always be unclean, filthy, etc. God could never want me after what has happened to me. My body parts are dirty. No one will ever really be able to love me."
6. Invalidation	"I am not loved, needed, wanted, cared for or important. They do not need me. I am worthless, have no value. I am unimportant. I was a mistake. I should have never been born. I am in the way. I am a burden. I was never liked by them because I was ________________. God could never love or accept me. I could never be as ________________ as he/she. I could never jump high enough to please him/her. I am not acceptable."
7. Hopeless	"It is never going to get any better. There is no way out. It will just happen again and again. There is no good thing for me. I have no reason to live. There are no options for me. I just want to die. Nothing good will ever come of this."
8. Confusion	"I don't know what is happening to me. Everything is confusing. This does not make any sense. Whey would they do this to me?" (This lie is sometimes confused with demonic interference. Demons will cause confusion in a memory which will feel much like a confusion lie.)

Made in the USA
Columbia, SC
16 September 2023